Canon® EOS® 77D

by Julie Adair King and Robert Correll

for
dummies®
A Wiley Brand

Canon® EOS® 77D For Dummies®

Published by: **John Wiley & Sons, Inc.**, 111 River Street, Hoboken, NJ 07030-5774, www.wiley.com

Copyright © 2017 by John Wiley & Sons, Inc., Hoboken, New Jersey

Published simultaneously in Canada

For general information on our other products and services, please contact our Customer Care Department within the U.S. at 877-762-2974, outside the U.S. at 317-572-3993, or fax 317-572-4002. For technical support, please visit https://hub.wiley.com/community/support/dummies.

Wiley publishes in a variety of print and electronic formats and by print-on-demand. Some material included with standard print versions of this book may not be included in e-books or in print-on-demand. If this book refers to media such as a CD or DVD that is not included in the version you purchased, you may download this material at http://booksupport.wiley.com. For more information about Wiley products, visit www.wiley.com.

Library of Congress Control Number: 2017947399

ISBN 978-1-119-42009-5 (pbk); ISBN 978-1-119-42012-5 (ebk); ISBN 978-1-119-42013-2 (ebk)

Manufactured in the United States of America

10 9 8 7 6 5 4 3 2 1

Contents at a Glance

Table of Contents

Introduction

n 2003, Canon revolutionized the photography world by introducing the first digital SLR (dSLR) camera to sell for less than $1,000, the EOS Digital Rebel/300D. The camera delivered exceptional performance and picture quality, earning it rave reviews and multiple industry awards. No wonder it quickly became a best seller.

That tradition of excellence and value lives on in the EOS 77D. Like its predecessors, this baby offers advanced controls for experienced photographers as well as features to help beginners be successful from the get-go. Adding to the fun, the camera also offers high-definition video recording and built-in Wi-Fi for easy connections to your computer, smartphone, or tablet.

In fact, the 77D is so feature-packed that sorting out everything can be a challenge. For starters, you may not even know what SLR means, let alone have a clue about all the other terms you encounter in your camera manual — resolution, aperture, and ISO, for example. If you're like many people, you may be so overwhelmed by all the camera controls that you haven't yet ventured beyond fully automatic picture-taking mode. That's a shame because it's sort of like buying a Porsche Turbo and never pushing it past 35 miles per hour.

About This Book

In this book, you discover not only what each bell and whistle on your camera does but also when, where, why, and how to put it to best use. Unlike many photography books, this one doesn't require any previous knowledge of photography or digital imaging. Everything is explained in easy-to-understand language, with lots of illustrations to help clear up any confusion.

In short, what you have in your hands is the paperback version of a photography workshop tailored specifically to your camera. Whether your interests lie in taking family photos, exploring nature and travel photography, or snapping product shots for your business, you'll get the help you need to capture the images you envision.

Within this book, you may note that some web addresses break across two lines of text. If you're reading this book in print and want to visit one of these web pages, simply key in the web address exactly as it's noted in the text, pretending as though the line break doesn't exist. If you're reading this as an e-book, you've got it easy — just click the web address to be taken directly to the web page.

Additionally, replicas of some of your camera's buttons and onscreen graphics appear throughout the book to help you locate the button or setting being discussed.

Foolish Assumptions

We don't assume much about you, the reader, but we do assume the following:

» You either have or are planning to acquire a Canon EOS 77D camera.

» You want to learn about the camera's features and how to use them.

» You would like to deepen your knowledge of photography so that you can take better still photos and movies with the 77D.

Icons Used in This Book

If this isn't your first *For Dummies* book, you may be familiar with the large round icons that decorate its margins. If not, here's your very own icon-decoder ring:

TIP

A Tip icon flags information that saves you time, effort, money, or another valuable resource, including your sanity.

WARNING

When you see this icon, look alive. It indicates a potential danger zone that can result in much wailing and teeth-gnashing if it's ignored.

TECHNICAL STUFF

Lots of information in this book is of a technical nature — digital photography is a technical animal, after all. But if we present a detail that's useful mainly for impressing your geeky friends, we mark it with this icon.

REMEMBER

This icon highlights information that's especially worth storing in your brain's long-term memory or to remind you of a fact that may have been displaced from that memory by another pressing fact.

Beyond the Book

In addition to the material in the print or e-book you're reading right now, this product also comes with some access-anywhere goodies on the web. Check out the free Cheat Sheet for a handy reference to your camera's buttons, controls, and exposure modes. To get this Cheat Sheet, simply go to www.dummies.com and type **Canon EOS 77D For Dummies Cheat Sheet** in the Search box.

Where to Go from Here

To wrap up this preamble, we want to stress that if you initially think that digital photography is too confusing or too technical for you, you're in good company. *Everyone* finds this stuff mind-boggling at first. Take it slowly, trying just one or two new camera settings or techniques each time you pick up your camera. With time, patience, and practice, you'll soon wield your camera like a pro, dialing in the necessary settings to capture your creative vision almost instinctively.

So, without further ado, we invite you to grab your camera and a cup of whatever it is you prefer to sip while you read and start exploring the rest of this book. Your EOS 77D is the perfect partner for your photographic journey, and we thank you for allowing us, through this book, to serve as your tour guides.

1

Fast Track to Super Snaps

Chapter **1**

Getting Up and Running

I f you're like many people, shooting for the first time with a single-lens reflex (SLR) camera produces a blend of excitement and anxiety. On the one hand, you can't wait to start using your new equipment, but on the other, you're a little intimidated by all its buttons, dials, and menu options.

Well, fear not: This chapter provides the information you need to start getting comfortable with your Canon EOS 77D. The first section walks you through initial camera setup. Following that, you get an overview of camera controls, discover how to view and adjust camera settings, work with lenses and memory cards, and get advice on some basic setup options.

Preparing the Camera for Initial Use

After unpacking your camera, you have to assemble a few parts. In addition to the camera body and the supplied battery (charge it before the first use), you need a lens and a memory card. Later sections in this chapter provide details about lenses and memory cards, but here's the short story:

>> **Lens:** Your camera accepts Canon EF and EF-S lenses; the 18–55mm or 18–135mm kit lenses sold as a bundle with the camera body falls into the EF-S category. If you want to buy a non-Canon lens, check the lens manufacturer's website to find out which lenses work with your camera.

>> **SD, SDHC, or SDXC memory card:** The SD stands for *Secure Digital;* the HC and XC stand for *High Capacity* and *eXtended Capacity.* The different labels reflect how many gigabytes (GB) of data the card holds. SD cards hold less than 4GB; SDHC, 4GB to 32GB; and SDXC, more than 32GB.

With camera, lens, battery, and card within reach, take these steps:

1. **Turn the camera off.**

2. **Attach a lens.**

   First, remove the caps that cover the front of the camera and the back of the lens. Then locate the proper *mounting index,* which is a mark on the camera's lens mount that indicates how to align the lens with the camera body. Your camera has two of these markers, one red and one white, as shown in Figure 1-1. Which marker you use depends on the lens type:

   - *Canon EF-S lens:* The white square is the mounting index.

   - *Canon EF lens:* The red dot is the mounting index.

   Your lens also has a mounting index; align that mark with the matching one on the camera body, as shown in Figure 1-1. Place the lens on the camera mount and rotate the lens toward the side of the camera that sports the white EOS logo (or, to put it another way, away from the shutter-button side of the camera). You should feel a solid click as the lens locks into place.

3. **Insert the battery.**

   The battery compartment is on the bottom of the camera. When inserting the battery, hold it with the contacts down and the Canon imprint facing out (toward the side of the camera with the memory card cover). Gently push the battery in until the gray lock clicks into place.

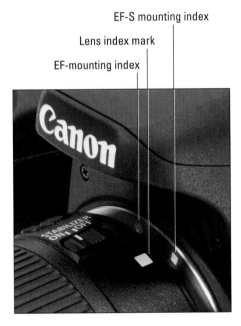

EF-S mounting index

Lens index mark

EF-mounting index

FIGURE 1-1:
Align the mounting index on the lens with the one on the camera body.

4. **Insert a memory card.**

   Open the memory card door and orient the card so that the notched corner is on top and the label faces the back of the camera, as shown in Figure 1-2. Push the card gently into the slot and close the card door.

   The memory-card access light (refer to Figure 1-2) blinks for few seconds to let you know that the camera recognizes the card. (The light appears even when the camera is turned off.)

REMEMBER

5. **Rotate the monitor to the desired viewing position.**

   When you first take the camera out of its box, the monitor is positioned with the screen facing inward, protecting it from scratches and smudges. Gently lift the right side of the monitor up and away from the camera back. You can then rotate the monitor to move it into the traditional position on the camera back, as shown on the left in Figure 1-3, or swing the monitor out to get a different viewing angle, as shown on the right.

Memory-card access light   Card slot

FIGURE 1-2:
Insert the memory card with the label facing the back of the camera.

FIGURE 1-3:
Here are just two possible monitor positions.

6. **Move the On/Off switch to the On position.**

   Okay, that's an odd way to say "Turn on the camera," right? Agreed, but there's good reason for it: This particular On/Off switch, shown in Figure 1-4, has three positions. When you rotate the switch to On, the camera comes to life and is ready to take still photos. When you move the switch one step further, to the movie camera symbol, the camera turns on and then sets itself to Movie mode. You can't take a still photograph in Movie mode; it's only good for recording video.

WARNING

It's easy to accidentally move the On/Off switch all the way to the Movie mode setting when you really want to take regular photos, so pay attention when turning the camera on until you get used to this arrangement. (One clue that you've rotated the switch too far is that the camera automatically engages Live View, which disables the viewfinder and presents a live preview of your subject on the camera monitor.)

7. **Set the language, time zone, and date.**

When you power up the camera for the first time, the monitor displays a screen asking you to set the date, time, and time zone. The easiest way to adjust these settings is to use the touch screen, which is enabled by default. Just tap an option to select it and then tap the up/down arrows at the bottom of the screen to set the value for that option. Finally, tap OK to exit the screen.

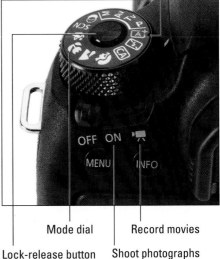

Scene Intelligent Auto exposure mode

Mode dial   Record movies

Lock-release button   Shoot photographs

FIGURE 1-4:
Rotate the switch to On to shoot photographs; move the switch one step further to set the camera to Movie mode.

You also can adjust settings by using the Set button and the four Quick Control keys surrounding it (these controls live just to the right of the monitor). Press the left/right keys to highlight a setting, press Set to activate the option, press the up/down keys to change the value, and press Set again to finalize the change.

TIP

The date/time information is included as *metadata* (hidden data) in the picture file. You can view metadata in some playback display modes (see Chapter 9) and in certain photo programs, including Canon Digital Photo Professional (see Chapter 10).

8. **Adjust the viewfinder to your eyesight.**

This step is critical; if you don't set the viewfinder to your eyesight, subjects that appear out of focus in the viewfinder might actually be in focus, and vice versa. If you wear glasses while shooting, adjust the viewfinder with your glasses on.

WARNING

You control viewfinder focus through the dial labeled in Figure 1-5. (In official lingo, it's called the *diopter adjustment dial*.) After taking off the lens cap, follow these steps:

1. *Look through the viewfinder, press the shutter button halfway, and then release it.*

   In dim lighting, the built-in flash may pop up; ignore it for now and concentrate on the lines that appear in the center of the frame and the row of data displayed at the bottom of the frame.

2. *Rotate the adjustment dial until the viewfinder markings and data appear sharpest.*

   Ignore the scene you see through the lens; that won't change because you're not actually focusing the camera. If the markings turn off before you finish making your adjustments, give the shutter button another quick half-press and release to redisplay them.

   Can't get the display sharp enough? You may need an adapter that enables further adjustment of the viewfinder. Look for an E-series dioptric adjustment lens adapter.

3. *If necessary, close the flash unit.*

Rotate to adjust viewfinder focus

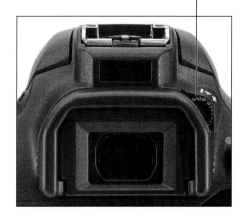

FIGURE 1-5:
Use this dial to adjust the viewfinder focus to your eyesight.

9. **Select an exposure mode by pressing and holding the lock-release button and rotating the Mode dial (refer to Figure 1-4).**

   The exposure mode determines how much control you have over various camera settings, as well as whether any special effects are applied. Chapter 2 explains the various exposure modes. For easiest operation, set the dial to Scene Intelligent Auto, as shown Figure 1-4. Be aware, though, that some camera features are available only in the four advanced shooting modes: P, Tv, Av, and M. The lock-release button is a handy feature that keeps you from accidentally turning the Mode dial when you aren't intending to.

That's all there is to it — the camera is now ready to go. The rest of this chapter familiarizes you with other major camera features and explains such basics as how to navigate menus, use the touch screen, and view and adjust camera settings.

REMEMBER

One more thing before you go: The official name for Canon's fully automatic exposure mode is Scene Intelligent Auto because, in this mode, the camera's brain analyzes the light and color information it picks up through the lens, consults an internal database to help it determine what type of scene you're shooting, and then adjusts picture settings as it deems necessary. In other words, Scene Intelligent Auto mode is intelligent enough to set up the camera to best capture the scene.

Exploring External Camera Features

Scattered across your camera's exterior are numerous features that you use to change picture-taking settings, review your photos, and perform various other operations. Later chapters explain how and when to use these tools; the following sections provide just a basic "What's this thing do?" introduction to them. (Don't worry about memorizing the button names; throughout the book, figures and margin symbols tell you exactly which button or switch to use.)

Topside controls

Your virtual tour begins on the top of the camera, shown in Figure 1-6.

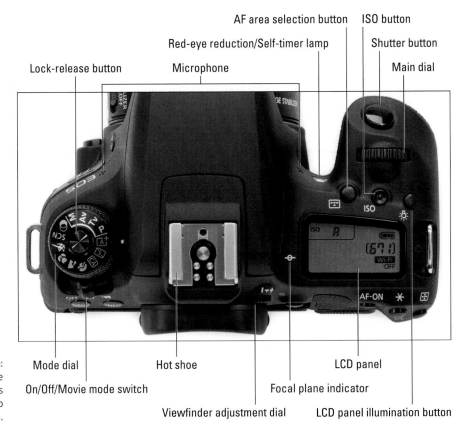

AF area selection button   ISO button

Red-eye reduction/Self-timer lamp   Shutter button

Lock-release button   Microphone   Main dial

FIGURE 1-6: Here's a guide to controls found on top of the camera.

Mode dial   Hot shoe   LCD panel

On/Off/Movie mode switch   Focal plane indicator

Viewfinder adjustment dial   LCD panel illumination button

Here are the items of note:

>> **On/Off/Movie mode switch:** As outlined in the preceding section, setting the switch to the movie-camera icon turns on the camera and sets it to Movie mode. Set the switch to On for still photography.

Even when the switch is in the On position, the camera automatically goes to sleep after a period of inactivity to save battery power. To wake the camera up, press the shutter button halfway and release it. See the section "Setup Menu 2" for help adjusting the timing of the automatic shutoff.

>> **Mode dial with lock-release button:** Press and hold the lock-release button in the center of the Mode dial, and then rotate the dial to select an *exposure mode,* which determines whether the camera operates in fully automatic, semi-automatic, or manual exposure mode when you take still pictures.

>> **Viewfinder adjustment dial:** Use this dial to adjust the viewfinder focus to your eyesight, as outlined in the preceding section.

>> **Main dial:** As its name implies, this dial is central to many camera functions, from scrolling through menus to changing certain shooting and playback settings.

TIP

On some camera screens, you see a symbol that resembles the top half of a dial that has notches around the edge. That's designed to remind you that you use the Main dial to adjust the setting.

>> **Red-Eye Reduction/Self-Timer Lamp:** When you set your flash to Red-Eye Reduction mode, this little lamp emits a brief burst of light prior to the real flash — the idea being that your subjects' pupils will constrict in response to the light, thus lessening the chances of red-eye. If you use the camera's self-timer feature, the lamp lights during the countdown period before the shutter is released. See Chapter 2 for more details about Red-Eye Reduction flash mode and the self-timer function.

>> **AF Area Selection button:** Press this button to access the AF Area Selection setting, which is related to autofocusing (see Chapter 5).

>> **ISO button:** True to its name, this button displays a screen where you can adjust the ISO setting, which determines how sensitive the camera is to light. Chapter 4 details this critical setting.

>> **LCD panel illumination button:** This button illuminates the top LCD panel with an amber backlight.

>> **Shutter button:** You no doubt already understand the function of this button, but you may not realize that when you use autofocus and

autoexposure, you need to use a two-stage process when taking a picture: Press the shutter button halfway, pause to let the camera set focus and exposure, and then press down the rest of the way to capture the image. You'd be surprised how many people mess up their pictures because they press that button with one quick jab, denying the camera the time it needs to set focus and exposure.

>> **Flash hot shoe:** This is the connection for attaching an external flash and other accessories such as flash adapters, bubble levels, flash brackets, off-camera flash cords, and the GP-E2 GPS Receiver.

TECHNICAL STUFF

>> **Focal plane indicator:** Should you need to know the exact distance between your subject and the camera, the *focal plane indicator*. This mark indicates the plane at which light coming through the lens is focused onto the camera's image sensor. Basing your measurement on this mark produces a more accurate camera-to-subject distance than using the end of the lens or some other point on the camera body as your reference point.

Back-of-the-body controls

Traveling over the top of the camera to its back, you encounter the smorgasbord of controls shown in Figure 1-7.

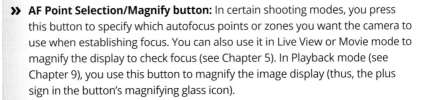

REMEMBER

Some buttons have multiple "official" names because they serve multiple purposes depending on whether you're taking pictures, reviewing images, recording a movie, or performing some other function. This book refers to these buttons by the first label you see in the following list (and in Figure 1-7) to simplify things. Again, though, the margin icons show you exactly which button you should press.

Starting at the top-right corner of the camera back and working westward (well, assuming that your lens is pointing north, anyway), here's an introduction to the buttons and other controls on this side of the camera:

>> **AF Point Selection/Magnify button:** In certain shooting modes, you press this button to specify which autofocus points or zones you want the camera to use when establishing focus. You can also use it in Live View or Movie mode to magnify the display to check focus (see Chapter 5). In Playback mode (see Chapter 9), you use this button to magnify the image display (thus, the plus sign in the button's magnifying glass icon).

>> **AE Lock/FE Lock/Index/Reduce button:** During shooting, press this button to lock autoexposure (AE) settings (see Chapter 4) and to lock flash exposure (FE), a feature detailed in Chapter 2.

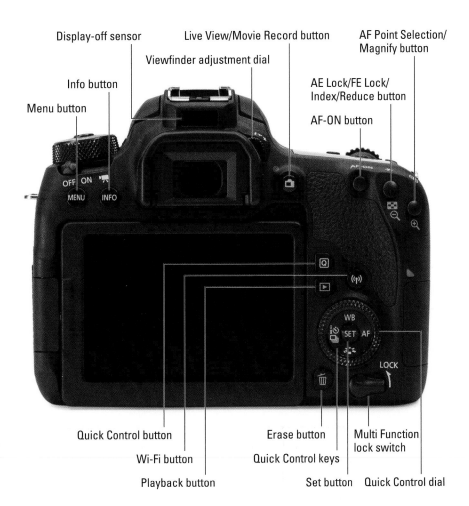

FIGURE 1-7:
Having lots of external buttons makes accessing the camera's functions easier.

This button also serves two image-viewing functions: It switches the display to Index mode, enabling you to see multiple image thumbnails at once. And if you magnify a photo, pressing the button reduces the magnification level.

» **AF-ON button:** Just like pressing the shutter button halfway, pressing this button initiates autofocus. See Chapter 5 for more information on focusing.

» **Live View/Movie button:** Press this button to shift to Live View mode, which enables you to compose your pictures using the monitor instead of the viewfinder. When shooting movies, press the button to start and stop recording. (You must first set the On/Off/Movie switch to the Movie position.)

» **Q (Quick Control) button:** Press this button to shift to Quick Control mode, which enables you to adjust major shooting settings quickly. See "Using Quick Control Mode," later in this chapter, for help.

» **Wi-Fi button:** Pressing this button enables certain wireless communication features. See the appendix for an explanation of Wi-Fi operations.

» **Playback button:** Press this button to switch the camera into picture-review mode.

» **Memory card access light:** This light glows while the camera is recording data to the memory card. Don't power off the camera while the light is lit, or you may damage the card or camera.

» **Set button and Quick Control keys:** The Set button and the four-way directional pad with buttons, known as *Quick Control keys,* team up to perform several functions, including choosing options from the camera menus. You use the Quick Control keys to navigate through menus and then press the Set button to select a specific menu setting.

REMEMBER

In this book, the instruction "Press the left Quick Control key" means to press the one to the left of the Set button; "press the right Quick Control key" means to press the one to the right of the Set button, and so on.

During viewfinder photography — that is, when you're using the viewfinder and not the monitor to frame your shots — the Quick Control keys also have individual responsibilities, which are indicated by their labels:

- *Press the up key to change the White Balance setting.* The White Balance control, explained in Chapter 6, enables you to ensure that colors are rendered accurately.

- *Press the right key to adjust the AF Operation mode.* This option controls one aspect of the camera's autofocus behavior, as outlined in Chapter 5.

- *Press the left key to change the Drive mode.* The Drive mode settings enable you to switch the camera from single-frame shooting to continuous capture or any of the other drive modes, including remote shooting. See Chapter 2 for details.

- *Press the down key to change the Picture Style.* Chapter 6 explains Picture Styles, which you can use to adjust the color, contrast, and sharpness of your pictures.

For Live View and Movie shooting, the Quick Control keys perform different actions. See Chapter 5 for help.

» **Quick Control dial:** The Quick Control dial surrounds the Set button and the Quick Control keys. Rotating the dial offers a handy way to quickly scroll through options and settings. It's a timesaver, so we point out when to use it as we provide instructions throughout the book.

» **Erase button:** Sporting a trash can icon, the universal symbol for delete, this button lets you erase pictures from your memory card during playback. Chapter 9 has specifics.

>> **Multi Function Lock switch:** You can rotate this switch up, in the direction of the arrow, to lock the Quick Control dial so that you don't accidentally move the dial and change a camera setting that you aren't intending to modify. If you want an even larger safety net, you can set things up so that the switch also locks the Main dial and the touch screen (when shooting). The section "Setup Menu 4," toward the end of this chapter, has details.

>> **Display-off sensor:** This handy gizmo senses when you bring your eye up to the viewfinder and turns the LCD monitor off so that the glare from the display doesn't bother you. When you pull your eye back, the LCD monitor comes back on.

>> **Info button:** In Live View, Movie, and Playback modes, pressing this button changes the picture-display style.

During viewfinder photography, you can press the Info button to toggle the display off or cycle between the Quick Control screen and electronic level. (These displays are explained later in this chapter.)

>> **Menu button:** Press this button to display camera menus; press a second time to exit the menus. See the upcoming section "Ordering from Camera Menus" for help navigating menus.

And the rest . . .

The remaining external features of note are shown in Figure 1–8 and described in the following list.

>> **Wireless remote-control sensor:** This sensor can pick up the signal from the optional Canon wireless remote-control unit. The part number is Canon RC-6, and sells for about $20.

You also have two other wireless remote-control options: If you have a smartphone or tablet that can run the Canon Connect app, you can use that device as a wireless remote. The appendix provides more information. Alternatively, you can buy the Canon Wireless Remote Control BR-E1 (about $50), which connects to your camera via Bluetooth, also detailed in the appendix. We bring them up now because unlike the RC-6 unit, these two tools don't need to be aimed at the camera's remote-control sensor to work.

>> **Lens-release button:** Press this button to disengage the lens from the lens mount so that you can remove it from the camera. While pressing the button, rotate the lens toward the shutter-button side of the camera to dismount the lens.

>> **Flash button:** Press this button to raise the built-in flash in the advanced exposure modes (P, Tv, Av, and M).

Digital terminal/HDMI port cover

Lens-release button   Left microphone

Wireless remote-control sensor   Flash button   Speaker

Depth-of-field Preview button   NFC antenna

Remote control/Microphone port cover

>> **Microphone:** You can record movie audio via the built-in microphone, which picks up sound from the two clusters of holes, one of which is labeled Microphone in Figure 1-8.

>> **Depth-of-Field Preview button:** When you press this button, the image in the viewfinder (or, in Live View mode, on the monitor) offers an approximation of the depth of field that will result from your selected aperture setting, or f-stop. *Depth of field* refers to the distance over which the scene appears to be in focus. Chapter 5 provides details.

>> **Speaker:** When you play a movie that contains audio, the sound comes wafting through these little holes.

>> **Connection ports:** Hidden under two covers on the left side of the camera, you find inputs for connecting the camera to various devices. Open the smaller cover to access the connections for a wired remote control or external

microphone. Under the larger door, you find a digital terminal for connecting the camera to your computer via USB and an HDMI out port that sends the signal from your camera to an HDMI TV. To use either feature, you need to purchase a cable to make the connection. For USB downloading, check the Canon website for the cables that will do the trick. For HDMI output, you can use any HD cable that has a Type-C connection on one end (the end that goes into the camera).

See Chapter 8 for help with displaying images on an HD television; Chapter 9 explains how to connect the camera via USB in order to download pictures to your computer. (Spoiler alert: Downloading via USB is probably not your cheapest or easiest option; instead, consider using a memory-card reader or taking advantage of wireless transfer.)

If you turn the camera over, you find a tripod socket, which enables you to mount the camera on a tripod that uses a ¼-inch screw, plus the chamber that holds the battery, as well as a connection port for attaching a Canon power adapter. See the camera manual for specifics on running the camera on AC power.

Changing from Standard to Guided Display Mode

By default, your camera is set to *Standard Display Mode.* Alternatively, you can set the camera to provide information to you in a *Guided Display Mode.* In this mode, designed for novices, camera screens are simplified and offer explanations and feedback when you adjust certain settings.

For example, the left side of Figure 1-9 shows the display when Tv exposure mode (shutter-priority auto-exposure) is selected. Likewise, the right side shows the guided menu with the Shooting settings menu selected.

FIGURE 1-9: In Guided Display and Menu modes, the camera offers simplified details about the feature you're currently using.

Guided mode is fine for users who need more of a helping hand than the standard screens provide. But assuming that you bought this book because you want to learn more about your camera and master the ins and outs of photography, you don't fall into that category. Standard mode is a better choice, for several reasons:

>> Although the Guided screens make understanding some options easier, in many cases, they can be just as baffling as the Standard screens.

>> The Guided screens often focus on one particular aspect of a camera setting without explaining how that setting affects other characteristics of your picture. When you change the shutter speed, for example, the camera has to make adjustments to one or two other critical settings — aperture and/or ISO — in order to properly expose the picture. Those settings, detailed along with shutter speed in Chapter 4, have their own impact on the look of your picture.

>> Standard mode also saves you some steps as you make certain camera adjustments.

>> The Guided screens limit your access to many shooting settings. In addition, when you use Guided mode, you can't access the My Menu feature, which enables you to create a custom menu that contains the menu options you use most.

>> Most other Canon dSLRs don't offer Guided mode, so if you're moving to the 77D from a previous Canon model that used standard displays, using Guided mode requires you to do unnecessary retraining. If you step up to a more advanced Canon model in the future, you also likely won't have the option to use Guided mode.

For these reasons, figures and instructions from this point forward relate to using the camera in the Standard mode instead of Guided mode.

If you want to experiment, navigate to the Display Level menu and play around with different settings. The Shooting screen and Menu display are set to Standard by default, as shown on the left in Figure 1-10. The Mode and Feature guides are enabled by default, as shown in the figure. To change settings, select the setting you want to change, tap OK or press the Set button, and then highlight a new option, as shown on the right in Figure 1-10. Tap OK or press Set to make the change.

We leave it up to you whether to disable these features. After you're familiar with the various exposure modes and camera settings, they simply slow you down, so we keep them off. But if you find them helpful, by all means leave them set to Enable. Just remember that instructions from here on out won't mention them.

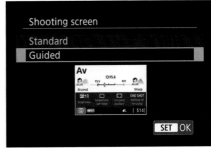

FIGURE 1-10:
Choose the
Display Mode
Settings menu
tab to turn the
Guided mode
features on
or off.

Ordering from Camera Menus

Although you can adjust some settings by using external controls, you access the majority of options via camera menus. The next section provides the basics you need to know to navigate menus and select menu options. Following that, you can find out how to deal with a special category of menu screens, the Custom Functions.

Again, figures from this point forward show menus as they appear in Standard mode. See the preceding section if you need help switching from Guided to Standard menu display.

Mastering menu basics

Here's how to display menus and adjust the options on those menus:

>> **Opening and closing menus:** Press the Menu button to display the menus; press again to exit the menu system and return to shooting. You also can just press the shutter button halfway and release it to exit to shooting mode.

>> **Understanding menu screens:** Which menus and menu screens appear depends on the exposure mode, which you set by rotating the Mode dial on top of the camera. Things also change when you switch from still photography to Movie mode, which you accomplish by rotating the On/Off switch to the movie-camera symbol. Figure 1-11 shows a menu screen as it appears for normal photography in the advanced exposure modes (P, Tv, Av, and M).

However, the following menu elements are common to all exposure modes:

● *Menu icons:* Along the top of the screen, you see icons representing individual menus. In the advanced exposure modes, you get the five menus labeled in Figure 1-11: Shooting, Playback, Setup, Display Level Settings, and My Menu. The My Menu feature, which enables you to build a custom menu, isn't available in other exposure modes.

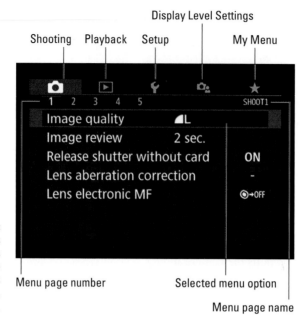

Display Level Settings

Shooting   Playback   Setup   My Menu

Image quality	◢L
Image review	2 sec.
Release shutter without card	ON
Lens aberration correction	-
Lens electronic MF	⊙→OFF

FIGURE 1-11:
You can access all menus only when the Mode dial is set to P, Tv, Av, or M.

Menu page number   Selected menu option

Menu page name

REMEMBER

- *Menu page numbers:* Some menus are multi-page (sometimes called tabs) affairs. The numbers under the menu icons represent the various pages of the current menu.

- This book takes the same approach to page references as the Canon instruction manual: *Shooting Menu 1* refers to page one of the Shooting menu, *Shooting Menu 2* to page 2, and so on. How many pages appear for each menu depends, again, on the exposure mode and whether the camera is set to still photography or Movie mode.

The highlighted menu icon marks the active menu; options on that menu appear automatically on the main part of the screen. In Figure 1-11, Shooting Menu 1 is active, for example.

» **Selecting a menu or menu page:** You have these options:

- *Touch screen:* Tap the menu icon to select that menu; tap a page number to display that page.

- *Quick Control keys or Main dial:* Press the right or left cross keys or rotate the Main dial to scroll through the menu icons. If you use this technique, you have to scroll through all pages of a menu to get to the neighboring menu.

- *Q button:* Press the Q button to cycle through menu icons.

TIP

As you scroll through the menus, notice the color coding: Red for the Shooting menu, blue for the Playback menu; orangey-yellow (ochre?) for the Setup menu, teal for Display Level Settings; and green for My Menu.

>> Select and adjust a menu setting: Again, you have a choice of techniques:

- *Touch screen:* Tap the menu item to display options for that setting. The current setting is highlighted; tap another setting to select it. On some screens, you see a Set icon; if it appears, tap that icon to lock in your selection and exit the settings screen.

- *Quick Control dial, Quick Control keys, and Set button:* Rotate the Quick Control dial or press the up or down Quick Control keys to highlight the menu setting and then press the Set button to display the available options for that setting. In most cases, you then use the Quick Control dial to highlight the desired option and press Set again. If you prefer, use the cross keys to highlight your preferred setting before pressing the Set button.

TIP

You can mix and match techniques, by the way: For example, even if you access a menu option via the control keys, you can use the touch-screen techniques to select a setting.

Instructions from this point forward assume that you don't need to be told the specifics of how to select menus and menu options at every turn. So instead of stepping you through each button press or touch-screen tap required to adjust a setting, instructions simply say something like "Choose Image Quality from Shooting Menu 1." If choosing a menu option involves any special steps, however, instructions offer guidance.

Navigating Custom Functions

Custom Functions are a group of advanced settings available only in the P, Tv, Av, and M exposure modes. (*Remember:* You set the exposure mode via the Mode dial on top of the camera.)

To explore Custom Functions, choose that item from Setup Menu 4, as shown on the left in Figure 1-12. You then see the options screen for a specific Custom Function, as shown on the right in the figure. Here's a guide to using the Custom Function screens, which work a little differently from other menu screens:

FIGURE 1-12:
Choose Custom Functions from Setup Menu 4 to access additional customization options.

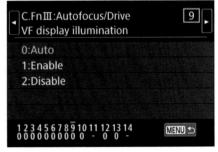

» **Interpreting the screens:** The Custom Functions screens are a little intimidating until you know what's what:

- *Custom Functions are grouped into four categories: Exposure, Image, Autofocus/Drive, and Operation/Others.* The category number and name appear in the upper-left corner of the screen. In Figure 1-12, for example, the label indicates that you're looking at a screen from the Autofocus/Drive category. (C.Fn III refers to Custom Functions group three.)

- *The number of the selected function appears in the upper-right corner.* Custom Function 9 is shown in Figure 1-12.

- *Settings for the current function appear in the middle of the screen.* Blue text indicates the current setting. The default setting is represented by the number 0. So in Figure 1-12, Auto is selected and is the default setting.

- *Numbers at the bottom of the screen show you the current setting for all Custom Functions.* The top row of numbers represents the Custom Functions, with the currently selected function indicated with a tiny horizontal bar over the number (9, in the figure). The lower row shows the number of the current setting for each Custom Function; again, 0 represents the default.

  For Custom Function 11, you instead see a dash, which is Canon's way of letting you know that this menu option controls more than one camera setting (thus, there isn't one single default setting).

» **Scrolling from one Custom Function to the next:** Use the Quick Control dial or press the left or right Quick Control keys or tap the left or right scroll arrows at the top of the screen. You can see the arrows in the right screen in Figure 1-12.

» **Changing the setting:** You first must activate the menu by pressing the Set button or tapping one of the available setting options. The screen then changes to look similar to the one shown on the left in Figure 1-13, with the currently selected option highlighted. To select a different option, highlight it by tapping it or pressing the up or down cross keys.

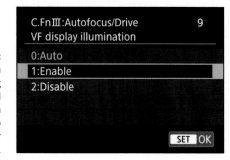
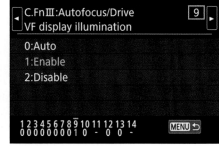

FIGURE 1-13: After you select a setting (left), the initial menu screen updates to reflect your choice (right).

To lock in your setting and deactivate the settings screen, tap the Set icon or press the Set button. The screen returns to its inactive state, as shown on the right in Figure 1-13, with the setting you selected appearing in blue and the row of digits at the bottom of the screen reflecting the number for that setting. Again, a blue number indicates that you chose a setting other than the default.

>> **Exiting the Custom Functions submenu:** Tap the Menu icon in the lower-right corner of the screen) or press the Menu button. Press Menu again to exit the menu system entirely and return to shooting.

Customizing the Touch Screen

Your camera's touch screen works much like the ones found on smartphones and other touch-based devices. When the touch screen is enabled, as it is by default, you can simply touch the monitor to choose menu commands, change picture settings, scroll through your pictures, and more.

How you touch the screen depends on the task at hand. Here's a rundown of the names assigned to various touch-screen moves, or *gestures:*

>> **Tap:** Tap a finger on the monitor. (Figures and instructions throughout the book indicate exactly where to tap.)

>> **Drag:** Using light pressure, drag your finger across the screen. On some menu screens, for example, you can drag up or down to scroll through a list of options.

>> **Swipe:** Drag one or two fingers quickly across the screen. You use this gesture, known in some circles as a *flick,* to scroll through your pictures in Playback mode, just as you do when showing off your photos on a smartphone.

>> **Pinch in/pinch out:** To pinch in, place your thumb at one edge of the screen and your pointer finger at the other. Then drag both toward the center of the screen. To pinch out, start in the center of the screen and swipe both fingers outward. Pinching is how you zoom in and out on pictures during playback.

TIP

You can customize two aspects of touch-screen behavior:

>> **Adjust (or disable) the touch-screen response:** You can choose from three settings, accessed via the Touch Control option, found on Setup Menu 3 and shown in Figure 1-14. Standard is the default, setting the screen to respond to a "normal" amount of pressure. Don't ask how the Powers That Be decided what that pressure level is — just know that if your normal pressure doesn't

evoke a response, you can change the setting from Standard to Sensitive. Choose Disable to make the touch screen totally inactive.

» **Silence the touch screen:** By default, the touch screen emits a tiny "boop" with every tap. If you find that annoying, choose the Beep option, found just beneath the Touch Control option on Setup Menu 3. The option that keeps the boop silent is Touch to Silence — silence indicated by a little speaker

FIGURE 1-14:
Control the touch-screen response through this menu item.

with a slash through it. The Disable setting turns off both touch-screen sounds and the beep the camera emits when focus is achieved.

TIP

CARING FOR THE CAMERA MONITOR

To keep the monitor in good working order, follow these precautions:

- **Don't use force when adjusting the monitor position.** Although the monitor assembly is sturdy, treat it with respect as you adjust the screen position. The monitor twists only in certain directions, and it's easy to forget which way it's supposed to move. So, if you feel resistance, don't force things — you could break the monitor. Instead, rely on that feeling of resistance to remind you to turn the screen the other way.

- **Use only your finger to perform touch-screen functions.** Use the fleshy part of your fingertip, not the nail or any other sharp object, and be sure that your fingers are dry because the screen may not respond if it gets wet.

- **Don't apply a screen protector.** Canon also advises against putting a protective cover over the monitor, such as the kind people adhere to their smartphones. Doing so can reduce the monitor's responsiveness to your touch.

- **Watch the crunch factor.** Before positioning the monitor back into the camera (whether face in or face out), use a lens brush or soft cloth to clean the back of the camera where the monitor folds in so there's nothing on it that could damage the monitor.

- **Clean smart.** To clean the screen, use only the special cloths and cleaning solutions made for this purpose. (You can find them in any camera store.) Do not use paper products such as paper towels because they can contain wood fibers that can scratch the monitor. And never use a can of compressed air to blow dust off the camera — the air is cold and can crack the monitor.

Viewing Shooting Settings

Your camera offers several displays that present the current picture-taking settings. The next sections explain the displays that are available during viewfinder photography. See the later section "Switching to Live View Mode" for information about displaying similar data when you use Live View, the feature that enables you to compose photos on the monitor instead of through the viewfinder.

REMEMBER

For still photography, you can use either the viewfinder or the Live View screen to compose your shots. But when you set the camera to Movie mode, you're limited to Live View.

Displaying the Quick Control screen

Shown in Figure 1-15, the Quick Control screen appears on the monitor when the camera is in shooting mode — that is, when you're not viewing menus, checking out your pictures in Playback mode, and so on. The screen displays different data depending on your exposure mode and whether features such as flash are enabled. The left side of Figure 1-15 shows the screen as it appears in Scene Intelligent Auto exposure mode; the right side, Tv mode (shutter-priority auto-exposure).

FIGURE 1-15: The data displayed on the Quick Control screen depends on your exposure mode.

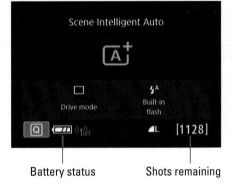

Battery status   Shots remaining

TIP

Here are the keys to taking advantage of this screen:

>> **Display and hide the Quick Control screen.** By default, the screen appears automatically when you turn on the camera and then turns off if no camera operations are performed for 30 seconds. You can turn the display on again by pressing the shutter button halfway and then releasing it. To turn off the display before the automatic shutoff occurs, press the Info button (on the back of the camera, just below the power switch). Press the Info button twice to cycle back to the Quick Control screen.

TIP

You can adjust the timing of the automatic shutdown of this screen and others via the Auto Power Off option on Setup Menu 2. We provide the details near the end of this chapter, in the section devoted to that menu.

>> **Keep an eye on the battery symbol and the shots remaining value.** A full battery like the one in the figure means that the battery is charged; as it runs out of power, bars disappear from the symbol. The shots remaining value indicates how many more pictures will fit in the free space available on your memory card. This value depends in large part on the Image Quality setting, which determines the resolution (pixel count) and file type (Raw or JPEG). If those terms are new to you, the next chapter explains them.

>> **You can replace the Quick Control screen with an electronic level by pressing the Info button.** This feature is useful when you use a tripod and want to ensure that the camera is level to the horizon. When the horizontal line appears green, as shown in Figure 1-16, you're good to go. Press Info again to return to the Quick Control screen. You can enable or disable the level and Quick Control screen from Setup Menu 3, as described in the Setup Menu 3 section later in this chapter.

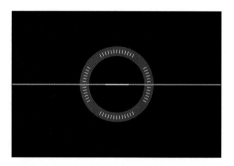

FIGURE 1-16:
Press the Info button to toggle between the Quick Control display and an electronic level.

Decoding viewfinder data

A limited assortment of shooting data, such as the shutter speed and f-stop, appears at the bottom of the viewfinder, as shown in Figure 1-17. In the framing area of the viewfinder, you may see marks that indicate the portion of the screen that contains autofocusing points. (The appearance of the autofocus markings depend on your autofocus settings, which you can explore in Chapter 5.) In the first screen in the figure, the four black brackets represent the autofocusing area.

In the following sections, we walk you through how to display and customize the viewfinder.

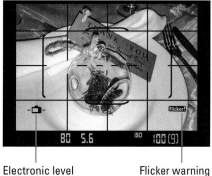

FIGURE 1-17: The default viewfinder display (left) can be customized to include a grid, electronic level, and flicker warning (right).

Electronic level   Flicker warning

Displaying viewfinder data

The markings in the framing area of the viewfinder appear automatically when you first turn on the camera; to display the shooting data, you must press the shutter button halfway. The display remains active for a few seconds after you release the button, and then the viewfinder display data shuts off to save battery power. To wake up the display, press the shutter button halfway and release it.

Adding a level and gridlines to the display

You can display gridlines in the viewfinder, as shown on the right in Figure 1-17, as well as a symbol that represents the electronic level. (When the lines at the sides of the symbol are horizontal, as in the figure, the camera is level.)

To hide or display these features, open Setup Menu 2 and choose Viewfinder Display. On the next screen, change the settings from Hide to Show. As you select each option, a preview appears at the bottom of the screen to remind you how enabling the feature affects the display.

Displaying a flicker-detection warning

When the Mode dial is set to an advanced exposure mode (P, Tv, Av, or M), the Viewfinder Display option offers a third setting, Flicker Detection. When the camera detects light sources that are blinking, which can mess up exposure and color, the word *Flicker!* appears in the area labeled in Figure 1-17. The biggest offenders are tubular fluorescent bulbs, which blink on and off so quickly that it's difficult for the human eye to detect them. When you see this warning, you may want to enable the Anti-flicker Shoot option on the Shooting Menu. This feature, covered in Chapter 4, also is available only in the advanced exposure modes.

Noting the number in brackets

The number in brackets does not represent the shots-remaining value, as it does in the Quick Control screen. Instead, that number — 9, in Figure 1-17 — represents the number of *maximum number of burst frames*. This number relates to shooting in the Continuous capture mode, where the camera fires off multiple shots in rapid succession as long as you hold down the shutter button. (Chapter 2 has details.) Although the highest number that the viewfinder can display is 9, the actual number of maximum burst frames may be higher. At any rate, you don't really need to pay attention to the number until it starts dropping toward 0, which indicates that the camera's *memory buffer* (its temporary internal data-storage tank) is filling up. If that happens, just give the camera a moment to catch up with your shutter-button finger.

REMEMBER

The maximum burst frames value also makes an appearance in the Quick Control screen, but only if the value drops to 9 or below. In that case, you see a single digit — not presented inside brackets — directly to the left of the shots-remaining value. The good news is that you rarely need to even worry about this number; we just bring it up so you don't scratch your head wondering what that value means when you see it on either display.

Reading the LCD panel

Another way to keep track of shooting information is through the LCD panel on top of the camera, shown in Figure 1-18. Don't see any data in the panel? The camera is probably in sleep mode; give the shutter button a half-press to wake it up.

As with the viewfinder and Shooting Settings display, the panel shows you the shots remaining value and battery status, as labeled in Figure 1-18. One other critical setting is also present: the status of the camera's built-in Wi-Fi feature. By default, it's turned off, as indicated in the figure.

Battery status

Shots remaining

Wi-Fi status

FIGURE 1-18:
The top LCD panel is another useful situational awareness tool.

REMEMBER

In dim lighting, you can press the little light bulb button above the right corner of the display to illuminate the panel. If you take a picture in B (Bulb) mode, the panel won't illuminate while the shutter button is down, however.

Switching to Live View Mode

Like most dSLRs sold today, your camera offers *Live View*, which disables the view-finder and instead displays a live preview of your subject on the camera monitor. The following list explains the basics of using Live View:

» **Switching to Live View for photography:** Press the Live View button, labeled in Figure 1-19, to shift from viewfinder shooting to Live View mode. You hear a clicking noise and then the viewfinder goes dark and the monitor displays the live scene. By default, some shooting data appears as well, with the amount and type of information varying depending on your exposure mode and a few other settings. The figure shows the display as it appears in the Scene Intelligent Auto exposure mode when the default picture-taking settings are used for that mode.

Live View/Movie Record button

FIGURE 1-19: In Live View mode, a live preview of your subject appears on the monitor, and the viewfinder is disabled.

TIP

The Live View button requires a firm push to turn the feature on and off. If nothing happens after one or two button presses, you may need to reset the Live View Shoot menu option to Enable. This is the default setting, but it's possible you or another user changed the setting to Disable at some point.

Where you find the Live View Shoot option depends on your exposure mode; in the advanced modes (P, Tv, Av, and M), go to Shooting Menu 5, as shown on the left in Figure 1-20. In other exposure modes, the option lives on Shooting Menu 1, as shown on the right.

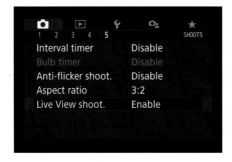
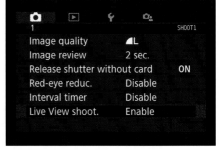

FIGURE 1-20:
To use Live View, make sure this menu option is set to Enable.

Why would Canon give you the option to disable Live View functionality? Because it's easy to accidentally press the Live View button and switch to that mode when you don't really want to go there.

» **Engaging Live View for movie recording:** For movie recording, simply moving the On/Off switch to the Movie mode setting, represented by the movie-camera symbol, engages Live View. You can't use the viewfinder in Movie mode, so the setting of the Live View Shoot menu option has no impact.

In Movie mode, pressing the Live View button starts and stops recording. To exit Movie mode, move the On/Off switch to On if you want to begin shooting stills or to Off if you're done shooting.

In many ways, shooting photos in Live View mode is the same as for viewfinder photography, but some important aspects, such as autofocusing, work very differently. Chapter 3 shows you how to take a picture in Scene Intelligent Auto exposure mode using Live View; Chapter 8 covers movie recording. Other chapters mention Live View variations related to specific picture-taking options.

Customizing the Live View display

By default, the Live View display offers the data shown on the left in Figure 1-21 when you're taking photographs; in Movie mode, the default display appears as shown on the right. Black bars appear at the top and bottom of the movie display to indicate the boundaries of the 16:9 movie frame. As is the case with other information displays, the type and amount of data that appears depends on your exposure mode and whether the camera is set to take still photos or shoot movies.

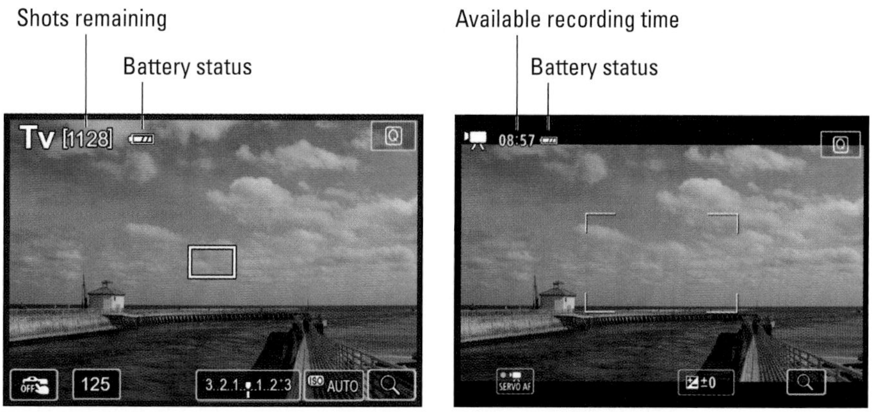

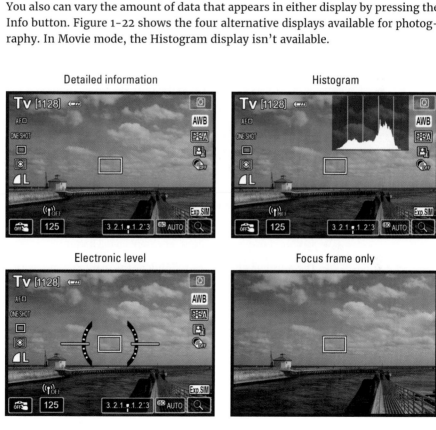

FIGURE 1-21: Here's a look at the default Live View display for photography (left) and movie recording (right).

Shots remaining

Battery status

Available recording time

Battery status

You also can vary the amount of data that appears in either display by pressing the Info button. Figure 1-22 shows the four alternative displays available for photography. In Movie mode, the Histogram display isn't available.

Detailed information

Histogram

Electronic level

Focus frame only

FIGURE 1-22: Press the Info button to change the type of data that appears during Live View shooting.

Additionally, you can add one of three grids to your screen, which can be helpful when checking alignment of objects in the frame. To enable or hide the grid, open the Shooting Menu and look for the Grid Display option, featured in Figure 1-23.

As with other menu options, where you find this one depends on your exposure mode: In P, Tv, Av, and M modes, the option lives on Shooting Menu 6, as shown in the figure. In other still photography modes, it's found on Shooting Menu 2; in Movie mode, Shooting Menu 2.

FIGURE 1-23:
Through this option, you can add one of three alignment grids to the screen.

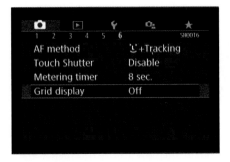

Although the various symbols and numbers on the displays won't make much sense until you explore the rest of the book, here are a few details that may give you a basic understanding of some of the common symbols:

TECHNICAL STUFF

>> **The white box or corner markings represent the autofocusing frame.** The appearance of the frame depends on the AF Method, which Chapter 5 explains. At the default setting, Face Priority + Tracking, the frame appears as you see on the right in Figure 1-24. In Live One-Point AF mode, the frame looks like the one on the left in Figure 1-21; in Smooth Zone mode, the frame appears as shown on the right in the same figure.

>> **Check the areas labeled in Figure 1-21 to view the battery status.** The symbol shown in the figure represents a full battery.

>> **The number of shots remaining or the available movie recording time appears next to the battery symbol.** Again, Figure 1-21 shows you where to look.

>> **You can't display the Electronic Level when the camera is set to the default AF Method setting (Face + Tracking).** To display the level, you must switch to Live One-Point AF or Smooth Zone mode. (You can do so via the Quick Control screen, as outlined a little later in this chapter.)

>> **The chart that appears in the histogram display (upper-right screen in Figure 1-22) is a tool you can use to gauge exposure.** See the discussion on interpreting a Brightness histogram in Chapter 9 to find out how to make sense of what you see. But note that when you use flash, the histogram is dimmed. The histogram can't display accurate information because the final exposure will include light from the flash and not just the ambient lighting.

In addition, the histogram dims when you use M (Manual) exposure mode and set the shutter speed to B (Bulb), which keeps the shutter open for as long as you hold down the shutter button. The camera can't predict how long you're going to hold that button down, so it can't create a histogram that will reflect your final exposure.

» **Also note the *Exposure Simulation* symbol that appears in the first three displays in Figure 1-22.** (Look in the lower-right corner of the frame.) This symbol indicates whether the monitor is simulating the actual exposure that you'll record. If the symbol blinks or is dimmed, the camera can't provide an accurate exposure preview, which can occur if the ambient light is either very bright or very dim. Exposure Simulation is also disabled when you use flash.

Staying safe with Live View

Take the following precautions when you use Live View and Movie modes:

» **Cover the viewfinder to prevent light from seeping into the camera and affecting exposure.** The camera ships with a cover designed just for this purpose. In fact, it's conveniently attached to the camera strap. To install it, first remove the rubber eyecup that surrounds the viewfinder by sliding it up and out of the groove that holds it in place. Then slide the cover down into the groove and over the viewfinder (Orient the cover so that the Canon label faces the viewfinder).

» **Using Live View or Movie mode for an extended period can harm your pictures and the camera.** Using the monitor full-time causes the camera's innards to heat up more than usual, and that extra heat can create the right conditions for noise, a defect that looks like speckles of sand. More critically, the increased temperatures can damage the camera.

» **A thermometer symbol appears on the monitor to warn you when the camera is getting too hot.** Initially, the symbol is white. If you continue shooting and the temperature continues to increase, the symbol turns red and blinks, alerting you that the camera soon will shut off automatically.

» **Aiming the lens at the sun or other bright lights also can damage the camera.** Of course, you can cause problems doing this even during normal shooting, but the possibilities increase when you use Live View and Movie modes.

» **Live View and Movie modes put additional strain on the camera battery.** The extra juice is needed to power the monitor for extended periods of time. If you do a lot of Live View or movie shooting, you may want to invest in a second battery so that you have a spare on hand when the first one runs out of gas.

Using Quick Control Mode

Earlier in this chapter, the section "Viewing Shooting Settings" introduces the Quick Control screen, which displays current picture settings when you use the viewfinder to compose pictures. Because digital photography isn't confusing enough, the 77D also offers Quick Control *mode,* which enables you to change certain settings without using the function buttons (the ISO button, Exposure Compensation button, and so on) or menus.

REMEMBER

Although the name implies that Quick Control mode is specific to the Quick Control screen, you can take advantage of this feature for Live View still photography and movie recording as well. Here's how it works:

1. Display the Quick Control or Live View screen.

If the monitor is asleep or the screen is showing menus or your existing photos, press the shutter button halfway and release it to redisplay the Quick Control or Live View screen. Figure 1-24 shows the default photography screens as they appear in the Scene Intelligent Auto exposure mode.

Tap to enter Quick Control mode

FIGURE 1-24:
To activate
Quick Control
mode, tap
the Q symbol
or press the
Q button.

Tap to enter Quick Control mode

2. Press the Q button or tap the Q icon to enter Quick Control mode.

If you're using the viewfinder to take pictures, the display changes to look similar to the one shown on the left in Figure 1-25. In Live View mode, the display appears as shown on the left in Figure 1-26.

3. Select the setting you want to adjust.

The currently selected setting is highlighted; in the figures, the Drive mode is active, for example. To choose a different setting, tap it or use the left/right Quick Control keys to highlight it.

FIGURE 1-25:
After highlighting the setting you want to adjust, rotate the Quick Control dial or Main dial to cycle through the available options (left) or press the Set button to display all options on a single screen (right).

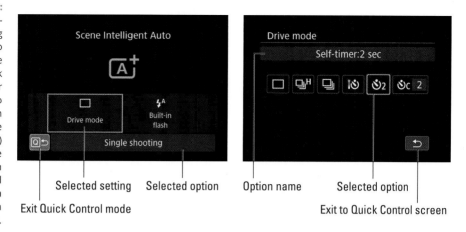

Selected setting   Selected option   Option name   Selected option

Exit Quick Control mode   Exit to Quick Control screen

FIGURE 1-26:
In Live View mode, tap or use the up/down Quick Control keys to highlight the setting you want to adjust, and then tap, use the left/right Quick Control keys, or rotate the Quick Control or Main dial to choose your desired option.

Selected setting   Setting name   Exit arrow   Option name

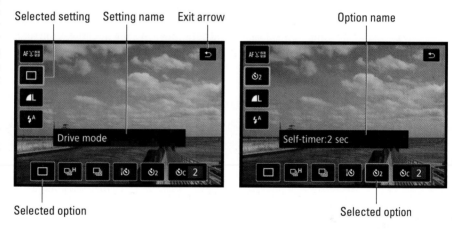

Selected option   Selected option

On the Quick Control screen, the name of the currently selected option for the setting appears at the bottom of the screen, as shown on the left in Figure 1-25. In Live View mode (refer to Figure 1-26), the text banner initially shows the name of the setting you're changing, with icons at the bottom of the screen representing the available options. The one surrounded by the orange box is the currently selected option.

4. **Rotate the Quick Control dial or Main dial to cycle through the available options for the setting.**

   As soon as you rotate the dial, the text label on the Quick Control screen updates to reflect the name of the each setting. And on the Live View screen, the name of the setting you're adjusting is replaced by the name of the selected option. In the right screen in Figure 1-26, for example, you can see how things look when you change the Drive mode from Single Frame to the 2-second Self-Timer option. (Chapter 2 explains these and other Drive mode options.)

TIP

During viewfinder photography, you can also tap the setting icon or press the Set button to display all the available options on a single screen, as shown on the right in Figure 1-25. Tap, use the left/right Quick Control keys, or rotate the Quick Control dial or Main dial to highlight the option you want to use, and then tap the exit arrow to exit the settings screen. (In Live View mode, tapping the icon on the sides of the screen simply selects the option represented by that symbol.)

5. **Repeat Steps 3 and 4 as needed to adjust other settings.**

6. **To exit Quick Control mode, press the Q button.**

In Live View mode, you also can tap the exit arrow in the upper-right corner of the screen.

TIP

A couple of final tips about taking advantage of Quick Control mode:

>> For some settings, the Live View preview updates to show the result of your choice. If you adjust the White Balance setting, which affects how colors are rendered, you see colors shift in the preview, for example.

>> After you choose some options, additional touch-control icons appear on the options screen. For example, you may see an icon bearing an Info label. By tapping that icon or pressing the Info button, you can access settings that enable you to modify the characteristics of the currently selected option. Instructions throughout the book alert you to these hidden settings.

REMEMBER

As with instructions for choosing menu items, the rest of this book assumes that you're now cool with the basics of using Quick Control mode. So, instead of repeating all the preceding steps for each feature that you can modify by using Quick Control mode, instructions merely say something like "Shift to Quick Control mode to adjust this setting." Just for good measure, though, the Q button symbol appears in the margin of paragraphs that discuss using Quick Control mode.

Familiarizing Yourself with the Lens

If you've never used a dSLR before, you may be unfamiliar with how to operate the lens. The following basics are specific to the 18–55mm kit lens sold with the 77D (shown in the figures), but they also apply to the alternate 18–135mm kit lens you can purchase with the 77D and many other lenses that support autofocusing with the camera. (You should explore the lens manual for specifics, of course.)

Focusing

Set the lens to automatic or manual focusing by moving the focus-method switch on the lens, labeled in Figure 1-27. Move the switch to the AF position for autofocusing and to MF for manual focusing. Then proceed as follows:

Auto/Manual focus switch

Focal-length indicator

Image Stabilizer switch

Manual focusing ring

Zoom ring

Lens-release button

FIGURE 1-27: Here are a few features that may be found on your lens.

>> **Autofocusing:** Press and hold the shutter button halfway. In Live View mode, you also have the option of tapping the touch screen to focus.

>> **Manual focusing:** After setting the focus method to MF, rotate the focusing ring on the lens barrel until your subject appears sharp in the viewfinder or on the Live View screen. The position of the focusing ring varies depending on the lens; again, Figure 1-27 shows the ring as it appears on the 18–55mm kit lens.

WARNING

To save battery power, the focus motor in STM (stepping motor) lenses such as the 18–55mm kit lens automatically goes to sleep after a period of inactivity. This also applies to the larger 18–135mm USM (ultrasonic motor) kit lens. While the lens is napping, manual focusing isn't possible (the focusing ring is free to turn, but the lens does not focus). The same is true if the camera itself goes into sleep mode, which is determined by the Auto Power Off feature on Setup Menu 2. Either way, wake up the camera and lens by pressing the shutter button halfway.

See Chapter 5 for more help with both automatic and manual focusing.

Zooming

If you bought a zoom lens, it has a movable *zoom ring.* The location of the zoom ring on the kit lens is shown in Figure 1-27. To zoom in or out, rotate the ring.

TIP

Zooming changes the lens *focal length.* (If you're new to that term, the sidebar "Focal length and the crop factor" explains the subject.) On the kit lenses, you can determine the focal length of the lens by looking at the number aligned with the bar labeled *focal length indicator* in Figure 1-27.

Enabling Image Stabilization

Many Canon lenses, including either kit lens, offer this feature, which compensates for small amounts of camera shake that can occur when you handhold the camera. Camera movement during the exposure can produce blurry images, so turning on Image Stabilization can help you get sharper handheld shots.

WARNING

However, when you use a tripod, Image Stabilization can have detrimental effects because the system may try to adjust for movement that isn't actually occurring. Although this problem shouldn't be an issue with most Canon IS lenses, if you do see blurry images while using a tripod, try turning the feature off. (You also save battery power by turning off Image Stabilization.) If you use a monopod, leave Image Stabilization turned on so it can help compensate for any accidental movement of the monopod.

FOCAL LENGTH AND THE CROP FACTOR

The angle of view that a lens can capture is determined by its *focal length,* or in the case of a zoom lens, the range of focal lengths it offers. Focal length is measured in millimeters. The shorter the focal length, the wider the angle of view. As focal length increases, the angle of view narrows, and the subject occupies more of the frame.

Generally speaking, lenses with focal lengths shorter than 35mm are considered *wide-angle lenses* and lenses with focal lengths greater than 80mm are considered *telephoto lenses.* Anything in the middle is a *normal lens,* suitable for shooting scenes that don't require either a wide or narrow angle of view.

Note, however, that the focal lengths stated in this book and elsewhere are *35mm-equivalent focal lengths.* Here's the deal: When you put a standard lens on most dSLR cameras, including the 77D, the available frame area is reduced, as if you took a picture on a camera that uses 35mm film negatives and cropped it. This *crop factor* varies depending on the camera, which is why the photo industry adopted the 35mm-equivalent measuring stick as a standard. With the 77D, the crop factor is roughly 1.6x. In the figure here, the red frame indicates the portion of a 35mm frame that is captured at that crop factor.

When shopping for a lens, it's important to remember this crop factor to make sure that you get the focal length designed for the type of pictures you want to take. Just multiply the lens focal length by 1.6 to determine the actual angle of view.

On non-Canon lenses, Image Stabilization may go by another name: *anti-shake, vibration compensation,* and so on. In some cases, the manufacturers recommend that you leave the system turned on or select a special setting when you use a tripod, so check the lens manual for information.

Whatever lens you use, Image Stabilization isn't meant to eliminate the blur that can occur when your subject moves during the exposure. That problem is related to shutter speed, a topic you can explore in Chapter 4.

Removing a lens

After turning the camera off, press and hold the lens-release button on the camera (refer to Figure 1-27), and turn the lens toward the shutter button side of the camera until the lens detaches from the lens mount. Put the rear protective cap onto the back of the lens and, if you aren't putting another lens on the camera, cover the lens mount with its cap, too.

WARNING

Always switch lenses in a clean environment to reduce the risk of getting dust, dirt, and other contaminants inside the camera or lens. Changing lenses on a sandy beach, for example, isn't a good idea. For added safety, point the camera body slightly down when performing this maneuver; doing so helps prevent any flotsam in the air from being drawn into the camera by gravity.

Decoding Canon lens terminology

When you shop for Canon lenses, you encounter these lens specifications:

>> **EF and EF-S:** *EF* stands for *electro focus;* the *S* stands for *short back focus.* And *that* simply means the rear element of the lens is closer to the sensor than with an EF lens. The good news is that your 77D works with both of these Canon lens types.

>> **IS:** Indicates that the lens offers image stabilization.

>> **STM:** Refers to *stepping motor technology,* an autofocusing system that's designed to provide smoother, quieter autofocusing.

>> **USM:** Refers to the *ultrasonic motor.* USM is an older technology than STM, but USM lenses still offers quick, professional-quality autofocusing.

The 18–55mm kit lens is an EF-S lens with both Image Stabilization and stepping motor technology. The 18–135mm kit lens is also an EF-S lens with Image Stabilization technology. Complete lens info can also be found on the ring surrounding the front element of the lens.

Working with Memory Cards

As the medium that stores your picture files, the memory card is a critical component of your camera. See the steps at the start of this chapter for help installing a card. Follow the tips in this section for buying and maintaining cards.

Buying SD cards

Again, you can use regular SD cards, which offer less than 4GB of storage space; SDHC cards (4GB–32GB); and SDXC cards (more than 32GB). Aside from card capacity, the other specification to note is card speed, which indicates how quickly data can be moved to and from the card.

Card speed is indicated in several ways. The most common spec is SD Speed Class, which rates cards with a number between 2 and 10, with 10 being the fastest. Most cards also carry another designation, UHS-1, -2, or -3; UHS (Ultra High Speed) refers to a new technology designed to boost data transmission speeds above the normal Speed Class 10 rate. The number 1, 2, or 3 inside a little U symbol tells you the UHS rating.

TIP

Your camera can use UHS-2 and -3 cards, but you won't get any extra speed benefit; the speed advantage with the 77D tops out at UHS-1.

Some SD cards also are rated in terms of how they perform when used to record video — specifically, how many frames per second the card can handle. As with the other ratings, a higher video-speed number indicates a faster card.

Formatting a card

The first time you use a new memory card, format it by choosing the Format Card option on Setup Menu 1. This step ensures that the card is properly prepared to record your pictures. See the upcoming section "Setup Menu 1" for more information about card formatting.

Removing a card

First, check the status of the memory card access light, found just above the card door on the right side of the camera. After making sure that the light is off, indicating that the camera has finished recording your most recent photo, turn off the camera. Open the memory card door, depress the memory card slightly, and then lift your finger. The card should pop halfway out of the slot, enabling you to grab it by the tail and remove it.

Handling cards

Don't touch the gold contacts on the back of the card (see the right card in Figure 1-28). When cards aren't in use, store them in the protective cases they came in or in a memory card wallet. Keep cards away from extreme heat and cold as well.

Locking cards

The tiny switch on the side of the card, labeled Lock switch in Figure 1-28, enables you to lock your card, which prevents any data from being erased or recorded to the card. If you insert a locked card into the camera, a message on the monitor alerts you to that fact.

TIP

You can safeguard individual images from accidental erasure by using the Protect Images option on the Playback menu; Chapter 9 tells you how. Note, though, that formatting the card *does* erase even protected pictures; the safety feature prevents erasure only when you use the camera's Delete function.

Lock switch   Don't touch!

FIGURE 1-28:
Avoid touching the gold contacts on the card.

Using Eye-Fi memory cards

Your camera works with *Eye-Fi memory cards,* which are special cards that enable you to transmit your files wirelessly to your computer and other devices. That's a cool feature, but unfortunately, the cards are more expensive than regular cards. And given that your camera offers built-in Wi-Fi, you probably don't need to invest in cards that also offer that feature. (If you already own Eye-Fi cards, you can use them in your 77D, however.) This book's appendix gets you started on using the camera's Wi-Fi features.

Reviewing Basic Setup Options

Your camera offers scads of options for customizing its performance. Later chapters explain settings related to picture-taking, such as those that affect flash behavior and autofocusing. The rest of this chapter offers a quick rundown of options on the Setup menu, which are mainly (but not all) related to general camera operations. Some of these features deserve only a brief glance; others may require your attention on a regular basis.

REMEMBER

If you've switched from Standard to Guided Display mode (discussed in the earlier section "Changing from Standard to Guided Display Mode"), switch back to Standard now. Otherwise, menus you see on your camera won't match the figures in this book and some instructions won't work as spelled out.

Also note that menu offerings change depending on your exposure mode — Scene Intelligent Auto, P, Creative Auto, and so on — and whether the camera is set to Movie mode, Live View mode, or viewfinder photography mode. For now, put the camera in still photo mode (the On/Off switch should be set to On) and exit Live View mode, if it's active (press the LV button to turn Live View on and off). Then rotate the Mode dial on top of the camera to the P position, which selects the Programmed Autoexposure mode, one of four advanced exposure modes. You can adjust all the camera's options only in these four exposure modes.

Setup Menu 1

Display Setup Menu 1, shown in Figure 1-29, to access the following options:

» **Select Folder:** By default, your camera creates an initial filestorage folder named 100Canon and puts as many as 9,999 images in that folder. When you reach image 9999, the camera creates a new folder, named 101Canon, for your next 9,999 images. The camera also creates a new folder if you perform a manual filenumbering reset.

FIGURE 1-29:
Setup Menu 1 contains the Format Card option with a handful of others.

Choose Select Folder to see the list of folders on your memory card. If the card contains multiple folders, the currently selected one is highlighted. The number to the right of the folder name shows you how many pictures are in the folder. You also see a thumbnail view of the first and last pictures in the folder, along with the file numbers of those two photos. To choose a different folder, tap it or use the up/down Quick Control keys or dial to select it and then press the Set button. You also can create a new folder by choosing the Create Folder setting; Chapter 11 provides details on this feature.

» **File Numbering:** This option controls how the camera names your picture files. After selecting File Numbering from the menu, choose the Numbering option to select one of these choices:

• *Continuous:* This is the default; the camera numbers your files sequentially, from 0001 to 9999, and places all images in the same folder (100Canon, by default) unless you specify otherwise using the Select Folder option. The numbering sequence is retained even if you change memory cards.

When you reach picture 9999, the camera automatically creates a new folder (101Canon, by default) and restarts the file numbering at 0001 — again, the folder issue being dependent on the status of the Select Folder option.

- *Auto Reset:* File numbering restarts at 0001 each time you put in a different memory card or create a new folder. It's easy to wind up with multiple photos that have the same file number if you're not careful about storing them in separate folders. So think twice — or maybe three times — about using this option.

You also find a separate option, Manual Reset. Select this setting to begin a new numbering sequence, starting at 0001. A new folder is automatically created to store your new files. The camera then returns to whichever Numbering mode is selected (Continuous or Auto Reset).

Beware of one gotcha that applies to both the Continuous and Auto Reset options: If you swap memory cards and the new card already contains images, the camera may pick up numbering from the last image on the new card, which throws a monkey wrench into things. To avoid this problem, format the new card before putting it into the camera, as explained later in this list.

» **Auto Rotate:** This option determines whether vertically oriented pictures are rotated to appear upright during picture playback or when you view them in a photo editor. Stick with the default setting, shown in Figure 1-29 until you explore Chapter 9, which discusses this and other playback issues.

» **Format Card:** Choose this option to wipe the installed memory card clean of all contents and ensure that it's properly prepared for use in the camera. For extra deep cleaning, select the Low-Level formatting box after you select the menu option. However, the standard formatting (Low-Level box unchecked) is usually adequate.

» **Wireless Communication Settings:** Choose this menu option to access settings related to using the camera's Wi-Fi and Bluetooth wireless features, which you can explore in this book's appendix.

» **Eye-Fi Settings:** If an Eye-Fi memory card is installed, this menu option appears and enables you to control the wireless transmission between the camera and your computer. When no Eye-Fi card is installed, the menu option is hidden, as it is in Figure 1-29. This book doesn't cover Eye-Fi cards, but if you want more details about the product, visit www.eye.fi.

Setup Menu 2

Setup Menu 2, posing in Figure 1-30, contains these options:

FIGURE 1-30:
Through the first option on this menu, you can adjust the delay time of the camera's automatic shutdown feature.

>> **Auto Power Off:** To save battery power, the camera automatically goes to sleep after a certain period of inactivity. At the default setting, the camera nods off after only ten seconds unless the camera is in Playback mode, Live View mode, or Movie mode, in which case it waits until 30 seconds have passed.

You can adjust this timing so that 30 seconds is the minimum delay time (the 10-second variation is disabled at the 30-second setting). Or you can extend the delay up to as long as 15 minutes. To disable auto shutdown altogether, select Off — but be aware that even at that setting, the monitor still turns off if you ignore the camera for 30 minutes.

Regardless of the shutoff time you select, you can bring the camera out of hibernation mode by giving the shutter button a quick half-press and release or pressing the Menu, Info, Playback, or Live View button.

>> **LCD Brightness:** This option enables you to make the camera monitor brighter or darker. But if you take this step, what you see on the display may not be an accurate rendition of exposure. The default setting is 4, which is the position at the midpoint of the brightness scale.

>> **LCD Auto Off:** This option enables or disables the display-off sensor, which is located above the camera's viewfinder. Turn to the section entitled "Back-of-the-body controls" for more information on the display-off sensor.

>> **Date/Time/Zone:** If you didn't do so when following the initial camera setup steps at the start of this chapter, enter the time, date, and time zone now. Keeping the date/time accurate is important because that information is recorded as part of the image file. In your photo browser, you can then see when you shot an image and, equally handy, search for images by the date they were taken. Chapter 9 shows you where to locate the date/time data when browsing your picture files.

TIP

When the Time Zone setting is active, the Time Difference value that's displayed is the difference between the time zone you select and Coordinated Universal Time, or UTC, which is the standard by which the world sets its clocks. For example, New York City is five hours behind UTC. This information is provided so that if your time zone isn't in the list of available options, you can select one that shares the same relationship to the UTC.

- » **Language:** This option determines the language of any text displayed on the camera monitor.

- » **Viewfinder Display:** Here's where you find the options that add a grid, electronic level, and/or a flicker detection warning to the viewfinder display. See the earlier section "Decoding viewfinder data" for details.

Setup Menu 3

Setup Menu 3, shown in Figure 1-31, contains the following offerings:

- » **GPS Device Settings:** If you attach the optional GP-E2 GPS device, this menu option offers settings related to its operation.

- » **Video System:** This option relates to viewing your images and movies on a television. Select NTSC if you live in North America or other countries that adhere to the NTSC video standard; select PAL for playback in areas that follow that code of video conduct. Your selection also determines what frame rate settings you can select when recording movies (refer to Chapter 8).

FIGURE 1-31:
Still more customization features await on Setup Menu 3.

- » **Touch Control:** Choose this setting to adjust the sensitivity of the touch screen or disable the touch screen altogether. (Julie often does this when wearing her camera on a neck strap so that she can't accidentally adjust a touch-screen-enabled setting if the monitor bumps against her chest as she walks.) See the earlier section "Customizing the Touch Screen" for more information.

- » **Beep:** Choose Enable if you want the camera to emit an audio cue when you select an option by tapping the touch screen and when the autofocusing system has found its focus point. The second option, Touch, disables touch-screen sounds only; choose Disable to turn off both sound effects.

- » **Battery Info:** Select this option to see battery information, such as the type of battery in the camera, how much battery juice is left, and the battery's recharge performance. For this last feature, three green bars means that the battery is working fine; two bars means that recharging is slightly below par; and one red bar means that you should invest in a new battery as soon as possible.

>> **Info Button Display Options:** This setting enables you to determine which information appears when you press the Info button during shooting. Your two options are the Electronic Level and Quick Control screen.

Setup Menu 4

Figure 1-32 shows Setup Menu 4, which you can access only in the advanced exposure modes: P, Tv, Av, and M.

FIGURE 1-32:
To display Setup Menu 4, you must set the Mode dial to P, Tv, Av, or M.

>> **Sensor Cleaning:** Choose this option to access features related to the camera's internal sensor-cleaning mechanism. These work like so:

- *Auto Cleaning:* By default, the camera's sensor-cleaning mechanism activates each time you turn the camera on and off. This process helps keep the image sensor — which is the part of the camera that captures the image — free of dust and other particles that can mar your photos. You can disable this option, but it's hard to imagine why you would choose to do so.

- *Clean Now:* Select this option and press Set to initiate a cleaning cycle. For best results, set the camera on a flat surface during cleaning.

- *Clean Manually:* In the advanced exposure modes, you can access this third option, which prepares the camera for manual cleaning of the sensor. Because you can easily damage the image sensor, rendering your camera a paperweight, use extreme caution if you decide to try cleaning the sensor yourself. You're really better off taking the camera to a good service center for cleaning.

>> **Multi Function Lock:** Control the behavior of the Multi Function Lock from this menu option. This setting (shown in Figure 1-33) is critical because it determines the results of moving the Lock switch on the back of the camera to the locked position.

By default, the switch only affects the Quick Control dial. When the dial is unlocked, rotating it while using the M exposure mode changes the aperture setting (f-stop), and spinning it while using the Av, Tv, or P mode changes the amount of Exposure Compensation after you meter the scene. (We explain these exposure controls in Chapter 4.) If you set the switch to the locked position, rotating it has no effect on those settings; a *Lock* alert appears in the Shooting Settings display, and an L appears in the viewfinder and

FIGURE 1-33:
This menu option determines what control is affected by the Lock switch on the back of the camera.

LCD panel to remind you that the dial is locked. You can still use the dial while navigating menus, selecting other camera settings, and while reviewing pictures.

If you prefer, you can also set the switch to lock the Main dial and even Touch control so that an errant movement or tap doesn't accidentally adjust a camera setting. A check mark above the control's symbol on the menu indicates that the lock will be in force; toggle the check mark on and off by tapping the item or highlighting it and pressing the Set button.

While using this book, stick with the default setup, shown in the figure. Otherwise, our instructions won't work.

WARNING

>> **Custom Functions:** Selecting this option opens the door to *Custom Functions,* which are a set of advance features. See "Navigating Custom Functions," earlier in this chapter, for tips on making your way through these screens.

>> **Clear Settings:** Via this option, you can restore the default menu settings. You also can reset all the Custom Functions settings to their defaults.

>> **Copyright Information:** Using this option, explained in Chapter 12, you can embed copyright information in your files.

>> **Manual/software URL:** Canon provides a hefty printed camera manual in the 77D shipping box. But you also can download an electronic version of the manual so that you can read it on your smartphone, tablet, or computer.

To make finding the download site easy, choosing this menu option displays a Quick Response (QR) code. If your smartphone or tablet has an app that can read these codes, you simply aim the device's camera at the code to display the download site's web address. The site also provides access to the Canon software that's available for free download to purchasers of the camera.

Setup Menu 5

Figure 1-34 shows Setup Menu 5, which you can access only in the advanced exposure modes.

>> **Certification Logo Display:** You have permission to ignore this screen, which simply displays logos for a couple of electronics-industry certifications claimed by the camera. You can find additional logos on the bottom of the camera.

>> **Firmware Ver.:** This screen tells you the version number of the camera firmware (internal operating software). At the time of publication, the current firmware version was 1.0.2.

FIGURE 1-34:
Set the Mode dial to an advanced exposure mode to display Setup Menu 5.

WARNING

Keeping your camera firmware up-to-date is important, so visit the Canon website (www.canon.com) regularly to find out whether your camera sports the latest version. Follow the instructions given on the website to download and install updated firmware if needed.

IN THIS CHAPTER

» Picking an exposure mode

» Changing the shutter-release (Drive) mode

» Understanding the Image Quality setting (resolution and file type)

» Choosing the image aspect ratio

» Illuminating with flash

Chapter **2**

Choosing Basic Picture Settings

E very camera manufacturer strives to ensure that your initial encounter with the camera is a happy one. To that end, the default camera settings are designed to make it as easy as possible to take a decent picture the first time you press the shutter button. However, the default settings don't produce optimal results in every situation. You may be able to shoot an acceptable portrait, for example, but adjusting a few options can greatly improve that picture.

So that you can start fine-tuning settings to your subject, this chapter introduces you to four basic options: exposure mode, Drive mode, Image Quality, and Aspect Ratio. Additionally, the last part of the chapter discusses how to add flash and modify flash results. These aren't the most exciting camera options to read about, but they make a big difference both in terms of photo quality and also how easily you can capture the image you have in mind.

Note: This chapter relates to still photography; for information about choosing settings for movies, see Chapter 8.

Choosing an Exposure Mode

The first picture-taking setting to consider is the *exposure mode,* also sometimes referred to as *shooting mode.* Whatever you call it (this book uses *exposure mode*), your choice determines how much control you have over certain picture settings, including those that determine exposure, color, and focus.

You choose an exposure mode via the Mode dial, found on top of the camera and shown in Figure 2-1. As labeled in the figure, exposure modes are grouped into categories, Basic Zone and Creative Zone. The next two sections provide a quick introduction to the exposure modes found in each zone.

Basic Zone exposure modes

These exposure modes provide almost fully automatic photography. Here's the scoop on what each mode offers:

Creative Zone (advanced) exposure modes

Basic Zone (automatic) exposure modes

FIGURE 2-1:
The exposure mode you choose determines how much control you have over picture settings.

>> **Scene Intelligent Auto:** The most basic mode, this is the closest you get to fully automatic shooting with the 77D. The name stems from the fact that the camera is smart enough to analyze the scene and select the settings it thinks would best capture that subject.

>> **Flash Off:** Just like Scene Intelligent Auto except that flash is disabled.

>> **Creative Auto:** A (small) step up from Scene Intelligent Auto, Creative Auto enables you to exercise a little creative control. For example, you can adjust how much the background blurs.

>> **Scene modes:** You also get an assortment of exposure modes designed to capture specific scenes according to traditional photography aesthetics. Four modes have their own settings on the Mode dial; you access the remaining ones by turning the dial to SCN.

• *Portrait:* For taking traditional portraits, with background blurring, soft skin tones, and slightly warmer (more reddish-yellow) colors.

- *Landscape:* For capturing scenic vistas; colors are given a boost and focus remains sharp over a long distance.

- *Close-up:* For shooting flowers and other subjects at close range. Backgrounds appear blurry, drawing more attention to the subject.

- *Sports:* Freezes motion of moving subjects, whether or not those subjects are athletes.

- *SCN:* Rotate the Mode dial to this setting to access the following additional scene modes: Group photo, Kids, Food, Candlelight, Night Portrait, Handheld Night Scene, and HDR Backlight Control.

- *Creative Filters:* Choose this mode to add special effects to a photo or movie as you shoot.

WARNING

Chapter 3 provides specifics on how and when to use all the Basic Zone modes except Creative Filters, which you can explore in Chapter 11. But be forewarned: To remain easy to use, all these modes prevent you from taking advantage of advanced exposure, color, and autofocusing features.

Creative Zone modes (P, Tv, Av, and M)

When you're ready to take more control over the camera, step up to the advanced modes found in the Creative Zone: P (programmed auto-exposure), Tv (shutter-priority auto-exposure), Av (aperture-priority auto-exposure), or M (manual exposure). All four modes give you control over exposure, color, focusing, and more.

Which of the four advanced modes is better? Well, the main difference between them is the level of input you have over two critical exposure settings: aperture and shutter speed. Chapter 4 explains in detail and shows you how to adjust those options and other exposure settings. Chapters 5 through 7 cover other features you can access in the Creative Zone modes.

REMEMBER

One often-misunderstood aspect about the M exposure mode: This M has nothing to do with manual focusing. You can choose from manual focusing or autofocusing in any exposure mode, assuming that your lens offers autofocusing. However, access to some options that modify how the autofocus system works is limited to P, Tv, Av, and M modes.

Changing the Drive Mode

Known generically as the *shutter-release mode*, the Drive mode determines how and when the camera records a picture when you press the shutter button. Here are your options:

>> **Single:** Records a single image each time you press the shutter button.

>> **Continuous:** Sometimes known as *burst mode,* this mode records a continuous series of images as long as you hold down the shutter button.

You can choose from two continuous modes:

- *High-speed continuous:* Captures about 6 frames per second (fps).

- *Low-speed continuous:* Captures about 3 fps.

Why would you ever choose the low-speed setting? Well, frankly, unless you're shooting something that's moving at an extremely fast pace, not too much is going to change between frames when you shoot at 6 fps. So you wind up with a ton of images that are exactly the same, wasting space on your memory card.

At either continuous setting, you may not be able to achieve the maximum frame rate. A number of picture settings can hamper the camera's frame rate, including shutter speed and autofocusing options, all covered in Part 2 of this book.

>> **10-Second Self-Timer/Remote Control:** Want to put yourself in the picture? Select this mode, depress the shutter button, and run into the frame. You have about 10 seconds to get yourself in place and pose before the image is recorded.

As an alternative to the press-and-run technique, you can connect the camera wirelessly to a smartphone or tablet and use that device to trigger the shutter release. The appendix talks more about this feature.

>> **Self-Timer: 2 Second:** This mode works just like the regular Self-Timer mode, but the capture happens 2 seconds after you press the shutter button.

TIP

Consider using this setting when you're shooting long exposures and using a tripod. In that scenario, the mere motion of pressing the shutter button can cause slight camera movement, which can blur an image. The ideal solution is to use a remote control to trigger the shutter release, but in a pinch, set the Drive mode to the 2-second self-timer mode, press the shutter button, and then take your hands off the camera.

>> **Self-Timer: Continuous:** With this option, the camera waits 10 seconds after you press the shutter button and then captures a continuous series of images. You can set the camera to record two to ten images per shutter release.

A symbol representing the current Drive mode appears in the Quick Control screen, but exactly where that symbol appears depends on your exposure mode. Figure 2-2 shows you where to find the symbol in Scene Intelligent Auto and Tv modes.

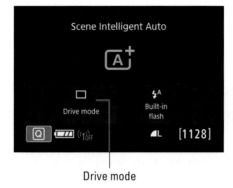

FIGURE 2-2: The Quick Control screen displays an icon indicating the current Drive mode.

Drive mode   Drive mode

When Live View is enabled, the Drive mode symbol doesn't appear in the default display. To see that symbol and other shooting data, press Info until you see the more detailed screens shown in Figure 2-3. Again, the left screen shows the display as it appears in Scene Intelligent Auto exposure mode; the right screen, Tv mode.

Drive mode

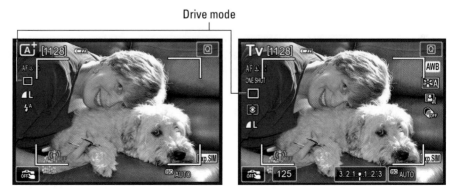

FIGURE 2-3: In Live View mode, press Info to display detailed settings data, including the Drive mode symbol.

You can change the Drive mode setting as follows:

>> **Quick Control method:** Press the Q button or tap the onscreen Q symbol to shift to Quick Control mode and then select the Drive mode icon, as shown in Figures 2-4 and 2-5. Rotate the Quick Control or Main dial to change the setting.

FIGURE 2-4: For viewfinder photography, you can rotate the Quick Control or Main dial to cycle through all options (left) or press Set to display all options on a single screen (right).

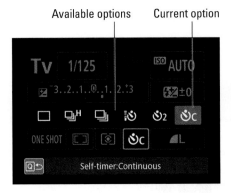

FIGURE 2-5: In Live View mode, rotate the Quick Control or Main dial to change the Drive mode (left); press the Info button to choose the number of shots you want the camera to take in Self-Timer Continuous mode (right).

For Self-Timer Continuous mode, the default number of frames that will be captured is two. To change that value, you have to take one more step:

● *Viewfinder photography:* Press Set to display all available settings on a separate screen, as shown on the right in Figure 2-4. Then press the up/down Quick Control keys or tap the arrows that appear above and below the current frame number. (The bottom arrow is dimmed in the figure because two frames is the lowest possible value.)

- *Live View shooting:* Press the Info button to display the screen shown on the right in Figure 2-5. Then adjust the frame number by rotating the Quick Control dial, pressing the left/right Quick Control keys, or tapping the arrow symbols.

>> **Press the left Quick Control key (viewfinder photography only).** You're whisked directly to the screen as shown in Figure 2-6. Here, you can change the Drive mode and set the number of continuous frames without changing screens. Tap Set or press the Set button to confirm your choice and exit the screen.

Press to access Drive mode settings

FIGURE 2-6: For viewfinder photography, a faster way to get to the Drive mode setting is to press the left Quick Control key.

TIP

When you use the Self-Timer modes for viewfinder photography or shoot in Live View mode, it's a good idea to use the cover provided on the camera strap to cover the viewfinder. Otherwise, light may seep in through the viewfinder and mess up the camera's exposure calculations.

Understanding the Image Quality Setting

Another critical camera option, the Image Quality setting determines two important aspects of your pictures: *resolution,* or pixel count; and *file type,* which refers to the kind of file used to store picture data (JPEG or Raw). The next section explains how to view and adjust the setting, which is a little more confusing than you may expect. Following that, you can get background information to help you figure out which is the best Image Quality option for your next shoot.

Adjusting the Image Quality setting

An icon representing the current Image Quality setting appears on the Quick Control and Live View displays. Figure 2-7 shows you where to find the symbols when shooting in the P, Tv, Av, and M modes. In other modes, the symbols appear elsewhere on the screen.

Image Quality setting (Large/Fine)

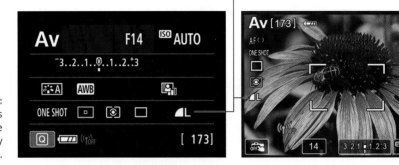

Help with understanding the symbols and other aspects of this setting arrives shortly. First, here are the ways you can access and adjust the setting, which depend on your exposure mode:

>> **Shooting Menu 1 (any exposure mode):** After selecting the Image Quality option, shown on the left in Figure 2-8, press Set to display the available settings, shown on the right.

Pixel dimensions

Megapixels   Shots remaining

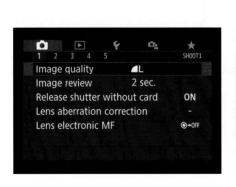

>> **Quick Control method (P, Tv, Av, and M modes only):** After choosing the Image Quality icon, as shown in Figure 2-9, rotate either the Quick Control or Main dial to cycle through the available settings. When not in Live View mode, you also can display all the options on a single screen by pressing the Set button or tapping the Image Quality icon.

FIGURE 2-9: In P, Tv, Av, and M exposure modes, you also can shift to Quick Control mode to change the Image Quality setting.

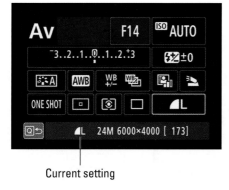

Current setting

Scroll arrows

If you're new to digital photography, the Image Quality settings won't make much sense until you read the next few sections, which explain resolution and file type in detail. But even if you're schooled in those topics, you may need some help deciphering the way that the settings are represented on your camera. As you can see from Figures 2-7 through 2-9, the options are presented in rather cryptic fashion, so here's your decoder ring:

>> At the top of the Shooting Menu's Image Quality selection screen, you see three bits of information, labeled in Figure 2-8: the *resolution,* or total pixel count (measured in megapixels), the *pixel dimensions* (the number of horizontal pixels, followed by the number of vertical pixels), and the number of subsequent shots you can fit on your current memory card at the current Image Quality setting. This same information appears at the bottom of the Quick Control screens, as shown in Figure 2-9, but only after you rotate the Main dial to change the current setting. Initially, the text label just indicates that the Image Quality option is active.

>> The settings marked with the arc symbols capture images in the JPEG file format. The arc icons represent the level of JPEG *compression,* which affects picture quality and file size. You get two options: Fine and Normal. The smooth arcs represent the Fine setting; the jagged arcs represent the Normal setting. As for the S2 setting, which for some reason appears without any symbol at all, it uses JPEG Fine. Check out the upcoming section "JPEG: The imaging (and web) standard" for details about all things JPEG.

» Within the JPEG category, you can choose from five resolution settings, represented by L, M, and S1 and S2 (large, medium, small, and smallest). See the next section for information that helps you select the right resolution.

» Raw refers to the other available file type on your camera. The upcoming section "Raw (CR2): The purist's choice" explains the Raw format. For now, just note that you don't see a size setting (L, M, S1, or S2) with the Raw option because Raw files are always created at the Large resolution setting. The Raw + JPEG Fine option records a JPEG Fine version of the image at the maximum resolution.

Which Image Quality option is best depends on several factors, including how you plan to use your pictures and how much time you care to spend processing images on your computer. The next several sections explain these and other issues related to the Image Quality setting.

Considering resolution: L, M, S1, or S2?

To choose an Image Quality setting, the first decision you need to make is how many pixels you want your image to contain. *Pixels* are the little square tiles from which all digital images are made; *pixel* is short for picture element. You can see some pixels close up in the right image in Figure 2-10, which shows a greatly magnified view of the eye area in the left image.

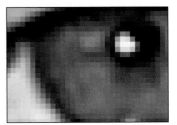

FIGURE 2-10: Pixels are the building blocks of digital photos.

When describing a digital image, photographers use the term *image resolution* to refer to the number of pixels it contains. Every image starts with a specific number of pixels, which you select via the Image Quality setting. Table 2-1 shows you the pixel count that results from the four options available on the 77D. However, understand that the table assumes that your camera is set to record pictures using the default aspect ratio of 3:2. If you change that setting, the resolution of the photo changes. See the upcoming section "Setting the Aspect Ratio" for details.

TABLE 2-1

The Resolution Side of the Image Quality Setting

Symbol	Setting	Pixel Count
L	Large	6,000 x 4,000 (24 MP)
M	Medium	3,984 x 2,656 (11 MP)
S1	Small 1	2,976 x 1,984 (5.9 MP)
S2	Small 2	2,400 x 1,600 (3.8 MP)

TECHNICAL STUFF

In the table, the first pair of numbers in the Pixel Count column represents the *pixel dimensions* — the number of horizontal pixels and vertical pixels. The values in parentheses indicate the total resolution, which you get by multiplying the horizontal and vertical pixel values. This number is usually stated in *megapixels*, or MP for short. The camera displays the resolution value using only one letter *M*, however. Either way, 1 MP equals 1 million pixels.

Resolution affects your pictures in three ways:

>> **Print size:** Pixel count determines the size at which you can produce a high-quality print. When an image contains too few pixels, details appear muddy, and curved and diagonal lines appear jagged. Such pictures are said to exhibit *pixilation*.

Depending on your photo printer, you typically need anywhere from 200 to 300 pixels per inch (ppi) for good print quality. To produce an 8-x-10-inch print at 200 ppi, for example, you need a pixel count of 1,600 x 2,000, or about 3.2 megapixels.

WARNING

Even though many photo-editing programs enable you to add pixels to an existing image — known as *upsampling* — doing so doesn't enable you to successfully enlarge your photo. In fact, upsampling typically makes matters worse.

To give you a better idea of the impact of resolution on print quality, Figures 2-11 through 2-13 show you the same image at 300 ppi, at 50 ppi, and then resampled from 50 ppi to 300 ppi. As you can see, there's no way around the rule: If you want quality prints, you need the right pixel count from the get-go.

>> **Screen display size:** Resolution doesn't affect the quality of images viewed on a monitor or television, or another screen device, the way it does for printed photos. Instead, resolution determines the *size* at which the image appears. Chapter 9 explains this issue in detail; for now, just know that you need *way* fewer pixels for onscreen photos than you do for prints. In fact, even the Small 2 Image Quality setting creates a picture too big to be viewed in its entirety in many email programs.

300 ppi

FIGURE 2-11:
A high-quality
print depends
on a high-
resolution
original.

50 ppi

FIGURE 2-12:
At 50 ppi,
the image
has a jagged,
pixelated look.

50 ppi resampled to 300 ppi

FIGURE 2-13:
Adding pixels
in a photo
editor doesn't
rescue a low-
resolution
original.

WARNING

» **File size:** Every additional pixel increases the amount of data required to create a digital picture file. So a higher-resolution image has a larger file size than a low-resolution image.

Large files present several problems:

- You can store fewer images on your memory card, your computer's hard drive, and removable storage media such as a DVD.

- The camera needs more time to process and store the image data, which can hamper fast-action shooting.

- When you share photos online, larger files take longer to upload and download.

- When you edit photos in your photo software, your computer needs more resources to process large files.

As you can see, resolution is a bit of a sticky wicket. What if you aren't sure how large you want to print your images? What if you want to print your photos *and* share them online? Well, if you want to take the better–safe–than–sorry route, follow these recommendations:

TIP

» **Shoot at a resolution suitable for print.** You then can create a low-resolution copy of the image for use online. In fact, your camera has a built-in Resize tool that can do the job. Chapter 10 shows you how to use that feature.

» **For everyday images, Medium is a good choice.** Even at the Medium setting, your pixel count (3,984 x 2,656) is far more than you need for an 8-x-10-inch print at 200 ppi, and a bit over what you need for an 8-x-10-inch print at 300 ppi.

» **Choose Large for an image that you plan to crop, print very large, or both.** The benefit of maxing out resolution is that you have the flexibility to crop your photo and still generate a decent-size print of the remaining image.

Consider Figure 2-14 as an example. When Julie took this shot, she couldn't get close enough to fill the frame with her main subject of interest, the two juvenile herons at the center of the frame. But because she took the picture using the Large resolution setting, she could crop the photo to eliminate everything but those birds and still have enough pixels left to produce a great print, as you see in the right image. In fact, the cropped version has enough pixels to print much larger than fits on this page.

FIGURE 2-14:
When you can't get close enough to fill the frame with the subject, capture the image at the Large resolution setting (left) and crop later (right).

Understanding file type (JPEG or Raw)

In addition to establishing the resolution of your photos, the Image Quality setting determines the *file type*, which refers to the kind of data file that the camera produces. Your camera offers two file types — JPEG and Raw (sometimes seen as *raw* or *RAW*), with a couple variations of each. The next sections explain the pros and cons of each setting.

JPEG: The imaging (and web) standard

This format is the default setting on your camera, as it is for most digital cameras. JPEG is popular for two main reasons:

» **Immediate usability:** JPEG is a longtime standard format for digital photos. All web browsers and email programs can display JPEG files, so you can share them online immediately after you shoot them. You also can get JPEG photos printed at any retail outlet, whether it's an online or local printer. Additionally, any program that has photo capabilities, from photo-editing programs to word-processing programs, can handle your files.

» **Small files:** JPEG files are smaller than Raw files. And smaller files mean that your pictures consume less room on your camera memory card and on your computer's hard drive.

The downside (you knew there had to be one) is that JPEG creates smaller files by applying *lossy compression*. This process actually throws away some image data. Too much compression produces a defect called *JPEG artifacting*. Figure 2-15 compares a high-quality original (left) with a heavily compressed version that exhibits artifacting (right).

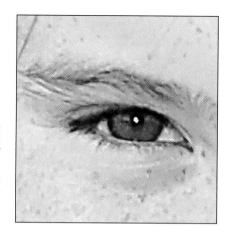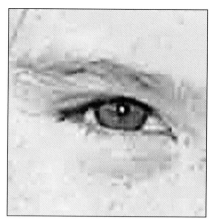

FIGURE 2-15:
The reduced
quality of
the image
on the right
is caused by
excessive JPEG
compression.

The amount of compression applied to your photos depends on whether you choose an Image Quality setting that carries the label Fine or Normal:

- >> **Fine:** At this setting, very little compression is applied, so you shouldn't see many compression artifacts, if any. Canon uses the symbol that appears in the margin here to indicate the Fine compression level; however, the S2 setting uses the Fine level even it doesn't sport the symbol.

- >> **Normal:** Switch to Normal, and the compression amount rises, as does the chance of seeing some artifacting. Notice the jagged edge of the Normal icon, shown in the margin? That's your reminder that all may not be "smooth" sailing when you choose a Normal setting.

Note, though, that the Normal setting doesn't result in anywhere near the level of artifacting that you see in the example in Figure 2-15. Again, that example is exaggerated to help you recognize artifacting defects and understand how they differ from other image-quality issues. In fact, if you keep your image print or display size small, you aren't likely to notice a great deal of quality difference between the Fine and Normal compression levels. The differences become apparent only when you greatly enlarge a photo.

Given that the differences between Fine and Normal aren't all that easy to spot until you really enlarge the photo, is it okay to shift to Normal and enjoy the benefits of smaller files? Well, only you can decide what level of quality your pictures demand. For most photographers, the added file sizes produced by the Fine setting aren't a huge concern, given that the prices of memory cards fall all the time. Long-term storage is more of an issue; the larger your files, the faster you fill your computer's hard drive and the more space you need for archiving purposes.

But in the end, the best practice is to take the storage hit in exchange for the lower compression level of the Fine setting. You never know when a casual snapshot is going to be so great that you want to print or display it large enough that even minor quality loss becomes a concern. And of all the defects that you can correct in a photo editor, artifacting is one of the hardest to remove. So stick with Fine when shooting in the JPEG format.

If you don't want *any* risk of artifacting, bypass JPEG and change the file type to Raw (CR2). The next section offers details.

Raw (CR2): The purist's choice

The other picture-file type that you can create is *Camera Raw,* or just *Raw* (as in uncooked) for short.

Each manufacturer has its own flavor of Raw files; Canon's are CR2 files (or, on some older cameras, CRW). You'll see that three-letter designation at the end of picture filenames.

Raw is popular with advanced photographers for these reasons:

>> **Greater creative control:** With JPEG, internal camera software tweaks your images, adjusting color, exposure, and sharpness as needed to produce the results that Canon believes its customers prefer (or according to certain camera settings you chose, such as the Picture Style). With Raw, the camera simply records the original, unprocessed image data. The photographer then copies the image file to the computer and uses software known as a *Raw converter* to produce the actual image, making decisions about color, exposure, and so on, at that point. The upshot is that "shooting Raw" enables you, not the camera, to have the final say on the visual characteristics of your image.

>> **More flexibility:** Having access to the Raw photo data means that you can reprocess the same photo with different settings over and over again without losing any quality.

>> **Higher bit depth:** *Bit depth* is a measure of how many color values an image file can contain. JPEG files restrict you to 8 bits each for the red, blue, and green color components, or *channels,* that make up a digital image, for a total of 24 bits. That translates to roughly 16.7 million possible colors. On your camera, a Raw file delivers a higher bit count, collecting 14 bits per channel.

Although jumping from 8 to 14 bits sounds like a huge difference, you may not ever notice any difference in your photos — that 8-bit palette of 16.7

million values is more than enough for superb images. Where having the extra bits can come in handy is if you really need to adjust exposure, contrast, or color after the shot in your photo-editing program. In cases where you apply extreme adjustments, having the extra original bits sometimes helps avoid a problem known as *banding* or *posterization,* which creates abrupt color breaks where you should see smooth, seamless transitions. (A higher bit depth doesn't always prevent the problem, however, so don't expect miracles.)

>> **Best picture quality:** Because Raw doesn't apply the destructive compression associated with JPEG, you don't run the risk of the artifacting that can occur with JPEG.

But just like JPEG, Raw isn't without its disadvantages:

>> **You can't do much with your pictures until you process them in a Raw converter.** You can't share them online, for example, or have them printed at a retail photo-printing kiosk or other common printing site. So when you shoot Raw, you add to the time you spend in front of the computer. Chapter 10 gets you started processing your Raw files using the in-camera Raw converter, as well as the one found in the Canon software that's available for free as part of your camera purchase.

>> **Raw files are larger than JPEG files.** Unlike JPEG, Raw doesn't apply lossy compression to shrink files, so Raw files consume more storage space.

Whether the upside of Raw outweighs the downside is a decision for you to ponder based on your photographic needs, schedule, and computer comfort level. If you opt for Raw, you can select from the two Image Quality options:

>> **RAW:** Produces one file at the Large resolution setting (24 MP).

>> **RAW+Large/Fine:** Produces two files: the Raw file plus a JPEG file captured at the Large/Fine setting. The advantage is that you can share the JPEG version online or get prints made immediately and then process the Raw file when you have time.

Of course, creating two files for every image eats up substantially more space on your memory card and your computer's hard drive. A single Raw file is just under 30 megabytes (MB) in size. The Large/Fine JPEG file adds another 7.6MB.

TIP

Final JPEG versus Raw recommendations

At this point, you may be finding all this technical goop a bit much, so here's a simplified summary of which option to choose:

» If you require the absolute best image quality and have the time and interest to do the Raw conversion process, shoot Raw.

» If great photo quality is good enough for you, you don't have wads of spare time, or you aren't that comfortable with the computer, stick with JPEG Fine (the setting that sports the smooth arc symbol).

» To enjoy the best of both worlds, consider RAW+Large/Fine — assuming, of course, that you have an abundance of space on your memory card and your hard drive.

» Avoid JPEG Normal (jagged-edge arc symbol) unless you're running critically low on memory-card space during a shoot. The smaller file size of the Normal option enables you to squeeze more frames into the remaining space. A better practice, however, is to carry a couple of spare cards so you don't have to make the tradeoff between file size and image quality.

Setting the Photo Aspect Ratio

Normally, photos have a 3:2 *aspect ratio* (the relationship of a photo's width to its height). But you can choose a different aspect ratio if you shoot in the P, Tv, Av, or M exposure mode.

Adjust the setting via the Aspect Ratio option, shown in Figure 2-16. For viewfinder photography, look on Shooting Menu 5 (left); if Live View is engaged, the option also appears on Shooting Menu 5 (right).

FIGURE 2-16:
The Aspect Ratio setting appears on Shooting Menu 5 for viewfinder shooting (left) and for Live View shooting (right).

In either mode, the possible aspect ratios are 4:3, 16:9, and 1:1. At any setting except 3:2, the viewfinder and Live View displays provide guides to indicate the framing area for the selected aspect ratio.

REMEMBER

How many pixels your image contains depends on the aspect ratio; at the 3:2 setting, you get the full complement of pixels delivered by your chosen Image Quality setting. Note, too, that if you set the Image Quality option to record JPEG pictures, the camera creates the different aspect ratios by cropping a 3:2 original, and the cropped data can't be recovered. Raw photos, although they appear cropped on the camera monitor, actually retain all the original data, which means you can change your mind about the aspect ratio later, when you process your Raw files. (Read about that subject in Chapter 10.)

Adding Flash

When the ambient light in a scene makes it hard to properly expose a photo, the built-in flash on your camera offers an easy, convenient solution.

Upcoming sections break down flash features into two groups: those you can use in the Basic Zone exposure modes and those available for Creative Zone shooting (P, Tv, Av, and M modes). Before you move on, though, note these basics:

>> **You can't use the built-in flash in certain Basic Zone exposure modes.** Those modes are: Flash Off (okay, that one's obvious), Landscape, Sports, Candlelight, and HDR Backlight Control. Hey, look at that, if you want to shoot in those modes, you're done with this chapter.

TIP

If you attach an external flash to the camera, you *may* be able to use flash in these exposure modes, though. Sorry, maybe you do have to pore over the rest of this chapter after all.

>> **The effective range of the built-in flash depends on the ISO setting.** The ISO setting affects the camera's sensitivity to light; Chapter 4 has details. At the lowest ISO setting, ISO 100, the maximum reach of the flash ranges from about 3 to 10 feet, depending on whether you're using a telephoto or wide-angle lens, respectively. To illuminate a subject that's farther away, use a higher ISO speed or an auxiliary flash that offers greater power than the built-in flash.

>> **Don't get too close.** Position the lens at a minimum distance of a little over 3 feet from the subject, or the flash may not illuminate the entire subject.

>> **Watch for shadows cast by the lens or a lens hood.** When you shoot with a long lens, you can wind up with unwanted shadows caused by the flash light hitting the lens. Ditto for a lens hood.

>> **While the flash is recycling, a "Busy" signal appears in the viewfinder and Live View display.** Figure 2-17 shows you how the signal appears in the viewfinder (look in the lower-left corner of the data display. The neighboring lightning bolt just indicates that flash is enabled.

FIGURE 2-17:
The "Busy" signal means that the flash is recharging.

REMEMBER

>> **Shutter speed affects flash results.** Detailed in Chapter 4, *shutter speed* determines how long the camera's shutter remains open, allowing light to hit the image sensor and expose the photo. In other words, shutter speed determines *exposure time,* which is measured in seconds.

Shutter speed has an impact on the overall image brightness and also determines whether action appears frozen (fast shutter speed) or blurry (slow shutter speed). But it also plays a role in how much flash power the camera uses to light your subject, which in turn affects the look of your flash pictures, as follows:

- *Slow shutter speeds produce softer flash lighting and brighter backgrounds.* The longer the shutter remains open, the more time the camera has to soak up the ambient light. And the more ambient light, the less flash light is needed to expose the image. Because light from the built-in flash is narrow and fairly harsh, reducing flash power typically results in softer, more flattering lighting. Additionally, objects beyond the reach of the flash are brighter than when you use a fast shutter speed.

  Figure 2-18 offers an example: The left image was taken at a shutter speed of 1/60 second; the right, at 1/8 second. How slow a shutter speed you need to get the background brightness you want depends on the amount of ambient light, so some experimentation is needed.

WARNING

  A slow shutter speed can produce blurring if the camera or subject moves during the exposure. So use a tripod and tell your subject to remain as still as possible.

Shutter speed: 1/60 second   Shutter speed: 1/8 second

FIGURE 2-18:
When you
use a slow
shutter speed
with flash,
backgrounds
are brighter
and the flash
light is softer.

- *With a fast shutter speed, flash is the primary light source, leaving objects beyond the flash range dark.* That result can be helpful when you want to diminish the impact of distracting background objects. Notice how the sand pit in the background of the first photo in Figure 2-18 nearly fades from view, for example. The down side is that because more flash power is needed, the light can appear harsh.

TIP

Unfortunately, you don't have control over shutter speed in Basic Zone modes; only the P, Tv, Av, and M modes provide that option. However, if you want the slow-shutter flash look and aren't ready for the advanced exposure modes, try Night Portrait mode. The camera automatically selects a slower shutter speed than in other Basic Zone modes.

» **The range of available shutter speeds for flash photography is more limited than when you go flash-free.** This restriction is due to the way the camera has to synchronize the flash firing with the opening of the shutter. Here are the numbers you need to know:

- *The fastest shutter speed you can use is 1/200 second.* Because a quickly moving subject may appear blurry even at 1/200 second, flash isn't a good tool for fast-action photography. Again, see Chapter 4 for help understanding the role of shutter speed in action photography.

- *The slowest shutter speed depends on the exposure mode.* In Basic Zone modes, the slowest setting is 1/60 second. The exception is Night Portrait mode (which purposely uses a slower speed to produce results similar to what you see on the right in Figure 2-18). In P, Tv, and Av modes, shutter speed can be as slow as 30 seconds. In M mode, you can also use a special shutter speed, *Bulb,* which keeps the shutter open as long as the shutter button is depressed.

REMEMBER

These guidelines, as well as other information presented in the rest of the chapter, apply to using the built-in flash. If you attach an external flash, things may work differently, so consult the flash unit's instruction manual. The camera's instruction manual also contains extensive flash information that may be of interest to advanced flash photographers; unfortunately, this book doesn't not have enough pages to cover all those features.

Using flash in Basic Zone modes

In the Basic Zone exposure modes that permit flash, you can set the flash behavior via the Flash mode setting, which is represented on the camera displays by the margin icons shown here. Here's how the various Flash modes work:

TIP

>> **Auto:** The camera measures the ambient light and then decides whether flash is needed. If the answer is yes, the built-in flash pops up automatically.

>> **On:** The flash pops up and fires regardless of the lighting conditions.

This setting is helpful when your subject is *backlit* — that is, the strongest light source is behind the subject. Without flash, your subject may appear underexposed. Using flash also helps eliminate facial shadows caused by the brim of a hat when you're shooting portraits in bright sunshine. It's also key to capturing a sunset portrait that properly exposes the subject without blowing out the colors of the sky.

>> **Off:** The flash does not fire, no way, no how, even if the flash is raised because you used it on the previous shot.

Which of the three Flash modes you can use, however, depends on the exposure mode, as follows:

>> **Scene Intelligent Auto, Creative Auto, Portrait, Close-up, and Kids modes:** You can choose from all three flash settings: Auto, On, or Off.

>> **Night Portrait mode:** Auto flash is the only option. Remember, too, that Night Portrait mode uses a slower-than-normal shutter speed; to avoid blurry photos, use a tripod and request that your subject remain as still as possible.

>> **Handheld Night Scene mode:** In this exposure mode, the camera takes four frames in rapid succession and merges them to get a sharper result than you might otherwise obtain when hand-holding the camera in dim lighting.

You have two Flash mode options: On and Off. By default, the Flash mode is set to Off, and this is the best choice if you're shooting landscapes. If you're photographing people or a close-up subject at night, you may want to change the Flash mode to On to help illuminate the subject. The flash will fire on the first shot only; warn people to keep smiling until all four frames are captured.

>> **Food Scene mode:** Auto Flash mode is off the table (see what we did there?). By default, the Flash mode is set to Off. To use flash, set the Flash mode to On. When you press the shutter button halfway, the flash unit pops up.

>> **Creative Filter mode:** Flash is unavailable for the four HDR Creative Filter effects; for other effects, you can choose from all three Flash modes. Turn to Chapter 11 for help with using this exposure mode.

You can view the current Flash mode setting in the Quick Control and Live View displays, as shown in Figure 2-19. To change the setting, shift to Quick Control mode, as shown in Figure 2-20. The left screen in the figure shows the Quick Control display for viewfinder shooting; the right screen shows the Live View version. In both cases, rotate the Quick Control or Main dial to change the Flash mode. When Live View isn't on, you also can press Set to display the available Flash mode settings on a separate screen.

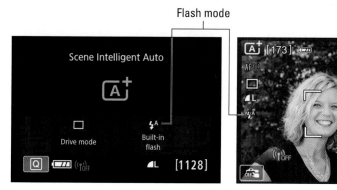

FIGURE 2-19: This symbol tells you that the flash is set to Auto mode.

FIGURE 2-20:
Change the
flash setting
via the Quick
Control screen.

RED-EYE REDUCTION: DOES IT WORK?

Red-eye, the phenomenon that turns eyes red in flash portraits, is caused when flash light bounces off a subject's retinas and is reflected back to the camera lens. Red-eye is a human phenomenon, though; with animals, the reflected light usually glows yellow, white, or green.

If you notice red-eye in your portraits, try enabling Red-Eye Reduction flash. When you turn on this feature, the Red-Eye Reduction Lamp on the front of the camera lights up when you press the shutter button halfway and focus is achieved. The purpose of this light is to shrink the subject's pupils, which helps reduce the amount of light that enters the eye and, thus, the chances of that light reflecting and causing red-eye. The flash itself fires when you press the shutter button the rest of the way. (Warn your subjects to wait for the flash, or they may stop posing after they see the light from the Red-Eye Reduction Lamp.)

You can enable Red-Eye Reduction in any exposure mode that permits flash. In the advanced exposure modes (P, Tv, Av, and M), the control lives on Shooting Menu 2, as shown in the left figure here; in all other exposure modes, it's found on Shooting Menu 1, as shown on the right.

Note the following tips:

- The camera doesn't display any symbols in the viewfinder or other displays to remind you that Red-Eye Reduction mode is in force.

- Changing the setting affects all exposure modes, regardless of which mode you were using when you turned the feature on or off.

- After you press the shutter button halfway, a row of vertical bars appears in the bottom of the viewfinder display. The bars quickly turn off, starting from the outside and working toward the center. For best results, wait until all the bars are off to take the picture. The delay gives the subject's pupils time to constrict in response to the Red-Eye Reduction Lamp. This feature isn't available for Live View shooting.

As to the question posed by the headline of this sidebar, the answer is a resounding "Sometimes!" ***Remember:*** The feature is named Red-Eye *Reduction,* not Red-Eye Elimination.

Even with the option turned on, you may still wind up with red-eye in some portraits. Fortunately, the problem can usually be fixed by using red-eye correction tools found in most photo-editing programs.

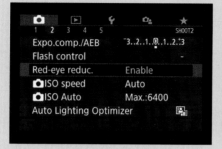
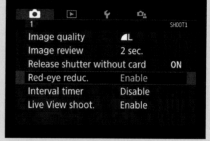

Using flash in P, Tv, Av, and M modes

These advanced exposure modes — Creative Zone modes, in Canon nomenclature — not only give you complete control over whether the flash fires but also enable you to modify flash performance. Keep reading to discover the possibilities.

Enabling and disabling flash

When the camera is set to P, Tv, Av, or M exposure mode, you don't control flash behavior via the Flash mode setting as you do in the Basic Zone modes. Instead, if you want to use the built-in flash, press the Flash button to raise the flash unit, as shown in Figure 2-21. (If the flash doesn't pop up, press the shutter button halfway and release it to wake up the camera. Then try again.)

Done with flash? Just close the flash unit by pressing down gently on the top of the flash assembly.

Flash button

FIGURE 2-21:
To use the built-in flash in P, Tv, Av, and M modes, press the Flash button to raise the flash unit.

There's no such thing as Auto flash in these exposure modes. But don't worry about that fact: Using flash (or not) is part of the decision that you, as the photographer, should make depending on your creative goals for the photo.

REMEMBER

If the flash doesn't fire, open Shooting Menu 2, select Flash Control, and make sure that the Flash Firing option is set to Enable. This is the default setting, but it's possible that you or someone else changed the setting to Disable and forgot to return it to the default. See the last section of this chapter for more information about the Flash Firing option (including why you would ever set it to Disable) and about other Flash Control options.

Adjusting shutter speed for flash photography

Your level of control over shutter speed and the range of available shutter speeds you can use with flash varies depending on which of the four Creative Zone modes you choose:

» **Tv and M modes:** You can choose any shutter speed between 30 seconds and 1/200 second. M mode also offers a shutter speed called *Bulb*, which keeps the shutter open as long as you keep the shutter button pressed. To change the shutter speed, just rotate the Main dial.

» **Av mode:** In this mode, you don't have direct control over shutter speed. Instead, you set a different exposure setting, aperture (f-stop), and the camera automatically selects a shutter speed that will properly exposure the image at that aperture.

By default, the camera can choose from shutter speeds ranging from 1/200 second to 30 seconds. However, if you want to avoid the potential problems that can arise with a slow shutter — camera shake and blurred moving subjects — you can bump up the slow limit of this range via the Flash Sync Speed in Av Mode option. To access the setting, open Shooting Menu 2 and choose Flash Control, as shown in Figure 2-22.

FIGURE 2-22:
In the Av exposure mode, you can limit the range of shutter speeds the camera can use when flash is enabled.

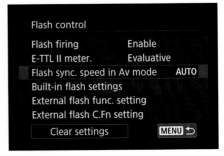

The default setting is Auto (the 1/200 second to 30 seconds range). Your other options are 1/200–1/60 Auto, which limits the slow end of the shutter speed range to 1/60 second; and 1/200 fixed, which forces the camera to use a shutter speed of 1/200 second for every flash shot.

» **P mode:** The camera selects an initial combination of aperture and shutter speed; rotate the Main dial to choose a different combination. Possible shutter speeds are the same as for Av mode, but you can't limit the slow end of the range as you can for Av mode.

Adjusting flash output with Flash Exposure Compensation

On some occasions, you may want a little more or less flash power than the camera thinks is appropriate. If so, take advantage of *Flash Exposure Compensation*. Like other advanced flash controls, this one is available only in P, Tv, Av, and M exposure modes.

REMEMBER

Flash Exposure Compensation settings are stated in terms of *exposure value* (EV) numbers. A setting of EV 0.0 indicates no flash adjustment; you can increase the flash power to EV +2.0 or decrease it to EV −2.0.

Figure 2-23 shows an example of the benefit of this feature. The left image shows you a flash-free shot. Clearly, a little more light was needed, but at normal flash power, the flash was too strong, blowing out the highlights in some areas, as shown in the middle image. Reducing the flash power to EV −1.3, resulted in a softer flash that straddled the line perfectly between no flash and too much flash, as shown in the third photo.

No flash   Flash EV 0.0   Flash EV -1.3

FIGURE 2-23: When normal flash output is too strong, lower the Flash Exposure Compensation value.

As for boosting the flash output, well, you may find it necessary on some occasions, but don't expect the built-in flash to work miracles even at a Flash Exposure Compensation of +2.0. Any built-in flash has a limited range, so the light simply can't reach faraway objects.

Here are the ways to enable Flash Exposure Compensation and set the level of adjustment:

>> **Quick Control method (not available for Live View shooting):** After shifting to the Quick Control display, highlight the Flash Exposure Compensation value, as shown on the left in Figure 2-24. Note that this value does not appear on the Quick Control display until you choose a setting other than 0 (no adjustment).

Flash Exposure Compensation setting

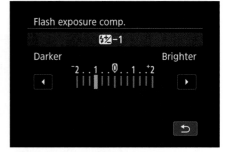

FIGURE 2-24:
For viewfinder photography, you can change the Flash Exposure Compensation from the Quick Control screen.

Rotate the Quick Control or Main dial to set the amount of flash adjustment. You also can display the screen shown on the right in the figure by tapping the Flash Exposure Compensation icon or pressing the Set button. On that screen, rotate the Quick Control dial or Main dial, press the right/left Quick Control keys, or tap the arrows at the ends of the setting scale. You also can drag your finger along the scale to adjust the setting. Tap the return arrow or press Set when you finish.

>> **Shooting Menu 2:** You also can get to the Flash Exposure Compensation setting via the menu. If you take the normal menu route, it's a long slog: Open Shooting Menu 2, choose Flash Control, and then choose Built-in Flash settings. On the next screen, shown in Figure 2-25, tap Flash Exp Comp (or highlight it and press Set) to display the screen shown on the right in the figure. You can then use the Quick Control dial, use the left/right Quick Control keys, or tap the Brighter and Darker arrows to adjust the setting. Tap the return arrow or press Set when you finish.

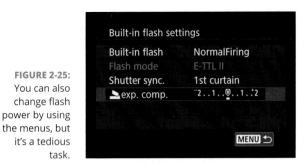
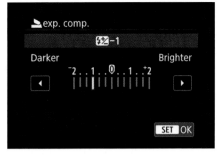

FIGURE 2-25:
You can also change flash power by using the menus, but it's a tedious task.

 » **Flash button:** When the flash is up, just press the Flash button to skip straight to the Built-in Flash Settings screen (left side of Figure 2-25). You don't even have to press the Menu button first to use this trick, and it works in Live View mode, as well as during viewfinder photography.

When the Flash Exposure Compensation option is set to any value except 0 (no adjustment), the value appears in the Quick Control display, in the area occupied by the icon in the left screen in Figure 2-24. In the Live View display, the setting appears in the area indicated on the left screen in Figure 2-26. In the viewfinder, you see a plus/minus flash symbol without the actual Flash Exposure Compensation value, as shown on the right in Figure 2-26.

FIGURE 2-26:
When flash compensation is enabled, the value appears in the detailed Live View display (left); the viewfinder just shows that the feature is enabled (right).

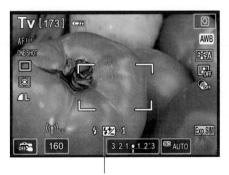
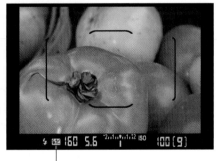

Flash Exposure Compensation setting   Flash Exposure Compensation enabled

WARNING

Any flash-power adjustment you make remains in force until you reset the control, even if you turn off the camera. So be sure to check the setting before using your flash. Additionally, the Auto Lighting Optimizer feature, covered in Chapter 4, can interfere with the effect produced by Flash Exposure Compensation, so you might want to disable it. (The setting is accessible via Shooting Menu 2.)

Locking the flash exposure

You might never notice it, but when you press the shutter button to take a picture with flash enabled, the camera emits a brief *preflash* before the actual flash. This preflash is used to determine the proper flash power needed to expose the image.

Occasionally, the information that the camera collects from the preflash can be off-target because of the assumptions the system makes about what area of the frame is likely to contain your subject. To address this problem, your camera has a feature called *Flash Exposure Lock*, or FE Lock. This tool enables you to set the flash power based on only the center of the frame.

Unfortunately, FE Lock isn't available in Live View mode. If you want to use this feature, you must use the viewfinder to frame and shoot your images.

Follow these steps to use FE Lock:

1. **With the flash raised, frame your photo so that your subject falls under the center autofocus point.**

    You want your subject smack in the middle of the frame. You can reframe the shot after locking the flash exposure, if you want.

2. **Press the shutter button halfway.**

    The camera meters the light in the scene. If you're using autofocusing, focus is set on your subject. (If focus is set on another spot in the frame, see Chapter 5 to find out how to select the center autofocus point.) You can now lift your finger off the shutter button, if you want.

3. **While the subject is still under the center autofocus point, press and release the FE Lock button.**

    You can see the button in the margin here. The camera emits the preflash, and the letters FEL display for a second in the viewfinder. (FEL stands for *flash exposure lock.*) You also see the asterisk symbol — the one that appears above the FE Lock button on the camera body — next to the flash icon in the viewfinder.

4. **If needed, reestablish focus on your subject.**

    In autofocus mode, press and hold the shutter button halfway. (Take this step only if you released the shutter button after Step 2.) In manual focus mode, rotate the focusing ring on the lens to establish focus.

5. **Reframe the image to the composition you want.**

    While you do, keep the shutter button pressed halfway to maintain focus if you're using autofocusing.

6. **Press the shutter button the rest of the way to take the picture.**

The image is captured using the flash output setting you established in Step 3.

TIP

Flash Exposure Lock is also helpful when you're shooting portraits. The preflash sometimes causes people to blink, which means that with normal flash shooting, in which the actual flash and exposure occur immediately after the preflash, their eyes are closed at the exact moment of the exposure. With Flash Exposure Lock, you can fire the preflash and then wait a second or two for the subject's eyes to recover before you take the actual picture.

Better yet, the flash exposure setting remains in force for about 16 seconds, meaning that you can shoot a series of images using the same flash setting without firing another preflash at all.

TIP

USING FLASH OUTDOORS

Although most people think of flash as a tool for nighttime and low-light photography, adding a bit of light from the built-in flash can improve close-ups and portraits that you shoot outdoors during the day. After all, your main light source — the sun — is over-head, so although the top of the subject may be adequately lit, the front typically needs some additional illumination. And if your subject is in the shade, getting no direct light, using flash is even more critical.

Be aware of a couple issues that arise when you supplement the sun with flash, however:

- You may need to make a white balance adjustment. Adding flash may result in colors that are slightly warmer (more yellow/red), or cooler (bluish) because the camera's white balancing system can get tripped up by mixed light sources. If you don't appreciate the shift in colors, see Chapter 6 to find out how to make a white balance adjustment to solve the problem.

- You may need to stop down the aperture (a fancy way of saying to make the aperture smaller) or lower ISO to avoid overexposing the photo. When you use flash, the fastest shutter speed you can use is 1/200 second, which may not be fast enough to produce a good exposure in very bright light when you use a wide-open aperture, even if you use the lowest possible ISO setting. If you want both flash and the short depth of field that comes with an open aperture, you can place a neutral-density filter over your lens. This accessory reduces the light that comes through the lens without affecting colors. In addition, some Canon external flash units enable you to access the entire range of shutter speeds on the camera.

Investigating other advanced flash options

In the P, Tv, Av, and M modes, selecting the Flash Control option on Shooting Menu 2, shown in Figure 2-27, enables you to take advantage of the following flash settings, shown on the right in the figure:

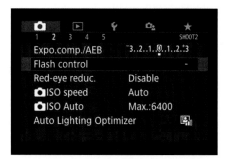

FIGURE 2-27:
You can customize additional flash options through the Shooting menu.

>> **Flash Firing:** Normally, this option is set to Enable. If you want to disable the flash, choose Disable instead. However, you don't have to take this step in most cases — just close the pop-up flash head on top of the camera if you don't want to use flash.

What's the point of this option, then? Well, if you use autofocusing in dim lighting, the camera may need some help finding its target. To that end, it sometimes emits an *AF-assist beam* from the flash head — the beam is a series of rapid pulses of light. If you want the benefit of the AF-assist beam, but you don't want the flash to fire, you can disable flash firing. Remember that you have to pop up the flash unit to expose the lamp that emits the beam. You also can take advantage of this option when you attach an external flash head.

>> **E-TTL II Meter:** The option name refers to the Canon flash metering system. The *E* stands for *evaluative, TTL* stands for *through the lens,* and *II* refers to the fact that this system is an update to the first version of the system.

This menu option enables you to choose from two flash metering setups. In the default mode, Evaluative, the camera exposes the background using ambient light when possible and then sets the flash power to serve as fill light on the subject. If you instead select the Average option, the flash is used as the primary light source, meaning that the flash power is set to expose the entire scene without relying on ambient light. Typically, this results in a more powerful (and possibly harsh) flash lighting and dark backgrounds.

>> **Flash Sync. Speed in Av Mode:** This option prevents the shutter speed from dropping beyond a certain level when you use flash in the Av exposure mode.

See the section "Adjusting shutter speed for flash photography," earlier in this chapter, for details.

» **Built-In Flash Settings:** Choose this option to access the following settings:

● *Built-in Flash:* This function enables you to configure the built-in flash for normal use or choose between two wireless flash methods, Easy Wireless or Custom Wireless. In both modes, the built-in flash is used to wirelessly trigger compatible off-camera flash units. (The remote units fire when they "see" the light from the built-in flash.)

The Canon wireless flash system is a great way to gain added lighting flexibility without having to carry around a lot of bulky studio lights. Although working with that system is beyond the scope (or page count!) of this book, the camera instruction manual has technical details, and you can find many tutorials and other useful information about multiple-flash photography online.

● *Flash Mode:* Ignore this option. It's related to using an external flash and isn't adjustable when you use the built-in flash.

● *Shutter Sync:* By default, the flash fires at the beginning of the exposure. This flash timing, known as *1st curtain sync,* is the best choice for most subjects. However, if you use a very slow shutter speed and you're photographing a moving object, 1st curtain sync causes the blur that results from the motion to appear in front of the object, which doesn't make much visual sense.

To make the motion trails actually trail the moving object, change the Shutter Sync option to *2nd curtain sync,* also known as *rear-curtain sync.* The flash fires twice in this mode when using E-TTL II metering (which is always on with the built-in flash): once when you press the shutter button and again at the end of the exposure.

● *Flash Exposure Compensation:* This setting adjusts the power of the built-in flash; see the earlier section "Adjusting flash power with Flash Exposure Compensation" for details.

Remember that you can get to this screen in a flash (sorry) by pressing the Flash button: Press once to raise the flash; press again to display the Built-in Flash Settings screen with the Flash Exposure Compensation setting already selected.

» **External Flash controls:** The last two options on the Flash Control list relate to external flash heads; they don't affect the performance of the built-in flash. However, they apply only to Canon EX-series Speedlites that enable you to control the flash through the camera. If you own such a flash, refer to the flash manual for details.

>> **Clear Settings:** Choose this option to access three settings that restore flash defaults. The first one, Clear Built-in Flash Set, restores the settings for the built-in flash. Sorry, you could have figured that out for yourself. The second option restores defaults for external flash settings, and the third restores the external flash head's Custom Function menu settings.

You can probably discern from these descriptions that most of these features are designed for photographers schooled in flash photography who want to mess around with advanced flash options. If that doesn't describe you, don't worry about it. The default settings selected by Canon will serve you well in most every situation. The exception is Flash Exposure Compensation, which comes in handy on many occasions.

Chapter **3**

Taking Great Pictures, Automatically

When you set your camera to a Creative Zone exposure mode (P, Tv, Av, or M), you can access a slew of features that enable you to precisely control exposure, color, focus, and more. But if you're not yet acquainted with those advanced options — or you're just not interested in "going there" right now — take advantage of Basic Zone exposure modes. In these modes, the camera selects most picture-taking settings for you, providing almost fully automatic photography.

Even in these modes, however, you can get better results by following the techniques outlined in this chapter. In addition to walking you through the steps of taking your first pictures in Scene Intelligent Auto mode, the pages to come contain tips for using scene modes (Portrait, Landscape, and so on), as well as Creative Auto mode. The one Basic Zone mode not covered in this chapter is Creative Filters mode; see Chapter 11 for help with that specialty shooting mode.

If what you see on your monitor looks vastly different from what you see in figures here and elsewhere, your camera is likely set to the Guided display level. To set your camera to match, open the Display Settings Options menu. Set the first two menu options to Standard and the other two to Disable, as shown in Chapter 1.

Using Scene Intelligent Auto Mode

For the simplest camera operation, set the Mode dial to Scene Intelligent Auto, as shown in Figure 3-1. Most people refer to this setting as simply *Auto,* but this book sticks with the official Canon name so that when you search the Canon website or the instruction manual, you're sure to land at the right spot. Remember to press and hold the lock-release button in the center of the Mode dial before trying to turn it.

Scene Intelligent Auto exposure mode

FIGURE 3-1:
Set the Mode dial to Scene Intelligent Auto for point-and-shoot simplicity.

REMEMBER The only tricky part about using Scene Intelligent Auto is that how you focus the camera varies depending on whether you use the viewfinder to compose your images or opt for Live View mode, which displays a live pre-view of your subject on the monitor. The next two sections provide specifics for each shooting option.

Viewfinder shooting

The following steps show you how to take a picture the "old-fashioned" way, looking through the viewfinder to frame your subject.

1. **Set the Mode dial to Scene Intelligent Auto (refer to Figure 3-1).**

   The Quick Control display appears, as shown in Figure 3-2.

FIGURE 3-2:
Even in Scene Intelligent Auto mode, you have control over the Drive mode and Flash mode.

2. **Set the lens focusing method (auto or manual).**

On the 18–55mm or 18–135mm kit lens, set the switch to AF, as shown in Figure 3-3, to take advantage of autofocusing. For manual focusing, set the switch to MF (and ignore upcoming instructions related to autofocusing). If you use a different Canon lens or third-party lens, check its instruction manual to find out how to set the lens to your preferred focusing method.

FIGURE 3-3: Set the lens switch to AF to use autofocusing; enable Image Stabilization for handheld shooting.

3. **If you're handholding the camera, set the Image Stabilizer switch to the On setting, as shown in Figure 3-3.**

TIP

Image stabilization helps produce sharper images by compensating for camera movement that can occur when you handhold the camera. If you're using a tripod, you can save battery power by turning stabilization off. Again, if you use a lens other than one of the two kit lenses, check your lens manual for details about its stabilization feature, if provided.

4. **Set the Drive mode to Single and the Flash mode to Auto.**

At these settings, which are the defaults, the camera takes a single picture each time you press the shutter button and fires the built-in flash if the ambient light is insufficient.

If necessary, you can adjust both options via the Quick Control method. Press the Q button or tap the Q symbol found in the lower-left corner of the display. Highlight the setting you want to change and then rotate the Quick Control or Main dial to adjust the setting. Press or tap Q again to return to shooting mode. You also can access the Drive mode setting by pressing the left Quick Control key.

5. **Looking through the viewfinder, frame the image so that your subject appears within the autofocus brackets.**

The brackets, labeled in Figure 3-4, represent the area of the frame that camera analyzes to set the focusing distance when you use autofocusing.

6. **Press and hold the shutter button halfway down.**

The camera's autofocus and autoexposure meters begin to do their thing, and the built-in flash pops up if the camera thinks additional light is needed to expose the subject. Additionally, the flash may emit an *AF*-assist beam, a few rapid pulses of light designed to help the autofocusing mechanism find its target. (The *AF* stands for autofocus.)

FIGURE 3-4:
Frame your subject so that it falls within the autofocus brackets.

When the camera establishes focus, one or more of the camera's autofocus points appear in the viewfinder and may blink red (if the scene is dark) to indicate which areas of the frame are in focus. For example, in Figure 3-5, which documents the year that pork products were celebrated at the Indiana State Fair, the camera focused on the front of the pig and other surfaces that were the same distance from the lens.

In most cases, you also hear a tiny beep, and the focus indicator in the lower-right corner of the viewfinder lights, as shown in Figure 3-5. Focus is locked as long as you keep the shutter button halfway down.

Focus achieved light

Focus points

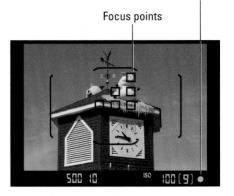

FIGURE 3-5:
When focus is achieved, you see the focus points the camera used to set the focusing distance.

REMEMBER

If the camera senses motion in the scene, however, you may hear a series of small beeps, and the focus lamp may not light. Both signals mean that the camera switched to continuous autofocusing and will adjust focus as necessary up to the time you take the picture. For this feature to work, you need to keep the subject within the autofocus brackets and keep the shutter button pressed halfway.

7. **Press the shutter button the rest of the way down to take the picture.**

After the camera records the picture data to the memory card, the image appears briefly on the camera monitor. If the picture doesn't appear or you want to take a longer look at the image, see Chapter 8, which covers picture playback.

As you can see, shooting in Scene Intelligent Auto is pretty much the same as taking a picture with any automatic camera. Here are a few additional pointers to make life even easier:

WARNING

» **Exposure:** After the camera meters exposure, it displays its chosen exposure settings at the bottom of the viewfinder, as shown in Figure 3-5, as well as on the LCD panel on top of the camera. (The 500 indicates a shutter speed of 1/500 second; the 10 indicates an aperture setting of f/10.) You can ignore all this data except for the shutter speed value. If that value blinks, the camera needs to use a slow shutter speed (long exposure time) to expose the picture. Because any movement of the camera or subject can blur the picture at a slow shutter speed, use a tripod and tell your subject to remain as still as possible.

Additionally, dim lighting may force the camera to use a high ISO setting, which increases the camera's sensitivity to light. Unfortunately, a high ISO can create *noise,* a defect that makes your picture look grainy. See Chapter 4 for tips on dealing with this and other exposure problems.

» **Flash:** The built-in flash has a relatively short reach, so if the flash fires but your picture is still too dark, move closer to the subject. If you don't want to use flash, press the Q button to shift to Quick Control mode and then change the flash mode to Off. Conversely, if the camera doesn't fire the flash in Auto Flash mode and you think that flash is needed, set the Flash mode to On.

When shooting portraits that require flash, you may want to enable Red-Eye Reduction to lessen the chances of the flash causing red-eye. Turn this feature on and off via Shooting Menu 1. Chapter 2 has details about how to get the best performance when using this flash feature.

» **Autofocusing tips:** Note these autofocusing pitfalls:

- *If the camera can't establish focus, you may be too close to your subject.* Check your lens instruction manual to find out its minimum close-focusing distance.

- *At the autofocus settings used by Scene Intelligent Auto, the camera focuses on the closest object.* So if you're shooting a portrait of someone standing behind a sign, the sign may appear in sharp focus but your subject may not.

- *Some subjects confuse autofocusing systems.* Water, highly reflective objects, and subjects behind fences are some problematic subjects. One trick is to find an object that's about the same distance from the camera as your subject, set focus on that object, and then reframe the scene — keeping the shutter button pressed halfway as you do. When you depress the shutter button fully, the camera will use the focusing distance you set on the stand-in object.

Chapter 5 discusses ways to modify the autofocusing system in ways that may solve some of these issues. But usually, a better option is to simply switch to manual focusing and set focus by rotating the focusing ring on the lens. (The lens's close-focus distance still applies.) The focusing ring on the 18–55mm kit lens is highlighted in Figure 3-3.

Live View photography

The initial steps for taking a picture in Live View mode are the same as for viewfinder photography: Rotate the Mode dial to the Scene Intelligent Auto setting (refer to Figure 3-1) and then set the focusing method (auto or manual) via the switch on the lens (see Figure 3-3). If handholding the camera, also enable image stabilization if your lens offers it. On the kit lenses and many other Canon models, you enable this feature by moving the IS switch to the On position.

From there, take this path:

1. **Press the Live View button to engage Live View.**

   The viewfinder pulls the blanket over its head and goes to sleep, and the scene in front of the lens appears on the monitor. What data you see superimposed on top of the scene depends on your display mode; Figure 3-6 shows the default display mode. Press Info to cycle through the available display options.

Focus area boundary mark Face detection frame

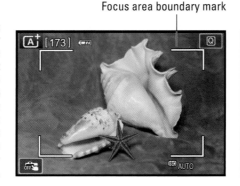 

FIGURE 3-6:
The corner marks indicate the area that will be used to set focus (left) unless a face is detected, in which case a focus frame appears over the face (right).

2. **Frame your subject so that it's inside the area marked by the four corner brackets, as shown in Figure 3-6.**

   These brackets appear only when you use the default Live View AF Method (autofocusing method) setting, called Face+Tracking. The idea behind this setting is that the camera assumes that if any people are in the scene, they are your subject of interest. So, if it detects a face, you see a focus frame over it, as shown on the right in Figure 3-6. Otherwise, you see only the corner brackets, as shown on the left.

   The Tracking part of the AF Method name refers to the fact that the camera uses continuous autofocusing. When that option is enabled, initial focusing begins automatically — you don't need to press the shutter button halfway as you do for viewfinder photography. But this initial focusing is only designed to get the scene in the focus ballpark so that your subject appears clearly on the monitor.

3. **Press the shutter button halfway to officially set focus.**

   When focus is achieved, one or more green focus points appear to indicate the area of the frame that the camera used to set the focusing distance, as shown on the left in Figure 3-7. Or, in a portrait, the frame over the face turns green, as shown on the right. You also hear a beep to signal that focus has been set.

Focus achieved Focus achieved

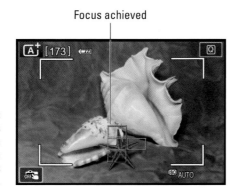 

FIGURE 3-7:
The focus points turn green when focus is achieved.

4. **Press the shutter button fully to take the shot.**

   You see your just-captured image on the monitor for a few seconds before the Live View preview returns.

5. **To exit Live View, press the Live View button again.**

   It's a good idea to exit Live View if you aren't going to continue taking photos or want to switch to using the viewfinder. This saves battery power and keeps your camera from overheating. Otherwise, leave Live View on and return to Step 2 to keep taking shots.

The tips on exposure, flash, and autofocusing at the end of the preceding section apply to Live View shooting as well. Also keep in mind these additional notes related only to Live View mode:

>> **Automatic scene selection:** See the little A+ symbol in the upper-left corner of the first screen in Figure 3-7? Notice that in the screen on the right, that symbol has changed. This shape shifting indicates that the camera analyzed the frame and determined the type of scene you're trying to shoot. There are dozens of possible scenes: portrait, portrait of a moving subject, portrait with blue sky included — and that's just for shots where people are detected. You can find a chart listing all the possible symbols in the Live View section of the camera manual, but it's pretty pointless to memorize them because you can't do anything to change the camera's mind about the scene type. In fact, the only reason this bullet point exists is so that when you see the icon changing, you don't worry that something is wrong.

>> **Tap to focus:** In Live View mode, you can tap your subject on the monitor to let the camera know where to set focus. However, if the touch shutter feature is turned on, your tap not only establishes a focus point but also triggers the shutter release, and the picture is recorded at that moment. If you want your tap to focus only, make sure the Touch Shutter icon, shown in the lower-left corner of both screens in Figure 3-7, is set to Off.

   To disable the Touch Shutter, the camera must be in Live View mode. You can then turn the feature on or off (it's disabled by default) via Shooting Menu 2.

>> **Enable/disable Live View:** If the camera doesn't engage Live View when you press the Live View button, open Shooting Menu 1 and set the Live View Shoot option to Enable. Should you decide to turn the feature off again, you need to exit Live View mode first; you can't disable Live View while using it.

Shooting in Flash Off Mode

You probably need a break after slogging through all the explanations just provided for shooting in Scene Intelligent Auto mode. So here's an easy-to-digest explanation about the next exposure setting on the Mode dial, Auto Flash Off, shown in Figure 3-8. This mode works just like Scene Intelligent Auto except that the flash is disabled. Choose this setting for occasions where flash is absolutely verboten and you're afraid that if you use Scene Intelligent Auto, you'll forget to set the Flash mode to Off.

FIGURE 3-8:
Flash Off mode works just like Scene Intelligent Auto but doesn't give you the option to use flash.

Taking Advantage of Scene Modes

In Scene Intelligent Auto and Flash Off modes, the camera tries to figure out what type of picture you want to take. If you don't want to rely on the camera to make that judgment, you can instead take advantage of *scene modes,* each of which is tailored to a specific type of photo. After you select a scene mode, the camera automatically selects picture settings that render the subject according to the photography style traditionally considered "best."

The next sections describe each scene mode and explain how to set your camera to use them. Before you dig into that information, though, you need to know that none of the scene modes can deliver its intended results all the time. How close the camera can hit the mark depends on the lighting conditions. Specifically, the amount of available light determines which shutter speed and aperture settings the camera needs to use to expose the picture. And those two settings, in turn, affect motion blur and whether the background appears sharp or blurry. Your lens also has an impact:

>> The range of available aperture settings varies depending on the lens.

>> Lens focal length (18mm, 55mm, 200mm, and so on) also affects *depth of field,* or the distance over which focus remains sharp.

To fully understand these issues, check out Chapter 4, which explains exposure, and Chapter 5, which covers ways to manipulate depth of field. In the meantime, just don't expect miracles from the scene modes.

As for actually taking a picture, the process is the same as spelled out for Scene Intelligent Auto mode, earlier in this chapter, for most scene modes. If you need to do anything differently, the description of the scene mode provides details.

Looking at the primary scene modes

Nearly every camera that offers scene modes provides the four scene types labeled in Figure 3-9: Portrait, Landscape, Close-up, and Sports.

Here's a quick description of each mode:

>> **Portrait:** Produces classic portraiture look featured in Figure 3-10: a sharply focused subject, blurry background, with skin enhanced to appear slightly softer and warmer (less blue, more amber).

>> **Landscape:** Again, takes the traditional approach to landscape photography, with both foreground and background appearing sharp and with blues and greens strengthened. Figure 3-11 shows an example.

>> **Close-up:** Like Portrait mode, Close-up mode blurs the background to draw the eye directly to the subject, as shown in Figure 3-12. Colors are not manipulated in Close-up mode as they are in Portrait mode.

REMEMBER

How close you can get to your subject depends on your lens; choosing Close-up mode has nothing to do with that limitation as it does on some compact cameras you may have used. Check your lens manual to find out its minimum focusing distance.

Landscape

Portrait

Sports   Close-up

Special scene modes

FIGURE 3-9:
Access the scene modes through these Mode dial settings.

FIGURE 3-10:
Portrait mode
produces a
soft-focus
background
and warmer,
softer skin.

FIGURE 3-11:
Landscape mode keeps both background and
foreground as sharply focused as possible
and boosts blue and green hues.

FIGURE 3-12:
Close-up mode also produces short depth
of field.

>> **Sports:** Sports mode freezes motion, as shown in Figure 3-13, whether you're actually photographing sports or some other moving subject.

To select one of these scene modes, just rotate the Mode dial to the corresponding icon. Depending on the scene mode, you may be able to tweak a couple of picture-taking settings. See the upcoming section "Adjusting a few settings" for details.

Accessing specialty scene modes

By setting the Mode dial to SCN, you can access additional scene modes, described in the following list. Some are either self–explanatory or "meh," but a few, most notably the last two on the list, are really helpful.

FIGURE 3-13:
To capture freeze the action of moving subjects, try Sports mode.

>> **Group Portrait:** Assumes that your subjects are standing at varying distances from the lens and so uses settings that ensure that the tall people relegated to the back row appear as sharply focused as the short ones hogging the front row.

>> **Kids:** Attempts to accommodate fidgety younger subjects by choosing a shutter speed that prevents motion blur. According to Canon, skin tones will appear "healthy" if you use this mode, although it's probably not the best idea to force a kid with the flu to pose for pictures anyway.

>> **Food:** Designed to make your dessert look especially appealing by brightening exposure a tad. Also removes any red tint that would otherwise affect image colors when your plate is lit by candlelight or tungsten lights.

>> **Candlelight:** Disables flash so that your subject is lit only by the warm glow of the candlelight and, unlike Food mode, leaves the reddish tint added by that light source intact. A slow shutter speed (long exposure time) is necessary, so use a tripod and ask your subjects to remain as still as possible. Otherwise, camera shake and subject motion can blur the image.

>> **Night Portrait:** Also uses a slow shutter and less flash power than normal, producing more flattering light on your subject. Again, you need a tripod and a subject that can remain still to avoid blurring.

REMEMBER

>> **Handheld Night Scene:** Designed to produce a sharper picture when you handhold the camera in dim lighting, which requires a slow shutter speed and, thus, increases the risk of picture-blurring camera shake.

To produce this result, the camera records four shots in quick succession when you press the shutter button. Then it blends the images in a way that reduces blurring.

You don't have to reserve this setting for nighttime shots, despite the mode name. For example, Julie used it to capture the shot in Figure 3-14, taken from the top flight of stairs inside a lighthouse. No way was she going to lug a tripod up 200-some steps to that vantage point, so she set the camera to Handheld Night Scene Mode, pointed the camera downward, held her breath, and pressed the shutter button. At a shutter speed of 1/40 second, that would normally be a recipe for a blurry image, but with the help of the Handheld Night Scene mode, the shot is acceptably sharp. (Enabling Image Stabilization, if available for your lens, also helps.)

FIGURE 3-14:
Handheld
Night Scene
captured this
handheld shot
from a vantage
point at the top
of a lighthouse.

WARNING

The angle of view of the final image may be smaller than what you see through the viewfinder. This occurs if the camera needs to crop the image in order to get the four shots to align properly in the merged image. Frame your subject a little loosely so that important parts of the scene aren't lost in the cropping process.

>> **HDR Backlight Control:** Try this mode when your subject is backlit — the light is behind the subject — which normally either leaves the subject too dark or the background too bright. This mode uses some digital voodoo to brighten

the darkest parts of the image while holding onto more highlight detail than is otherwise possible. Figure 3-15 offers an example of the difference this mode can make. Both the highlight and the shadow areas in the HDR version (shown on the right in the figure) contain more detail than the one shot in Scene Intelligent Auto (shown on the left). To achieve this result, the camera records three images each time you press the shutter button, adjusting exposure between each frame. Then the three frames are merged into one final HDR image.

Scene Intelligent Auto

HDR Backlight Control

FIGURE 3-15: Try shooting high-contrast scenes in HDR Backlight Control mode to retain more detail in both shadows and highlights.

TECHNICAL STUFF

HDR stands for *high dynamic range. Dynamic range* refers to the range of brightness values that a device can record. HDR refers to an image that contains a greater spectrum of brightness values than can normally be captured by a camera.

As with the Handheld Night Scene, the camera needs to crop the image a little in order to properly align the multiple frames into one. So frame your subject a little loosely so that important areas of the scene don't get cropped out of the final HDR image. Also use a tripod; this ensures that each frame records the same image area, helping the camera to properly align frames when merging them. Finally, keep in mind that anything that's moving in the scene usually appears at partial opacity in different parts of the frame in the merged image. (On the other hand, you may be able to claim that you captured a ghost in your picture. . . .)

To select the specialty scene mode you want to use, set the Mode dial to SCN and then press the Q button or tap the Q symbol on the touchscreen. Then highlight the Choose Scene symbol, which appears in different places depending on whether you're using the viewfinder or are shooting in Live View mode. Figure 3-16 shows you where to look. After selecting the symbol, press the Set button or tap Set on the touchscreen to display the selection screen shown in Figure 3-17. Press the up/down Quick Control keys or tap the up/down arrows to scroll through the list of scene types. Tap OK or press the Set button again to exit the selection screen and return to shooting mode.

Choose Scene

Choose Scene

FIGURE 3-16: When the Mode dial is set to SCN, press the Q button and select the Choose Scene option to access the available scene types.

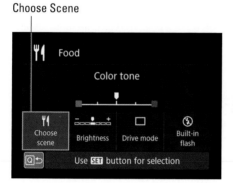

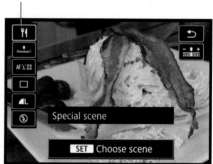

Adjusting a few settings

Whether you're using the four main scene modes or one of the specialty modes described in the preceding section, you may be able to adjust a few picture taking settings, detailed in the upcoming list.

Unless otherwise noted, you change the settings by using the Quick Control method: Press the Q button or tap the Q touchscreen symbol to put the camera

FIGURE 3-17: On the selection screen, highlight the scene type you want to use and then tap OK or press the Set button.

in that mode and then select the option you want to change. When you're using the viewfinder, the settings appear with a text label, as shown on the left in Figure 3-18; in Live View mode, they're represented by the symbols labeled on the right screen in the figure. If a particular option doesn't appear, the current scene mode doesn't enable you to play with that setting. (In both figures, the Choose Setting option is currently selected; that option applies only when you use the SCN exposure mode.)

>> **Brightness:** True to its name, this option enables you to request a brighter or darker exposure on your next shot. After selecting the option, rotate the Quick Control or Main dial to move the marker along the brightness scale. In Live View mode, the preview updates to provide an approximation of how the scene will look at the new setting.

>> **Color Tone:** This setting enables you to request a warmer (more amber) or cooler (more blue) rendition of your subject on the next shot. Again, rotate the Quick Control or Main dial to move the marker on the scale toward the red or blue end of the scale. If you're using Live View, the onscreen colors change to reflect the new setting.

>> **Flash mode:** For modes that permit flash, you may be able to choose from these flash modes: Auto flash (the camera decides when it's needed), On (the flash always fires), and Off. See Chapter 2 for a flash photography primer.

REMEMBER

When flash is enabled, you can also enable or disable Red-Eye Reduction flash. Adjust this option through Shooting Menu 1 instead of the Quick Control screen.

>> **Drive mode:** Before taking your first shot, check the Drive mode symbol to see which setting the camera uses by default in the current scene mode. In most cases, the default setting is Single (one shot for each press of the shutter button). But a few scene modes use one of the Continuous settings instead (the camera records a series of frames as long as you hold down the shutter button). Chapter 2 explains how each Drive mode works.

When the camera isn't in Live View mode, you can access the Drive mode setting by pressing the left Quick Control key instead of going the Quick Control route.

>> **Image Quality:** For viewfinder photography, you can access this setting only via Shooting Menu 1. As detailed in Chapter 2, your selection determines the picture resolution (pixel count) and file type (JPEG or Raw.) In Live View mode, you can adjust the setting through the Quick Control display (the setting is labeled in Figure 3-18), as well as through Shooting Menu 1.

You can't use the Raw or Raw+JPEG Image Quality setting in the HDR Backlight Control and Handheld Night Scene modes.

>> **Autofocusing:** For viewfinder photography, you can't deviate from the default autofocusing settings, which work as outlined in the earlier section "Viewfinder shooting." In Live View mode, you can vary the autofocusing behavior by adjusting the AF Method, labeled in Figure 3-18. But until you have time to read the section of Chapter 5 that explains how those options work, stick with the default settings and set focus as detailed in section "Live View photography," also found earlier in this chapter.

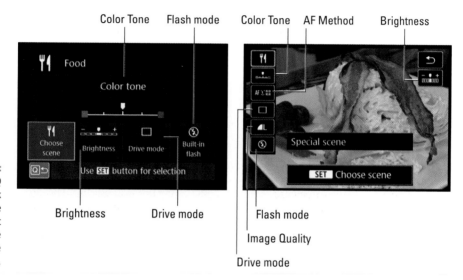

FIGURE 3-18:
Press or tap Q
to enter Quick
Control mode
and adjust
settings for the
scene you've
chosen.

Gaining More Control with Creative Auto

Creative Auto mode, represented on the Mode dial by the letters CA, offers a bit more control over the look of your pictures than the rest of the Basic Zone exposure modes. As in Scene Intelligent Auto, you can choose any Drive mode, Image Quality setting, or Flash mode (Auto, On, and Off). Additionally, Creative Auto provides two other settings, Ambience and Background Blur, which affect your picture as follows:

>> **Ambience:** You can exert some control over color, contrast, or exposure by choosing one of these Ambience options:

- *Standard:* Renders the image the same way as Scene Intelligent Auto. This setting is the default.

- *Vivid:* Increases contrast, color saturation, and sharpness.

- *Soft:* Creates the appearance of slightly softer focus.

- *Warm:* Warms colors (adds a reddish-orange color cast).

- *Intense:* Boosts contrast and saturation to a greater degree than Vivid.

- *Cool:* Adds a cool (blue) color cast.

- *Brighter:* Lightens the photo.

- *Darker:* Darkens the photo.

- *Monochrome:* Creates a black-and-white photo, with the option to add a sepia or cyan (bluish) tint.

Figure 3-19 offers a look at three variation on the same scene, captured at the Standard, Warm, and Intense settings.

Standard Ambience   Warm Ambience   Vivid Ambience

FIGURE 3-19: Here are examples of how the camera renders the same scene using the Standard, Warm, and Vivid Ambience settings.

Unfortunately, you can apply only one ambience adjustment at a time. You can't make your image both brighter and warmer, for example. For that kind of flexibility, you need to use the Creative Zone modes (P, Tv, Av, and M), as outlined in Part 2.

» **Background Blur:** This feature is somewhat mislabeled. Yes, you can use it to affect the extent to which background objects blur. But the adjustment also affects objects in front of your subject. Still, it's nice to be able to play with this characteristic of your photo, known in professional circles as *depth of field.*

REMEMBER

There's an "unfortunately" attached to this setting as well: Background Blur is disabled when the Flash mode is set to Auto or On. Again, to use flash *and* manipulate the amount of background and foreground blurring, step up to P, Tv, Av, or M exposure mode. The last section of Chapter 5 details ways to affect depth of field. Chapter 2 covers flash.

Now for the how-to's of viewing and adjusting settings in Creative Auto mode. If you're using the viewfinder, the Quick Control display appears as shown on the left in Figure 3-20. In Live View mode, all the adjustable settings don't appear by default, so press the Info button to cycle to the detailed Live View display shown on the right in the figure.

Background Blur setting

Ambience setting

Ambience setting

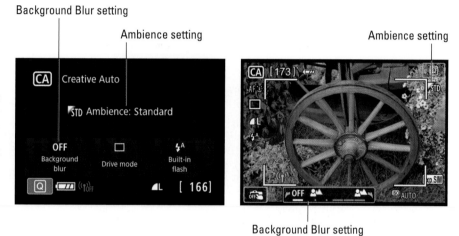

FIGURE 3-20:
Creative Auto mode offers two picture settings not available in other Basic Zone modes: Ambience and Background Blur.

Background Blur setting

 To adjust the Ambience, Background Blur, Drive mode, or Flash mode settings, use the Quick Control technique: Press the Q button or tap the Q symbol on the touchscreen. Then highlight the option you want to change and then rotate the Quick Control or Main dial to cycle through the available settings. If you're not in Live View mode, you also can display all available options for the selected setting by pressing the Set button.

As is the case with the other Basic Zone modes, you can choose the Image Quality setting via Shooting Menu 1. In Live View mode, you also can use the Quick Control screen to handle that task.

The way that the Ambience and Background Blur settings are presented are a little less than clear, so before moving on to another chapter, note these final bits of information:

>> **For Ambience options other than Standard, you can set the level or type of adjustment.** As soon as you rotate the Quick Control or Main dial to select a setting other than Standard, a second option appears under the Ambience option, as shown in Figure 3-21. Select that option and rotate the Quick Control or Main dial to change the setting. In most cases, the adjustment merely increases or decreases the impact of the setting. For example, the screen on the left in Figure 3-21 shows the Vivid level set to medium; the second screen, strong. If you set the Ambience option to Monochrome, you instead rotate the Quick Control or Main dial to set the effect to straight-up black-and-white picture or one that has a amber or blue tint.

FIGURE 3-21: For any Ambience setting except Standard, you get a second setting that adjusts the level or type of image adjustment.

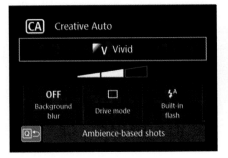
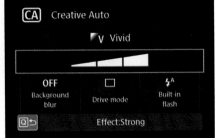

>> **When Background Blur is turned off, as shown on the left in Figure 3-22, select the option and then rotate the Quick Control or Main dial to enable the feature.** You then see a scale of sorts, as shown on the right in the figure. Rotate the Quick Control or Main dial to the right to increase the level of blur; rotate either dial to the left to lower it. If you go one step beyond the lowest blur level, you set the option back to Off.

If the Flash mode is set to Auto, as it is by default, the camera automatically changes it to Off. (Note the appearance of the Flash mode symbols in Figure 3-22.)

Understand, though, that turning off Background Blur doesn't mean that the background or foreground won't appear blurry. Whether it appears sharp or softly focused depends on the lighting conditions. That's because one of the exposure settings the camera selects for you — aperture — affects depth of field. In bright light, backgrounds are likely to appear sharper than in dim lighting. Again, check out the first part of Chapter 4 for information about the aperture setting.

» **In Live View mode, the preview displays an approximation of how your image will be affected by your chosen settings.** The color and exposure shifts applied by the Ambience settings usually are pretty close to what the final image shows, but the amount of background blurring may be more or less than the camera is able to simulate on the monitor.

FIGURE 3-22:
In Quick Control mode, select the Background blur option and then rotate the Quick Control or Main dial to change settings.

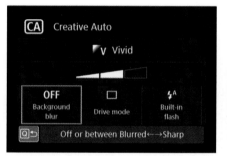
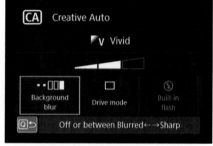

2
Taking Creative Control

IN THIS CHAPTER

» Getting a grip on exposure settings: aperture, shutter speed, and ISO

» Exploring advanced exposure modes: P, Tv, Av, and M

» Choosing a metering mode

» Tweaking autoexposure results

» Taking advantage of Automatic Exposure Bracketing (AEB)

Chapter **4**

Taking Charge of Exposure

Understanding exposure is one of the most intimidating challenges for a new photographer. Discussions of the topic are loaded with technical terms — *aperture, metering, shutter speed, ISO,* and the like. Add the fact that your camera offers many exposure controls, all sporting equally foreign names, and it's no wonder that many people decide to stick with Auto exposure mode and let the camera take care of all exposure decisions.

We fully relate to the confusion you may be feeling — we've been there. But we can also promise that when you take things nice and slow, digesting a piece of the exposure pie at a time, the topic is *not* as complicated as it seems on the surface. The payoff will be worth your time, too. You'll not only gain the know-how to solve most exposure problems but also discover ways to use exposure to put your creative stamp on a scene.

To that end, this chapter provides everything you need to know about controlling exposure, from a primer in exposure terminology (it's not as bad as it sounds) to tips on using the P, Tv, Av, and M exposure modes, which are the only ones that offer access to all exposure features.

Note: The one exposure-related topic not covered in this chapter is flash, which is covered in Chapter 2 because it's among the options you can access even in Auto mode. Also, this chapter deals with still photography; Chapter 7 covers movie exposure.

Introducing the Exposure Trio: Aperture, Shutter Speed, and ISO

Any photograph, whether taken with a film camera or digital camera, is created by focusing light through a lens onto a light-sensitive recording medium. In a film camera, the unexposed film serves as the medium; in a digital camera, it's the image sensor, which is an array of light-responsive computer chips.

Between the lens and the sensor are two barriers, the aperture and shutter, which together control how much light makes its way to the sensor. The actual design and arrangement of the aperture, shutter, and sensor vary depending on the camera, but Figure 4-1 offers an illustration of the basic concept.

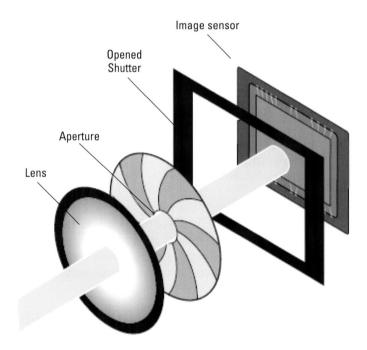

FIGURE 4-1: The aperture size and shutter speed determine how much light strikes the image sensor.

The aperture and shutter speed, along with a third feature, ISO, determine *exposure* — what most people would describe as picture brightness. This three-part exposure formula works as follows:

» **Aperture (controls amount of light):** The *aperture* is an adjustable hole in a diaphragm set inside the lens. By changing the size of the aperture, you control the size of the light beam that can enter the camera. Aperture settings are stated as *f-stop numbers,* or simply *f-stops,* and are expressed with the letter *f* followed by a number: f/2, f/5.6, f/16, and so on. The smaller the f-stop number, the larger the aperture, as illustrated in Figure 4-2. The range of available aperture settings varies from lens to lens.

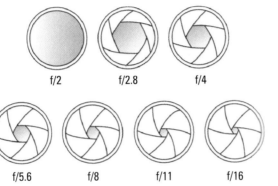

f/2   f/2.8   f/4

FIGURE 4-2: The smaller the f-stop number, the larger the aperture.

f/5.6   f/8   f/11   f/16

» **Shutter speed (controls duration of light):** Set behind the aperture, the shutter works something like shutters on a window. When you aren't taking pictures, the camera's shutter stays closed, preventing light from striking the image sensor. When you press the shutter button, the shutter opens briefly to allow light that passes through the aperture to hit the image sensor. The exception to this scenario is when you compose in Live View mode — the shutter remains open so that your image can form on the sensor and be displayed on the monitor. When you press the shutter release in Live View mode, the shutter first closes and then reopens for the actual exposure.

The length of time that the shutter is open is the *shutter speed* and is measured in seconds: 1/60 second, 1/250 second, 2 seconds, and so on.

» **ISO (controls light sensitivity):** ISO, which is a digital function rather than a mechanical structure on the camera, enables you to adjust how responsive the image sensor is to light. The term *ISO* is a holdover from film days, when an international standards organization rated each film stock according to light sensitivity: ISO 100, ISO 200, ISO 400, ISO 800, and so on. A higher ISO rating means greater light sensitivity.

On a digital camera, the sensor doesn't actually get more or less sensitive when you change the ISO. Instead, the light "signal" that hits the sensor is either amplified or dampened through electronics wizardry, sort of like how raising the volume on a radio boosts the audio signal. But the upshot is the same as changing to a more light-reactive film stock: A higher ISO means that less light is needed to produce the image, enabling you to use a smaller aperture, faster shutter speed, or both.

Distilled to its essence, the image-exposure formula is this simple:

>> Aperture and shutter speed together determine the quantity of light that strikes the image sensor.

>> ISO determines how much the sensor reacts to that light.

The tricky part of the equation is that aperture, shutter speed, and ISO settings affect your pictures in ways that go *beyond* exposure:

>> Aperture affects *depth of field,* or the distance over which focus appears acceptably sharp.

>> Shutter speed determines whether moving objects appear blurry or sharply focused.

>> ISO affects the amount of image *noise,* a defect that looks like grains of sand.

You need to be aware of these side effects, explained in the next sections, to determine which combination of the three exposure settings will work best for your picture. If you're already familiar with this stuff and you just want to know how to adjust exposure settings, skip ahead to the section "Setting ISO, Aperture, and Shutter Speed."

Aperture affects depth of field

The aperture setting, or f-stop, affects *depth of field* (the distance over which focus appears sharp). With a shallow depth of field, your subject appears more sharply focused than faraway objects; with a large depth of field, the sharp-focus zone spreads over a greater distance.

When you reduce the aperture size — "stop down the aperture," in photo lingo — by choosing a higher f-stop number, you increase depth of field. As an example, see Figure 4-3. For both shots, focus was set on the fountain statue. Notice that the background in the first image, taken at f/13, is sharper than in the right example, taken at f/5.6. Aperture is just one contributor to depth of field, however; the focal length of the lens and the distance between that lens and your subject also affect how much of the scene stays in focus. See Chapter 5 for the complete story. Also be aware that depth of field affects not only objects behind your subject, but also those in front of it.

f/13, 1/25 second, ISO 200

f/5.6, 1/125 second, ISO 200

FIGURE 4-3: Widening the aperture (choosing a lower f-stop number) decreases depth of field.

TIP

One way to remember the relationship between f-stop and depth of field, or the distance over which focus remains sharp, is to think of the *f* as *focus:* The higher the *f*-stop number, the greater the zone of sharp *focus.* (Please *don't* share this tip with photography elites, who will roll their eyes and inform you that the *f* in *f-stop* most certainly does *not* stand for focus but, rather, for the ratio between aperture size and lens focal length — as if *that's* helpful to know if you aren't an optical engineer. Chapter 1 explains focal length, which *is* helpful to know.)

Shutter speed affects motion blur

At a slow shutter speed, moving objects appear blurry, whereas a fast shutter speed captures motion cleanly. This phenomenon has nothing to do with the actual focus point of the camera but rather with the movement occurring — and being recorded by the camera — while the shutter is open.

Compare the photos in Figure 4-3, for example. The static elements are perfectly focused in both images, although the background in the left photo appears sharper because that image was shot using a higher f-stop, increasing the depth of field. But how the camera rendered the moving portion of the scene — the fountain water — was determined by shutter speed. At 1/25 second (left photo), the water blurs, giving it a misty look. At 1/125 second (right photo), the droplets appear more sharply focused, almost frozen in midair. How fast a shutter speed you need to freeze action depends on the speed of your subject.

WARNING

If your picture suffers from overall image blur, like the picture shown in Figure 4-4, where even stationary objects appear out of focus, the camera moved during the exposure. This movement, or *camera shake,* is always a danger when you hand-hold the camera at slow shutter speeds. The longer the exposure time, the longer you have to hold the camera still to avoid the blur caused by camera shake.

How slow a shutter speed can you use before camera shake becomes a problem? The answer depends on a couple factors, including your physical abilities and your lens — the heavier the lens, the harder it is to hold steady. Camera shake also affects your picture more when you shoot with a lens that has a long focal length. You may be able to use a slower shutter speed with a 55mm lens than with a 200mm lens, for example. Finally, it's easier to detect slight blurring in an image that shows a close-up view of a subject than in one

FIGURE 4-4:
If both stationary and moving objects are blurry, camera shake is the usual cause.

that captures a wider area. Moral of the story: Take test shots to determine the slowest shutter speed you can use with each of your lenses.

Of course, to avoid the possibility of camera shake altogether, mount your camera on a tripod. If you must handhold the camera, investigate whether your lens offers Image Stabilization, a feature that helps compensate for small amounts of camera shake. The 18–55mm and 18–135mm kit lenses do provide that feature; enable it by moving the Stabilizer switch on the lens to the On position.

Freezing action isn't the only way to use shutter speed to creative effect. When shooting waterfalls, for example, many photographers use a slow shutter speed to give the water even more of a blurry, romantic look than you see in the fountain example. With colorful subjects, a slow shutter can produce some cool abstract effects and create a heightened sense of motion. Chapter 7 offers examples of both effects.

ISO affects image noise

As ISO increases, making the image sensor more reactive to light, you increase the risk of *noise.* Noise is similar in appearance to film *grain,* a defect that often mars pictures taken with high-ISO film. Figure 4-5 offers an example of digital noise.

FIGURE 4-5: Noise is caused by a very high ISO or long exposure time, and it becomes more visible as you enlarge the image.

Ideally, then, you should always use the lowest ISO setting on your camera to ensure top image quality. But sometimes the lighting conditions don't permit you to do so. Take the rose photos in Figure 4-6 as an example. When Julie shot these pictures, she didn't have a tripod, so she needed a shutter speed fast enough to allow a sharp handheld image. She opened the aperture to f/5.6, which was the widest setting on the lens she was using at that focal length, to allow as much light as possible into the camera. At ISO 100, the camera needed a shutter speed of 1/40 second to expose the picture, and that shutter speed wasn't fast enough for a successful handheld shot. You see the blurred result on the left in Figure 4-6.

Raising the ISO to 200 allowed a shutter speed of 1/80 second, which was fast enough to capture the flower cleanly, as shown on the right in the figure.

ISO 100, f/5.6, 1/40 second

ISO 200, f/5.6, 1/80 second

FIGURE 4-6:
Raising the ISO allowed a faster shutter speed, which produced a sharper handheld shot.

Fortunately, you don't encounter serious noise on the 77D until you really crank up the ISO. In fact, you may get away with a fairly high ISO if you keep your print or display size small. Some people probably wouldn't even notice the noise in the left image in Figure 4-5 unless they were looking for it, for example. But as with other image defects, noise becomes more apparent as you enlarge the photo, as shown on the right in that same figure. Noise is also easier to spot in shadow areas of your picture and in large areas of solid color.

How much noise is acceptable — and, therefore, how high of an ISO is safe — is your choice. Even a little noise isn't acceptable for pictures that require the highest quality, such as images for a product catalog or a travel shot that you want to blow up to poster size.

WARNING

A high ISO isn't the only cause of noise: A long exposure time (slow shutter speed) can also produce the defect. So, how high you can raise the ISO before the image gets ugly varies depending on shutter speed.

Your camera offers tools that combat both types of noise; check out the section "Looking at a few other exposure solutions," later in this chapter, for information.

Doing the exposure balancing act

Aperture, shutter speed, and ISO combine to determine image brightness. So changing any one setting means that one or both of the others must also shift to maintain the same image brightness.

Suppose that you're shooting a soccer game and you notice that although the overall exposure looks great, the players appear slightly blurry at the current shutter speed. If you raise the shutter speed, you have to compensate with either a larger aperture, to allow in more light during the shorter exposure, or a higher ISO setting, to make the camera more sensitive to the light. Which way should you go? Well, it depends on whether you prefer the shallower depth of field that comes with a larger aperture or the increased risk of noise that accompanies a higher ISO. Of course, you can also adjust both settings to get the exposure results you need, perhaps upping ISO slightly and opening the aperture just a bit as well.

All photographers have their own approaches to finding the right combination of aperture, shutter speed, and ISO, and you'll no doubt develop your own system when you become more practiced at using the advanced exposure modes. In the meantime, here are some handy recommendations:

>> Use the lowest possible ISO setting unless the lighting conditions are so poor that you can't use the aperture and shutter speed you want without raising the ISO.

>> If your subject is moving, give shutter speed the next highest priority in your exposure decision. Choose a fast shutter speed to ensure a blur-free photo or, on the flip side, select a slow shutter speed to intentionally blur that moving object, an effect that can create a heightened sense of motion.

>> For nonmoving subjects, make aperture a priority over shutter speed, setting the aperture according to the depth of field you have in mind. For portraits, for example, try using a wide-open aperture (a low f-stop number) to create a shallow depth of field and a nice, soft background for your subject.

WARNING

Be careful not to go too shallow with depth of field when shooting a group portrait — unless all the subjects are the same distance from the camera, some may be outside the zone of sharp focus. A shallow depth of field also makes action shots more difficult because you have to be absolutely spot on with focus. With a larger depth of field, the subject can move a greater distance toward or away from you before leaving the sharp-focus area, giving you a bit of a focusing safety net.

Keeping all this information straight is a little overwhelming at first, but the more you work with your camera, the more the whole exposure equation will make sense to you. You can find tips in Chapter 7 for choosing exposure settings for specific types of pictures; keep moving through this chapter for details on how to monitor and adjust aperture, shutter speed, and ISO settings.

Stepping Up to Advance Exposure Modes (P, Tv, Av, and M)

With your camera in certain Basic Zone modes, including Creative Auto and certain Scene modes, you can affect exposure and depth of field to some extent. But if you're really concerned with these picture characteristics — and you should be — set the Mode dial to one of the four Creative Zone exposure modes highlighted in Figure 4-7. In these modes, you get more precise control over aperture, shutter speed, and other exposure features.

Each of the four exposure modes — known collectively as Creative Zone modes in Canon lingo — offers a different level of control over aperture and shutter speed. Chapter 2 introduced the differences between the four modes, but here's a recap and a few additional details:

Creative Zone (advanced) exposure modes

FIGURE 4-7:
To fully control exposure and other picture properties, choose one of these exposure modes.

TECHNICAL
STUFF

>> **P (programmed autoexposure):** The camera selects both the aperture and shutter speed to deliver a good exposure at the current ISO setting. But you can choose from different combinations of the two for creative flexibility by rotating the Main dial. This is called Program shift, and is sometimes referred to generically as *flexible programmed autoexposure.*

>> **Tv (shutter-priority autoexposure):** You select a shutter speed, and the camera chooses the aperture setting that produces a good exposure at that shutter speed and the current ISO setting.

Why *Tv?* Well, shutter speed controls exposure time; *Tv* stands for time value.

>> **Av (aperture-priority autoexposure):** The opposite of shutter-priority autoexposure, this mode gives you control over the aperture setting — thus, *Av,* which stands for aperture value. The camera then selects the appropriate shutter speed to properly expose the picture — again, based on the selected ISO setting.

>> **M (manual exposure):** In this mode, you specify both shutter speed and aperture.

REMEMBER

To sum up, the first three modes are semiautomatic modes that offer exposure assistance while still providing some creative control. Note one important point about these modes, however: In extreme lighting conditions, the camera may not be able to select settings that will produce a good exposure, and it doesn't stop you from taking a poorly exposed photo. You may be able to solve the problem by using features designed to modify autoexposure results, such as Exposure Compensation (explained later in this chapter) or by adding flash, but you get no guarantees.

Manual mode puts all exposure control in your hands. If you're a longtime photographer who comes from the days when manual exposure was the only game in town, you may prefer to stick with this mode. If it ain't broke, don't fix it, as they say. And in some ways, manual mode is simpler than the semiautomatic modes — if you're not happy with the exposure, you just change the aperture, shutter speed, or ISO setting and shoot again. You don't have to fiddle with features that enable you to modify the results delivered by the modes that use autoexposure (P, Tv, and Av).

Whichever mode you choose, check out the next several sections to find out how to view and adjust the various exposure settings.

Monitoring Exposure Settings

When you press the shutter button halfway, the current f-stop, shutter speed, and ISO speed appear in the viewfinder display, as shown in Figure 4-8.

REMEMBER

Don't confuse the number in brackets — 9, in the figure — for the ISO value. The bracketed value reflects the buffer value, which is relevant only when you shoot in one of the Continuous Drive modes. The *buffer* is a bit of internal memory the camera uses to temporarily store image data until it has time to record the data to the memory card. When the buffer value drops to 0, the buffer is full and the camera won't take any more pictures until it catches up with its data-recording work.

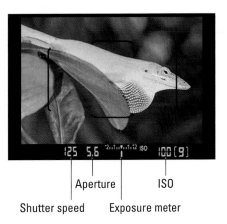

Aperture   ISO

Shutter speed   Exposure meter

FIGURE 4-8:
The shutter speed, f-stop, and ISO speed appear in the viewfinder.

You also can view exposure settings in the Quick Control and Live View displays, as shown in Figure 4-9. In those displays, the buffer value only appears when the buffer value drops to 9 or below. (The buffer actually can hold more than nine shots, but there's only room in the viewfinder readout for a single-digit value, so that display always shows 9 even when more storage is available.) Exposure settings are also displayed on the LCD panel, as shown in Figure 4-10.

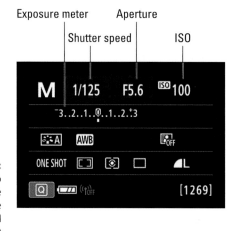

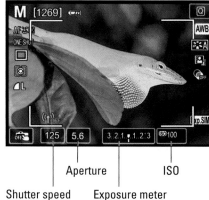

FIGURE 4-9: You also can view the settings in the Quick Control display (left) and Live View display (right).

REMEMBER

In the viewfinder and on the monitor in Live View mode, shutter speeds are presented as whole numbers, even if the shutter speed is set to a fraction of a second. For example, for a shutter speed of 1/125 second, you see just the number 125 in the displays, as shown in the figures. When the shutter speed slows to 1 second or more, you see quotation marks after the number in all three displays — 1″ indicates a shutter speed of 1 second, 4″ means 4 seconds, and so on.

The viewfinder, Quick Control display, LCD panel, and Live View display also offer an *exposure meter*, labeled in

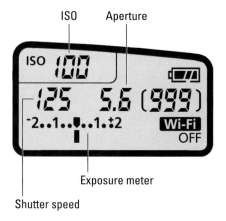

FIGURE 4-10: The top LCD panel also shows important exposure information.

Figures 4-8 through 4-10. This graphic serves two different purposes, depending on the exposure mode:

>> **In M mode, the meter indicates whether your settings will properly expose the image.** Figure 4-11 gives you three examples. When the *exposure indicator* (the bar under the meter) aligns with the center point of the meter, as shown in the middle example, the current settings will produce a proper exposure. If the indicator moves to the left of center, toward the minus side of the scale, as in the left example in the figure, the camera is alerting you that the image will be underexposed. If the indicator moves to the right of center, as in the right example, the image will be overexposed. The farther the indicator moves toward the plus or minus sign, the greater the potential exposure problem.

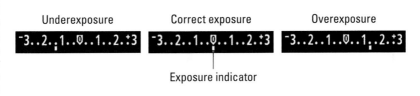

Underexposure   Correct exposure   Overexposure

Exposure indicator

REMEMBER

Keep in mind that the information reported by the meter is dependent on the *metering mode,* which determines what part of the frame the camera uses to calculate exposure. You can choose from four metering modes, as covered in the next section. But regardless of metering mode, consider the meter a guide, not a dictator — the beauty of manual exposure is that *you* decide how dark or bright an exposure you want, not the camera.

>> **In the other modes (P, Tv, and Av), the meter displays the current Exposure Compensation setting.** Remember, in those modes the camera sets either the shutter speed or the aperture, or both, to produce a good exposure — again, depending on the current metering mode. Because you don't need the meter to tell you whether exposure is okay, the meter instead indicates whether you enabled *Exposure Compensation,* a feature that forces a brighter or darker exposure than the camera thinks is appropriate. (Look for details later in this chapter.) When the exposure indicator is at 0, no compensation is being applied. If the indicator is to the right of 0, you applied

compensation to produce a brighter image; when the indicator is to the left, you asked for a darker photo.

WARNING

In some lighting situations, the camera *can't* select settings that produce an optimal exposure in the P, Tv, or Av modes. Because the meter indicates the exposure compensation amount in those modes, the camera alerts you to exposure issues as follows:

- *Av mode (aperture-priority autoexposure):* The shutter speed value blinks to let you know that the camera can't select the shutter speed that will produce a good exposure at the aperture you selected. Choose a different f-stop or adjust the ISO.

- *Tv mode (shutter-priority autoexposure):* The aperture value blinks to tell you that the camera can't open or stop down the aperture enough to expose the image at your selected shutter speed. Your options are to change the shutter speed or ISO.

- *P mode (programmed autoexposure):* In P mode, both the aperture and shutter speed values blink if the camera can't select a combination that will properly expose the image. Your only recourse is to either adjust the lighting or change the ISO setting.

Choosing an Exposure Metering Mode

The *metering mode* determines which part of the frame the camera analyzes to calculate the proper exposure. Your camera offers four metering modes, described in the following list and represented in the Quick Control and Live View displays by the icons you see in the margin.

REMEMBER

You can access all four metering modes only in the advanced exposure modes (P, Tv, Av, and M). In Basic Zone modes, the camera selects the metering mode, with the Evaluative mode used in most cases.

>> **Evaluative metering:** The camera analyzes the entire frame and then selects exposure settings designed to produce a balanced exposure.

>> **Partial metering:** The camera bases exposure only on the light that falls in the center 6 percent of the frame. In the Live View display, a circle appears to indicate the size of the metering area, as shown on the left in Figure 4-12.

FIGURE 4-12:
The Live
View screen
displays circles
representing
the area
measured
in Partial
metering mode
(left) and Spot
metering mode
(right).

Partial metering symbol

Partial metering circle

Spot metering symbol

Spot metering circle

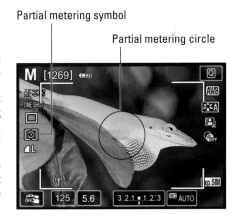
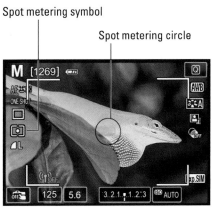

>> **Spot metering:** This mode works like Partial metering but uses a smaller region of the frame to calculate exposure. For Spot metering, exposure is based on just the central 3.5 percent of the frame. Again, a circle marking appears in the Live View display to indicate the metering area. For this setting, you also see the circle in the viewfinder.

>> **Center-Weighted Average metering:** The camera bases exposure on the entire frame but puts extra emphasis — or *weight* — on the center.

In most cases, Evaluative metering does a good job of calculating exposure. But it can get thrown off when a dark subject is set against a bright background, or vice versa. For example, in the left image in Figure 4-13, the amount of bright background caused the camera to select exposure settings that underexposed the statue, which was the point of interest for the photo. Switching to Partial metering properly exposed the statue. (Spot metering would produce a similar result for this particular subject.)

TIP

Of course, if the background is very bright and the subject is very dark, the exposure that does the best job on the subject typically overexposes the background. You may be able to reclaim some lost highlights by turning on Highlight Tone Priority, a Custom Function explored later in this chapter. Also, if you want to use spot or partial metering but you don't want your subject to appear in the center of the frame, see the later section "Locking Autoexposure Settings" to find out how to accomplish that goal when you shoot in the P, Tv, or Av exposure modes.

Evaluative | Partial

FIGURE 4-13:
In Evaluative
mode, the
camera
underexposed
the statue;
switching to
Partial metering
produced a
better result.

To change the metering mode, use either of these two options:

>> **Quick Control method:** After shifting to Quick Control mode, choose the icon labeled in Figure 4-14 and rotate the Quick Control or Main dial to cycle through the four modes. Note that in Live View mode, the text label initially identifies the setting you're adjusting, as shown in the figure. But as soon as you rotate the either dial, the text identifies the selected metering mode option.

Metering mode symbol

FIGURE 4-14:
You can
quickly adjust
the Metering
mode in Quick
Control mode.

For viewfinder photography, you can display all four metering mode settings on a separate screen by pressing the Set button after you highlight the metering mode option on the Quick Control screen. If you go that route, tap the exit arrow or press the Set button to return to the initial Quick Control screen.

>> **Shooting Menu 3:** Look for the Metering mode option at the top menu, as shown in Figure 4-15.

FIGURE 4-15:
You also can access the Metering mode from Shooting Menu 3.

TIP

In theory, the best practice is to check the Metering mode before each shot and choose the mode that best matches your exposure goals (when in Live View, the monitor shows you the anticipated results of the current exposure settings). But in practice, it's a pain, not just in terms of having to adjust yet one more setting but also in terms of having to *remember* to adjust one more setting. So, until you're comfortable with all the other controls on your camera, just stick with Evaluative metering. It produces good results in most situations, and after all, you can see in the monitor whether you like your results and, if not, adjust exposure settings and reshoot. This option makes the whole Metering mode issue a lot less critical than it is when you shoot with film.

The exception might be when you're shooting a series of images in which a significant contrast in lighting exists between subject and background. Then, switching to Spot or Partial metering may save you the time spent having to adjust the exposure for each image. Many portrait photographers, for example, rely on Spot metering exclusively because they know their subject is usually going to be hovering near the center of the frame. Use Spot metering is also helpful when you need a very accurate metering of a specific element in the photo to keep it from being over- or underexposed.

Setting ISO, Aperture, and Shutter Speed

REMEMBER

If you want to control ISO, aperture (f-stop), or shutter speed, set the camera to P, Tv, Av, or M exposure mode. Then check out the next several sections to find the exact steps to follow in each mode.

Controlling ISO

To refresh your memory about the ISO information presented at the start of this chapter: The ISO setting controls how sensitive the camera's image sensor is to light. At higher ISO values, you need less light to expose an image correctly. But the downside to raising ISO is a greater possibility of image noise. Refer to Figure 4-5 for a reminder of what that defect looks like.

In Basic Zone modes, the camera controls ISO. But in the advanced exposure modes, you have the following ISO choices:

>> **Select a specific ISO setting.**
Normally, you can choose ISO settings ranging from 100 to ISO 25600. But if you really want to push things, you can amp ISO up to 51200. To take advantage of that option, navigate to Custom Function 2, ISO Expansion, shown in Figure 4-16. If you set the option to On, the list of possible ISO values for photography includes an H (High) setting, which delivers 51200 ISO.

FIGURE 4-16:
By enabling Custom Function 2, you can push the available ISO range to 51200 for still photography.

As the Custom Function screen indicates, the expanded ISO range varies for movie shooting. In Movie mode, the ISO range tops out at 25600. (The highest ISO setting normally available for Movie mode is 12800.)

REMEMBER

One complication: If you enable Highlight Tone Priority, an exposure feature covered later in this chapter, you lose the option of using ISO 100 as well as the H setting.

>> **Let the camera choose (Auto ISO).**
You can ask the camera to adjust ISO for you if you prefer. And you can specify the highest ISO setting that you want the camera to use, which you can limit to as little as ISO 400 or as much as ISO 25600. Set the top ISO limit via the ISO Auto setting on Shooting Menu 2, as shown in Figure 4-17. The default maximum is ISO 6400.

FIGURE 4-17:
This setting enables you to specify the maximum ISO setting the camera can use in Auto ISO mode.

Using Auto ISO is especially handy when the light is changing fast or your subject is moving from light to dark areas quickly. In these situations, Auto ISO can save the day, giving you properly exposed images without any ISO futzing on your part.

You can view the current ISO setting in Quick Control and Live View displays, as well as in the viewfinder. (Refer to Figures 4-8 through 4-10 if you need a reminder of where to look.)

To adjust the ISO setting, you have these options:

>> **Press the ISO button (top of the camera, labeled in Figure 4-18).** You then see the screen shown on the right, where you can choose your desired setting by rotating the Quick Control or Main dial, pressing the left/right Quick Control keys, or tapping the left/right arrows.

Press to access ISO setting screen   Reset to Auto ISO   Current setting

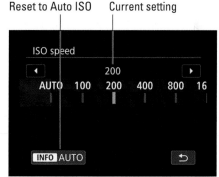

FIGURE 4-18: The fastest route to the ISO setting screen is to press the ISO button.

To quickly return to the Auto ISO setting, press the Info button or tap the Info symbol on the touchscreen.

>> **Quick Control method (not available in Live View mode).** After choosing the ISO option, as shown in Figure 4-19, rotate the Quick Control or Main dial to cycle through the ISO settings. You also can tap the icon or press Set to display the same settings screen shown on the right in Figure 4-18.

FIGURE 4-19:
For viewfinder shooting, you also can adjust the ISO setting through the Quick Control screen.

TIP

When the camera is set to Auto ISO, the ISO value in the Quick Control and Live View displays initially show Auto as the ISO value, as you would expect. But when you press the shutter button halfway, which initiates exposure metering, the value changes to the specific ISO value the camera selected. In the viewfinder, the specific ISO value always appears, whether you dialed that setting in yourself or the camera selected it in Auto ISO mode.

When you view shooting data during playback, you may see a value reported that isn't on the list of "official" ISO settings — ISO 320, for example. This happens because, in Auto mode, the camera can select values all along the available ISO range, whereas if you select a specific ISO setting, you're restricted to specific notches within the range.

Adjusting aperture and shutter speed

Which Creative Zone exposure mode you use determines your level of control over aperture and shutter speed and also the method you use to adjust the setting(s) you can change. Here's how things work in each mode:

» **P:** You can choose from different combinations of aperture and shutter speed, but you have no direct control over either. To view the camera's recommended combination, compose your shot and then press the shutter button halfway to meter the scene. To select a different combination of the two settings, rotate the Main dial.

If you need a reminder of where to find the f-stop and shutter speed in the various displays, refer to Figures 4-8 through 4-10.

» **Tv:** You control shutter speed; adjust that setting by rotating the Main dial. After selecting the shutter speed, frame your shot and press the shutter button halfway to initiate autoexposure metering. The displays then show the aperture setting that the camera selected to expose the picture at your chosen shutter speed and the current ISO.

» **Av:** The opposite of Tv mode, Av mode enables you to set the f-stop while the camera selects the shutter speed. Again, rotate the Main dial to set the aperture setting you want to use. Then frame your subject and press the shutter button halfway. The camera then displays the shutter speed it selected.

WARNING

Even though you're in aperture-priority mode and so concentrating on the f-stop, always check the shutter speed that the camera selected for you. If the shutter speed drops so low that handholding the camera or capturing a moving subject won't be possible, you can either open the aperture (choose a lower f-stop number) or dial in a higher ISO setting, which will enable the camera to select a faster shutter speed at your preferred f-stop.

>> **M (manual exposure):** You set both aperture and shutter speed. Use these techniques:

- *Adjust shutter speed.* Rotate the Main dial.

  In M mode, you have access to Bulb mode, which keeps the shutter open as long as you keep the shutter button pressed fully down. To get to the Bulb setting, go one step past the slowest possible normal shutter speed (30 seconds).

- *Adjust aperture.* Rotate the Quick Control dial.

REMEMBER

In M, Tv, and Av modes, the settings that are available for adjustment appears in the Quick Control and Live View displays in light gray boxes before you've metered the scene. This is a subtle reminder that you can change the settings without metering or entering Quick Control mode. Figure 4-20 shows shutter speed and aperture settings entered in Manual exposure mode.

You do have a couple other options for adjusting settings in the M, Tv, and Av exposure modes:

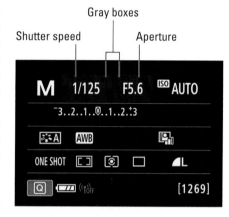

FIGURE 4-20:
In Manual mode, both shutter speed and aperture are immediately adjustable. Rotate the Main dial to change shutter speed; rotate the Quick Control dial to change aperture.

>> **For viewfinder photography, use Quick Control mode.** After pressing the Q button or tapping the Q touchscreen symbol, highlight the setting you want to change and then rotate the Main or Quick Control dial. The Quick Control method doesn't work in Live View mode, unfortunately.

>> **In Live View mode, use the touchscreen.** Just tap the setting on the touchscreen to display a screen that offers the available values for that setting.

A few more words of wisdom related to aperture and shutter speed:

>> When using M exposure mode, don't forget that you can check the exposure meter to get the camera's take on your exposure settings. Of course, you don't have to follow the camera's guidance — you can take the picture using any settings you like, even if the meter indicates that the image will be under- or overexposed.

REMEMBER

» In Live View mode, the preview updates as you adjust exposure settings to show you the change in image brightness. If the camera can't display an accurate preview, the Exp Sim (which stands for *Exposure Sim*ulation) symbol in the lower-right corner of the screen appears dimmed. (This happens, for example, when you use flash.)

» In P, Tv, and Av mode, the shutter speed or f-stop value blinks if the camera isn't able to select settings that produce a good exposure. If the problem is too little light, try raising the ISO or adding flash to solve the problem. If there's too much light, lower the ISO value or attach a *neutral density* (ND) filter, which is sort of like sunglasses for your lens — it simply cuts the light entering the lens. (The *neutral* part just means that the filter doesn't affect image colors, just brightness.)

» Keep in mind that when you use P, Tv, and Av modes, the settings that the camera selects are based on what it thinks is the proper exposure. If you don't agree with the camera, you have two options. Switch to manual exposure (M) mode and simply dial in the aperture and shutter speed that deliver the exposure you want, or if you want to stay in P, Tv, or Av mode, try using exposure compensation, one of the exposure-correction tools described in the next section.

Sorting Through Your Camera's Exposure-Correction Tools

In addition to the normal controls over aperture, shutter speed, and ISO, your camera offers a collection of tools that enable you to solve tricky exposure problems. The next sections give you the lowdown on these features.

Overriding autoexposure results with Exposure Compensation

REMEMBER

In the P, Tv, and Av exposure modes, you have some input over exposure: In P mode, you can rotate the Main dial to choose from different combinations of aperture and shutter speed; in Tv mode, you can dial in the shutter speed; and in Av mode, you can select the aperture setting. But because these are semiautomatic modes, the camera ultimately controls the final exposure. If your picture turns out too bright or too dark in P mode, you can't simply choose a different f-stop/

shutter speed combo because they all deliver the same exposure — which is to say, the exposure that the camera has in mind. And changing the shutter speed in Tv mode or adjusting the f-stop in Av mode won't help either because as soon as you change the setting that you're controlling, the camera automatically adjusts the other setting to produce the same exposure it initially delivered.

Not to worry: You actually do have final say over exposure in these exposure modes. The secret is Exposure Compensation, a feature that tells the camera to produce a brighter or darker exposure on your next shot, whether or not you change the aperture or shutter speed (or both, in P mode).

Best of all, this feature is probably one of the easiest on the camera to understand. Here's all there is to it:

>> Exposure compensation is stated in EV values, as in +2.0 EV. Possible values range from +5.0 EV to –5.0 EV. A setting of EV 0.0 results in no exposure adjustment.

TECHNICAL STUFF

>> Each full number on the EV scale represents an exposure shift of one *stop*. In photography lingo, a *stop* refers to an increment of exposure adjustment. If you adjust the aperture or shutter speed to allow half as much light to hit the image sensor as the current settings, you're decreasing exposure by one stop. Allowing twice as much light increases exposure by one stop.

Back to Exposure Compensation: If you change the Exposure Compensation setting from EV 0.0 to EV –1.0, you're asking for a one-stop decrease in exposure, resulting in a darker image. If you instead raise the value to EV +1.0, the camera increases exposure by one stop, producing a brighter photo.

>> Exposure Compensation isn't possible in the M exposure mode because there are no automatic exposure settings to override. You have to set the exposure settings that produce the desired result yourself.

>> As you adjust the Exposure Compensation, the notch under the meter indicates the amount of adjustment. For example, in Figure 4-21, the adjustment is set to EV +1.0. The meter in the viewfinder also indicates the amount of Exposure Compensation. Figure 4-22 shows how Exposure Compensation is displayed on the top LCD panel.

Even though the meters initially show a range of just +/– three stops (two in the case of the viewfinder), you can access the entire five-stop range. Just keep rotating the Quick Control dial to display the far ends of the range. Remember, you have to press the Shutter button halfway to meter first. Otherwise, rotating the Quick Control dial will have no effect.

Exposure Compensation EV +1.0

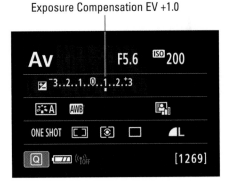

Exposure Compensation symbol

Exposure Compensation EV +1.0

Notice, too, the +/– symbol at the left end of the meters in the figure; that's the universal symbol for exposure compensation, the same one that marks the Exposure Compensation button. The symbol appears in the displays to remind you that the adjustment is being applied; if you reset the value to EV 0.0, the symbol disappears.

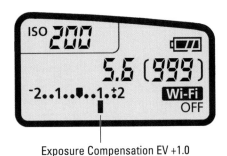

Exposure Compensation EV +1.0

FIGURE 4-22:
The Exposure Compensation amount is also displayed on the top LCD panel.

TIP

Exposure compensation is especially helpful when your subject is much lighter or darker than an average scene. For example, take a look at the image on the left in Figure 4-23. Because of the very bright sky, the camera chose an exposure that made the tree too dark. Setting the Exposure Compensation value to EV +1.0 resulted in a properly exposed image.

Sometimes you can cope with situations like this one by changing the Meter-ing mode, as discussed earlier in this chapter. The images in Figure 4-23 were metered in Evaluative mode, for example, which meters exposure over the entire frame. Switching to Partial or Spot metering probably wouldn't have helped in this case because the area the camera meters in those modes — the center of the frame — are bright. In any case, it's usually easier to simply adjust exposure com-pensation than to experiment with metering modes.

EV 0.0   EV +1.0

FIGURE 4-23:
For a brighter exposure than the autoexposure mechanism chooses, dial in a positive Exposure Compensation value.

REMEMBER

You can take several roads to applying exposure compensation:

>> **Quick Control mode (not available in Live View mode):** Highlight the exposure meter in the Quick Control display and rotate the Quick Control dial to move the exposure indicator left or right along the meter, as shown on in Figure 4-24. If you accidentally rotate the Main dial, you will add autoexposure brackets, which tells the camera to shoot more than one photo — each with a different exposure.

FIGURE 4-24:
When Live View is not engaged, you also can set the Exposure Compensation amount via the Quick Control screen.

>> **Touchscreen (Live View only):** Tap the exposure meter at the bottom of the Live View screen to display a separate screen where you can set the amount of adjustment.

>> **Shooting Menu 2:** Select Expo Comp/AEB, as shown on the left in Figure 4-25, to display the screen shown on the right in the figure. You can access this same screen in Quick Control mode by pressing Set when the meter is highlighted.

FIGURE 4-25:
If you go
the menu
route, adjust
Exposure
Compensation
by rotating the
Quick Control
dial, pressing
the left/right
Quick Control
keys, or tap-
ping the left/
right arrows —
not by rotating
the Main dial.

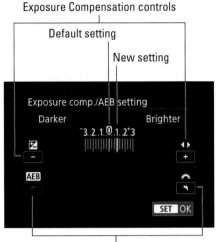

Whichever way you choose, this is a tricky screen, so pay attention:

- The screen has a double purpose: You use it to enable automatic exposure bracketing (AEB), as well as exposure compensation. So, if you're not careful, you can wind up changing the wrong setting. The labels on the second screen in Figure 4-25 show which of the screen's controls affect which setting. When AEB isn't in force, you see only a single meter, as shown in the figure; that meter represents the exposure compensation setting.

- To apply exposure compensation, *don't rotate the Main dial.* On this screen, rotating the Main dial adjusts the AEB setting. Instead, rotate the Quick Control dial, press the left or right Quick Control keys, or tap the plus or minus signs at the ends of the exposure compensation meter. The blue marker indicates the default setting (EV 0.0); the marker labeled *New Setting* in the figure shows the amount of adjustment that will be applied if you go forward.

- Tap the Set touchscreen symbol or press the Set button to lock in the amount of exposure compensation and exit the screen.

REMEMBER

When you dial in an adjustment of greater than two stops in either direction, the notch under the viewfinder meter disappears and is replaced by a triangle at one end of the meter — at the right end for a positive Exposure Compensation value and at the left for a negative value. However, the meter on the Quick Control and Live View screens and on Shooting Menu 2 adjust to show the actual setting.

Whatever setting you select, the way that the camera arrives at the brighter or darker image you request depends on the exposure mode:

>> In Av (aperture-priority) mode, the camera adjusts the shutter speed but leaves your selected f-stop in force.

>> In Tv (shutter-priority) mode, the opposite occurs: The camera opens or stops down the aperture, leaving your selected shutter speed alone.

>> In P (programmed autoexposure) mode, the camera decides whether to adjust aperture, shutter speed, or both to accommodate the Exposure Compensation setting.

These explanations assume that you have a specific ISO setting selected rather than Auto ISO. If you do use Auto ISO, the camera may adjust that value instead.

Keep in mind, too, that the camera can adjust the aperture only so much, according to the aperture range of your lens. The range of shutter speeds is limited by the camera. So, if you reach the end of those ranges, you have to compromise on either shutter speed or aperture, or adjust ISO.

REMEMBER

By default, the Exposure Compensation value is reset to EV 0.0 when you turn the camera off. If you don't want the reset to happen, head for Setup Menu 4, choose Custom Functions, and change the setting for Custom Function 3 to Disable. Just don't forget that the compensation is still in force the next time you use the camera.

Improving high-contrast shots with Highlight Tone Priority

When a scene contains both very dark and very bright areas, achieving a good exposure can be difficult. If you choose exposure settings that render the shadows properly, the highlights are often overexposed, as in the left image in Figure 4-26. Although the dark lamppost in the foreground looks fine in the first shot, the white building behind it became so bright that all detail was lost. The same thing occurred in the highlight areas of the church steeple.

To produce a better image in this situation, try enabling Highlight Tone Priority, which helps keep highlight areas intact without darkening shadows. The feature did the trick for the scene in Figure 4-26; the results appear in the second image in the figure. The difference is subtle, but the windows in the building are at least visible, the steeple regained some of its color, and the sky, too, has a bit more blue.

REMEMBER

Highlight Tone Priority is available only in the P, Tv, Av, and M modes. It's turned off by default, which may seem like an odd choice after looking at the improvement it made to the scene in Figure 4-26. What gives? The answer is that in order to do its thing, Highlight Tone Priority needs to play with a few other camera settings, as follows:

Highlight Tone Priority off

Highlight Tone Priority on

FIGURE 4-26:
Highlight Tone Priority can help prevent overexposed highlights.

>> **The ISO range is reduced to ISO 200–25600.** The camera needs the more limited range in order to favor the image highlights. (If you enable the feature for movie recording, the top end of the ISO range is 12800.)

>> **Auto Lighting Optimizer is disabled.** This feature, which attempts to improve image contrast, is incompatible with Highlight Tone Priority. So, read the next section, which explains Auto Lighting Optimizer, to determine which of the two exposure tweaks you want to use.

>> **You can wind up with more noise in shadow areas of the image.** Again, noise is the defect that looks like grains of sand.

REMEMBER

The only way to enable Highlight Tone Priority is via Custom Function 4, shown in Figure 4-27. To access this setting, open Setup Menu 4 and choose Custom Functions. Scroll to Custom Function 4 by rotating the Quick Control dial, pressing the left/right Quick Control keys, or tapping the left/right triangles at the top of the screen. When you get to the screen shown in the figure, press Set and highlight Enable, as shown in the figure, and then press Set again or tap the Set touchscreen symbol. You also can simply tap the Enable option twice: once to highlight it and a second time to select it.

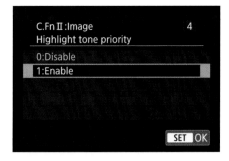

FIGURE 4-27:
Enable Highlight Tone Priority from Custom Function 4.

As a reminder that Highlight Tone Priority is enabled, a D+ symbol appears near the ISO value in the Quick Control and Live View displays, as shown in Figure 4-28. The same symbol appears with the ISO setting in the viewfinder, on the top LCD panel, and in the shooting data that appears in Playback mode. (See Chapter 9 to find out more about picture playback.) Notice that the symbol that represents Auto Lighting Optimizer, also labeled in the figure, is dimmed because that feature is disabled automatically as soon as you turn on Highlight Tone Priority.

Highlight Tone Priority on   Auto Lighting Optimizer off

FIGURE 4-28:
These symbols indicate that Highlight Tone Priority is enabled and Auto Lighting Optimizer is disabled.

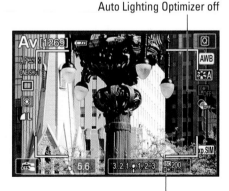

Auto Lighting Optimizer off   Highlight Tone Priority on

Experimenting with Auto Lighting Optimizer

When you select an Image Quality setting that results in a JPEG image file — that is, any setting other than Raw — the camera tries to enhance your photo while it's processing the picture. Unlike Highlight Tone Priority, which concentrates on preserving highlight detail only, Auto Lighting Optimizer adjusts both shadows and highlights to improve the final image tonality (range of darks to lights). In other words, it's a contrast adjustment.

In the Basic Zone exposure modes, you have no control over how much adjustment is made. But in P, Tv, Av, and M modes, you can decide whether to enable Auto Lighting Optimizer. You also can request a stronger or lighter application of the effect than the default setting, which is Standard. Figure 4-29 offers an example of the impact of each Auto Lighting Optimizer setting.

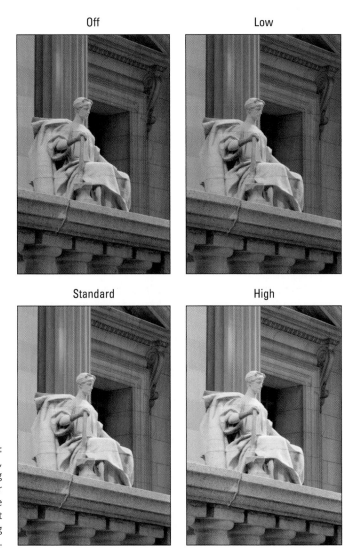

FIGURE 4-29: For this image, Auto Lighting Optimizer brought more life to the shot by increasing contrast.

Given the level of improvement that the Auto Lighting Optimizer correction made to this photo, it may seem crazy to ever disable the feature. But it's important to note a few points:

>> **The level of shift that occurs between each Auto Lighting Optimizer setting varies depending on the subject.** This particular example shows a fairly noticeable difference between the High and Off settings. But you don't always see this much impact from the filter. Even in this example, it's difficult to detect much difference between Off and Low.

>> **Although the filter improved this particular scene, at times you may not find it beneficial.** For example, maybe you're purposely trying to shoot a backlit subject in silhouette or produce a low-contrast image. Either way, you don't want the camera to insert its opinions on the exposure or contrast you're trying to achieve.

>> **Enabling Auto Lighting Optimizer may slow your shooting rate.** That slowdown occurs because the filter is applied after you capture the photo, while the camera is writing the data to the memory card.

>> **In some lighting conditions, Auto Lighting Optimizer can produce an increase in image noise.** As shown near the start of this chapter, in Figure 4-5, noise becomes more apparent when you enlarge a photo. It also tends to be most visible in areas of flat color.

WARNING

>> **The corrective action taken by Auto Lighting Optimizer can make some other exposure-adjustment features less effective.** So turn it off if you don't see the results you expect when you're using the following features:

   • Exposure compensation, discussed earlier in this chapter

   • Flash compensation, discussed in Chapter 2

   • Automatic exposure bracketing, discussed later in this chapter

>> **You can't use this feature while Highlight Tone Priority is enabled.** In fact, as soon as you turn on that feature, explained in the preceding section, the camera automatically disables Auto Lighting Optimizer.

>> **By default, the Auto Lighting Optimizer is disabled when the camera is in Manual (M) exposure mode.**

You can view the current Auto Lighting Optimizer setting in the Quick Control and Live View displays; look for the icon representing the setting in the areas labeled in Figure 4-30.

TIP

Notice the vertical bars in the graphic — the number of bars tells you how much adjustment is being applied. Two bars, as in Figure 4-30, represent the Standard setting; three bars, High; and one bar, Low. The bars are replaced by the word *Off* when the feature is disabled.

Auto Lighting Optimizer symbol (Standard setting)

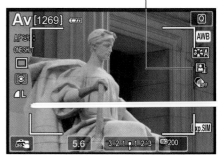

FIGURE 4-30:
These symbols
tell you the
status of the
Auto Lighting
Optimizer
setting.

You can adjust the setting in two ways:

» **Quick Control method:** Figure 4-31 shows the process for viewfinder shooting: After pressing Q to shift to Quick Control mode, highlight the Auto Lighting Optimizer symbol and then rotate the Quick Control or Main dial to adjust the level of adjustment.

To access an additional option that enables you to choose to control the feature separately for the M exposure mode, press Set or tap the Auto Lighting Optimizer icon. You then see the second screen in the figure. If you want the camera to apply the setting you select only when you shoot in the P, Tv, and Av exposure modes, put a check mark in the box labeled Disable during manual exposure. You can either tap the check box or press the Info button to toggle the adjustment on and off for M exposure mode.

FIGURE 4-31:
After
highlighting the
Auto Lighting
Optimizer
option (left);
press Set to
access the
option that
disables the
feature when
you shoot in
the M exposure
mode (right).

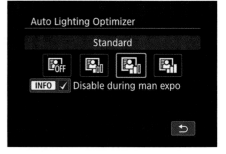

Things work the same way in Live View mode except that you can adjust the Auto Lighting Optimizer level and toggle the Manual exposure mode adjustment from one screen, as shown in Figure 4-32.

>> **Shooting Menu 2:** Figure 4-33 shows the menu versions of the Auto Lighting Optimizer settings screens.

TIP

If you're not sure what level of Auto Lighting Optimizer might work best or you're concerned about the other drawbacks of enabling the filter, consider shooting the picture in the Raw file format. For Raw pictures, the camera applies no post-capture tweaking, regardless of whether this filter or any other one is enabled. Then, by using Canon Digital Photo Professional, the software provided free with the camera, you can apply the Auto Lighting Optimizer effect when you convert your Raw images to a standard file format. (See Chapter 10 for details about processing Raw files.)

FIGURE 4-32:
In Live View mode, all the options are available from the main Quick Control screen.

FIGURE 4-33:
You can also adjust Auto Lighting Optimizer settings through Shooting Menu 2.

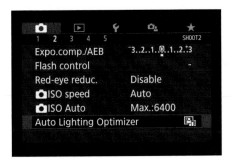

Looking at a few other exposure solutions

In addition to the exposure correction tools covered in the preceding sections, you may find the following features helpful on occasion:

>> **Peripheral Illumination Correction:** Some lenses produce pictures that appear darker around the edges of the frame than in the center, even when the lighting is consistent throughout. This phenomenon is commonly known as *vignetting,* and your camera offers a tool that may help correct the problem. To check it out, open Shooting Menu 1, choose Lens Aberration Correction, and then select Peripheral Illumination Correction, as shown in Figure 4-34.

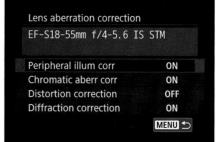

FIGURE 4-34:
Peripheral Illumination Correction works to combat vignetting, which makes the corners of an image appear unnaturally dark.

REMEMBER

This adjustment is available in your camera's advanced exposure modes (P, Tv, Av, and M), but it only works when the Image Quality option (also on Shooting Menu 1) is set to capture the photo in the JPEG file format — in other words, any setting but Raw. However, if you prefer to shoot in the Raw format, most Raw-processing tools offer a tool for correcting vignetting, often with more precision than the camera's automated version. Chapter 10 explains how to use Canon Digital Photo Professional software to do the job.

A few other points about Peripheral Illumination Correction:

- *The feature is enabled by default if the camera's firmware (internal software) contains data about your lens.* The second screen in Figure 4-34 shows that the data is available for the 18–55mm kit lens, for example. (The lens model appears above the list of menu options.)

TECHNICAL STUFF

If you use a Canon lens and the screen indicates that the camera doesn't have data for that lens, you may be able to add its information to the camera. Canon calls this step *registering your lens,* a process you accomplish by connecting the camera to your computer and then using a registration tool included with Canon EOS Utility software. That software, along with others covered in Chapter 10, is available for free with your camera purchase. See the EOS Utility instruction manual, available for download from the Canon support pages, if you're interested in registering a lens.

- *For non-Canon lenses, Canon recommends disabling Peripheral Illumination Correction even if correction data is available.* You can still apply the correction in Digital Photo Professional when you shoot in the Raw format.

WARNING

- *The correction may produce increased noise at the corners of the photo.* This problem occurs because exposure adjustment can make noise more apparent.

>> **Long Exposure Noise Reduction:** A long exposure time can result in *noise,* the digital defect that gives your pictures a grainy look (refer to Figure 4-5). You may be able to reduce the appearance of noise created by a long

exposure by enabling — surprise — a tool called Long Exposure Noise Reduction. In Basic Zone modes, the camera determines when to use this tool; in the P, Tv, Av, and M modes, you can make the call. Look for the setting on Shooting Menu 4, as shown in Figure 4-35.

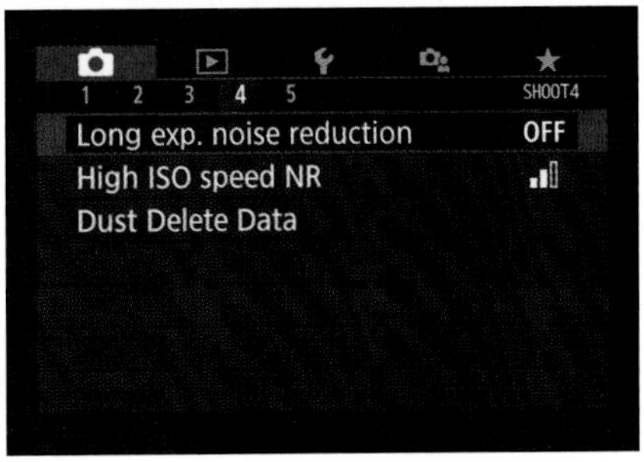

Long Exposure Noise Reduction offers three settings:

- *Off:* No noise reduction is applied. This setting is the default.

FIGURE 4-35:
This filter attacks noise that can occur when you use a slow shutter speed.

- *Auto:* Noise reduction is applied when you use a shutter speed of 1 second or longer, but only if the camera detects the type of noise that's caused by long exposures. (The other common cause of noise, a high ISO setting, creates a slightly different type of noise.)

- *On:* Noise reduction is always applied at exposures of 1 second or longer. (**Note:** Canon suggests that this setting may result in more noise than either Off or Auto when the ISO setting is 1600 or higher.)

WARNING

Although Long Exposure Noise Reduction can be fairly effective, it has a significant downside because of the way it works. Say that you make a 30-second exposure. After the shutter closes at the end of the exposure, the camera takes a *second* 30-second exposure to measure the noise by itself, and then subtracts that noise from your *real* exposure. So, your shot-to-shot wait time is twice what it would normally be. For some scenes, that may not be a problem, but for shots that feature action, such as fireworks, you definitely don't want that long wait time between shutter clicks.

» **High ISO Speed Noise Removal:** Also found on Shooting Menu 4 and adjustable only in P, Tv, Av, and M modes, this tool attempts to conquer the second type of noise, a high ISO setting, just as its name implies. After choosing the option, as shown in Figure 4-36, you can select from these settings:

- *Off:* Turns off the filter.

- *Low:* Applies a little noise removal.

- *Standard:* Applies a more pronounced amount of noise removal; this setting is the default.

- *High:* Goes after noise in a more dramatic way.

FIGURE 4-36:
Activate High
ISO Speed NR
to tame noise
from high
ISO settings;
the Multi
Shot setting
captures four
images and
merges them
into a single
JPEG file.

- *Multi Shot:* Tries to achieve a better result than High by capturing four frames in a quick burst and then merging them together into a single image. The final image is saved in the JPEG format, even if the Image Quality option is set to Raw or Raw+JPEG.

As with the Long Exposure Noise Reduction filter, this filter is applied after you take the shot, slowing your capture rate. The High and Multi Shot settings cause the most significant delay.

A few other caveats apply:

- *High ISO noise-reduction filters work primarily by applying a slight blur to the image.* Don't expect this process to eliminate noise entirely, and expect some resulting image softness.

- *The Multi Shot Setting has several limitations.* It's not available when any of the following are enabled: Long Exposure Noise Reduction, Auto Exposure Bracketing, or White Balance Bracketing. Additionally, you can't use flash or the Bulb shutter speed.

- *For best results, use a tripod to avoid camera shake and to ensure that each frame covers the same area.* Otherwise, your image may exhibit blur or ghosting. Moving objects may also appear blurry, so this feature works best with still-life and landscape shots.

Finally, remember that the High ISO Noise Reduction setting automatically reverts to Standard if you turn off the camera, switch to a fully automatic exposure mode or Movie mode, or set the shutter speed to Bulb.

» **Anti-Flicker Shooting:** Some types of lights, by design, cycle on and off rapidly. It usually happens too quickly for the human eye to detect, but the camera's exposure system may be affected nonetheless. If the camera meters the light during an on cycle and takes the photo in an off cycle, the exposure will be too dark, and vice versa.

As mentioned in Chapter 1, you have the option of enabling Flicker Detection from the Viewfinder Display option in Setup Menu 2. If you do, the word

FLICKER appears in the viewfinder if the camera detects the type of lighting that can cause problems.

When the warning appears, you can set the camera to work around the on/off cycles by opening Shooting Menu 5 and setting the Anti-Flicker Shooting option to Enable. (The feature is disabled by default, as shown in Figure 4-37.) Unfortunately, you don't have access to this option in Live View or Movie mode or when the exposure mode is set to any setting other than P, Tv, Av, or M. Also understand that Anti-Flicker Shooting may create some lag between the time you press the shutter button and the time the picture is recorded because the camera has to wait to accommodate the on/off cycle of the lights.

FIGURE 4-37:
Anti-Flicker Shooting may produce more consistent exposures when you shoot under certain types of lights.

Locking Autoexposure Settings

To help ensure a proper exposure, your camera continually meters the light until the moment you press the shutter button fully to shoot the picture. In autoexposure modes — that is, any mode but M — the camera also keeps adjusting exposure settings as needed.

For most situations, this approach works great, resulting in the right settings for the light that's striking your subject when you capture the image. But on occasion, you may want to lock in a certain combination of exposure settings. For example, perhaps you want your subject to appear at the far edge of the frame. If you were to use the normal shooting technique, you would place the subject under a focus point, press the shutter button halfway to lock focus and set the initial exposure, and then reframe to your desired composition to take the shot. The problem is that exposure is then recalculated based on the new framing, which can leave your subject under- or overexposed.

The easiest way to get around this issue is to switch to M (manual exposure) mode and select the exposure settings that work best for your subject, regardless of composition. But if you prefer to use autoexposure, you can use AE Lock (autoexposure lock), which prevents the camera from adjusting exposure when you reframe your shot. To put it another way, you can interrupt the normal continuous exposure adjustment at any point before you take the picture. This option is available only for the P, Tv, and Av exposure modes.

REMEMBER

To use AE Lock successfully, you need to know that the camera establishes and locks exposure differently depending on the metering mode, the focusing mode (automatic or manual), and on an autofocusing setting called AF Point Selection. (Chapter 5 explains this option.) Here's the scoop:

>> **Evaluative metering and automatic AF Point Selection:** Exposure is based on the focusing point that achieved focus.

>> **Evaluative metering and manual AF Point Selection:** Exposure is locked on the autofocus point you select.

>> **All other metering modes:** Exposure is based on the center autofocus point, regardless of the AF Point Selection mode.

>> **Manual focusing:** Exposure is based on the center autofocus point.

This information is critical because you need to compose your shot initially so that your subject falls under the area of the frame the camera will use to meter exposure. For example, if you use Spot metering, place your subject at the center of the frame, set and lock exposure, and then reframe as desired.

If you can keep those details in mind, using AE Lock is easy. After framing your shot according to the guidelines just presented, press and hold the shutter button halfway to initiate exposure metering and autofocusing. Then, keeping the shutter button pressed halfway, press the AE Lock button. Exposure is now locked and remains locked for 4 seconds, even if you release the AE Lock button. Reframe to your desired composition and then press the shutter button the rest of the way to take the picture.

To remind you that AE Lock is in force, the camera displays an asterisk at the left end of the viewfinder or, in Live View mode, in the lower-left corner of the display.

Note: If your goal is to use the same exposure settings for multiple shots, you must keep the AE Lock button pressed during the entire series of pictures. Every time you let up on the button and press it again, you lock exposure anew based on the light that's in the frame. (Really, switching to manual exposure is much easier in this situation.)

Bracketing Exposures Automatically

Exposure bracketing simply means to capture several shots of your subject, using different exposure settings for each shot. The idea is to give yourself a safety net when you're shooting in tricky lighting or just aren't sure what exposure result will work best artistically.

Bracketing is also key to *HDR photography.* HDR stands for *high dynamic range,* which refers to an image that contains a greater range of brightness values than the camera can record in a single exposure. To produce an HDR image, the photographer records the same scene multiple times, again using different exposure settings for each image. The images are then combined using special computer software, often called *tone mapping software,* to combine the exposures in a way that uses specific brightness values from each shot.

TIP

With the HDR Backlight Control scene mode, covered in Chapter 3, you can create limited HDR effects; that mode captures three frames and merges the result into a single JPEG image. But capturing the bracketed frames yourself gives you control over how many frames are recorded and how great an exposure shift occurs between each frame. You also wind up having access to all the captured frames, whereas HDR Backlight Control only creates one composite image.

Whether you're interested in exposure bracketing for HDR or you just want to cover your bases to make sure that at least one frame is exposed to your liking, your camera offers a tool that simplifies the process. Called Automatic Exposure Bracketing (AEB), this feature captures three frames, shooting the first one at the current exposure settings and then automatically capturing two additional frames, one darker and one brighter.

Upcoming steps show you how to shoot a bracketed series; first, here are a few things you need to know about the AEB feature:

>> **AEB is available only in P, Tv, Av, and M exposure modes.** In M mode, you can't set the shutter speed to Bulb (the setting that keeps the shutter open as long as you hold down the shutter button).

>> **You can request an exposure change of up to two stops between frames.** Two stops doesn't sound like very much, but in fact, it's a fairly large jump between exposures. You may even wind up with one frame that's seriously overexposed and one that's just as underexposed, so experiment to find the magic number that gives you the exposure shift you're after.

>> **How the camera delivers the darker and brighter shots depends on your exposure mode and whether Auto ISO is enabled.** Here's how things work in each exposure mode:

- *P:* If the ISO setting is Auto, the camera adjusts ISO between frames. Otherwise, it adjusts both aperture and shutter speed to produce the different exposures.

- *Tv:* The camera respects your selected shutter speed and instead adjusts the ISO setting if Auto ISO is enabled. If not, the ISO remains the same between frames and the camera achieves the exposure shift by changing the aperture setting.

- *Av:* The camera uses your selected f-stop for all three frames. Again, if Auto ISO is enabled, the camera changes the ISO setting between frames. But if you dialed in a specific ISO setting, the shutter speed varies between shots instead.

- *M mode:* ISO is adjusted between frames if Auto ISO is enabled. Otherwise, the camera assumes that you want to maintain the same depth of field between shots and adjusts shutter speed to produce the various exposures.

TIP

If you want to keep the depth of field constant between shots — especially important when you plan to combine bracketed frames into an HDR image — shoot in M or Av mode so that the camera uses the same f-stop for all frames. (Remember that aperture affects depth of field.) If anything in the scene is moving, though, you also want the shutter speed to remain consistent, so in that case, the best option is to use M exposure mode and enable Auto ISO adjustment.

REMEMBER

>> **AEB isn't available when you use flash.** In fact, if you set up the camera to record a bracketed series and then enable flash, all your bracketing settings are undone.

>> **You can combine AEB with exposure compensation if you want.** The camera simply applies the compensation amount when it calculates the exposure for the three bracketed images. For example, if Exposure Compensation is set to EV +1.0 and the bracketing amount is set to one stop, you get one frame exposed at EV +1.0, one at EV 0.0 (darkest shot), and a third at EV +2.0 (brightest shot).

>> **Because Auto Lighting Optimizer adjusts contrast after the shot, it can render AEB ineffective.** So, it's best to disable the feature when bracketing. You can turn it off in Quick Control mode or via the Auto Lighting Optimizer option on Shooting Menu 2.

>> **A couple other features put AEB off limits.** Specifically, if you shoot in Live View mode and enable the Creative Filters, you can't use AEB. Additionally, automatic bracketing doesn't work if you set the High ISO Noise Reduction filter to the Multi Shot setting.

With those preliminaries out of the way, the following steps explain how to set up and shoot a bracketed series of photos:

1. **Display Shooting Menu 2 and choose Expo Comp/AEB, as shown in Figure 4-38.**

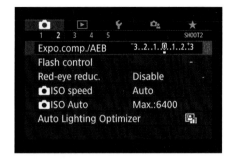

   After you select the menu option, you see the first screen shown in Figure 4-39, which is the same one that appears when you apply Exposure Compensation, explained earlier in this chapter.

   At first, you see only the Exposure Compensation controls, labeled in the figure. (If you're shooting in the M exposure mode, you have no

   FIGURE 4-38:
   Automatic Exposure Bracketing records your image at three exposure settings.

   need to use Exposure Compensation, so those controls appear dimmed on the screen.)

Exposure Compensation controls

FIGURE 4-39: The top controls adjust Exposure Compensation (left); the bottom controls set up Automatic Exposure Bracketing (right).

Bracketing controls

TIP

When you're not using Live View, you can use the Quick Control feature to get to the settings screen instead of using the menus. Press Q or tap the Q touchscreen symbol, highlight the exposure meter, and press Set.

2. **Rotate the Main dial to enable Automatic Exposure Bracketing and establish the amount of exposure change you want between images.**

   As soon as you rotate the dial (or tap the AEB touchscreen arrows), the AEB portion of the screen comes to life, displaying the meter shown on the right in Figure 4-39. This meter represents the maximum two-stop exposure shift available through AEB. The meter is set up in one-third stop increments; the tall lines represent the full stop positions (+/–1 or 2 stops). The smaller lines represent third-stop positions.

The three colored lines represent the three frames the camera will capture. The first shot, represented by the middle line, is always taken at the current exposure setting. The left line represents the second shot, which will be darker; the right line, the third shot, which will be brighter. In the figure, the meter shows bracketing set to produce a one-stop shift between the neutral, darker, and brighter exposure. Keep rotating the Main dial or tapping the AEB arrows until the bars indicate the amount of exposure shift you have in mind.

TIP

If you're familiar with the Exposure Compensation feature, you may notice something different about the top meter in the right screen in Figure 4-39: It indicates a maximum Exposure Compensation adjustment of +/–7 stops instead of the usual 5. What gives? Well, if you set Exposure Compensation to +5.0 and set the bracketing amount to +2.0, your brightest shot is captured at EV +7.0; the neutral shot at EV +5.0; and the darkest shot at EV +3.0.

To adjust the Exposure Compensation setting, rotate the Quick Control dial, press the right/left Quick Control keys, or tap the plus/minus signs at the end of the meter. The bracketing meter scoots left or right in tandem as you adjust the Exposure Compensation setting.

3. **Tap Set or press the Set button.**

AEB is now enabled. To remind you of that fact, the exposure meter on Shooting Menu 2 and on the Quick Control screen now includes three markers, one representing each of the three bracketed frames, as shown in Figure 4-40. You see the same markers on the viewfinder meter, as well as on the meter that appears at the bottom of the screen in Live View mode, and on the LCD panel (see Figure 4-41).

Neutral exposure

Bracketing settings   Darkest exposure | Brightest exposure

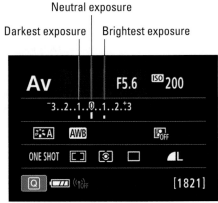

FIGURE 4-40:
The three lines under the exposure meter indicate that bracketing is in force.

4. **Shoot the bracketed series.**

How you do this depends on which Drive mode you're using, as follows:

- *Single Drive mode:* You take each exposure separately, pressing the shutter button fully three times to record your trio of images. After you take the first shot, the indicators under the exposure meter in the displays blink to remind you that you're in the middle of a three-frame series. When the blinking stops, you've captured that last frame in the series.

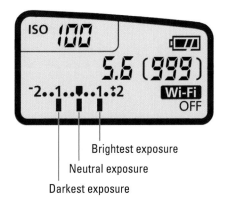

Brightest exposure
Neutral exposure
Darkest exposure

FIGURE 4-41:
Brackets also appear under the exposure meter on the LCD panel.

- *Continuous Drive mode:* Press and hold the shutter button down to record a burst of three frames. (Be sure to wait for the camera to record all three frames before you release the shutter button.) To record another series, release and then press the shutter button again. When AEB is enabled, you can't capture more than three frames with each shutter button press as you normally can.

- *Self-Timer modes:* All three exposures are recorded with a single press of the shutter button. But you don't need to hold down the shutter button as you do in Continuous mode — just press and release.

Along with the blinking exposure meter indicators, an asterisk blinks in the viewfinder display between frames.

5. **To turn off Automatic Exposure Bracketing, change the AEB setting back to 0.**

Just repeat Steps 1 and 2, rotating the Main dial or tapping the AEB arrows until the AEB meter disappears. Be sure to also follow Step 3, pressing the Set button or tapping Set on the touchscreen. Otherwise, the change won't stick.

REMEMBER

AEB is also turned off when you power down the camera, enable the flash, replace the camera battery, replace the memory card, or shoot in M exposure mode and set the shutter speed to Bulb.

Chapter **5**

Controlling Focus and Depth of Field

To many people, the word *focus* has just one interpretation when applied to a photograph: Either the subject is in focus or it's blurry. But an artful photographer knows that there's more to focus than simply getting a sharp image of a subject. You also need to consider *depth of field,* or the distance over which other objects in the scene appear sharply focused.

This chapter explains how to manipulate both aspects of an image. After a reminder of how to set your lens to auto or manual focusing, the first part of the chapter details focusing options available for viewfinder photography; following that, you can get help with focusing during Live View photography and movie recording.

A word of warning: The two systems are different, and mastering them takes time. If you start feeling overwhelmed, simplify things by following the steps laid out at the beginning of Chapter 3, which show you how to take a picture using the default autofocus settings. Then return another day to study the focusing options discussed here.

Things get much easier (and more fun) at the end of the chapter, which covers ways to control depth of field. Thankfully, the concepts related to that subject apply no matter whether you're using the viewfinder, taking advantage of Live View photography, or shooting movies.

Setting the Lens to Automatic or Manual Focusing Mode

REMEMBER

Regardless of whether you're using the viewfinder, Live View, or Movie mode, your first focus task is to set the lens to auto or manual focusing (assuming that your lens supports autofocusing with the 77D). On most lenses, including the 18–55mm or 18–135mm kit lenses, you find a switch with two settings: AF for autofocusing and MF for manual focusing, as shown in Figure 5-1. The position of the manual focusing ring varies from lens to lens; Figure 5-1 shows you where to find it on the kit lenses.

Manual focusing ring   Auto/Manual Focus switch

FIGURE 5-1: On the kit lenses, as on many Canon lenses, you set the switch to AF for autofocusing and to MF for manual focusing.

Depending on your lens, you may be able to adjust focus manually even when the lens switch is set to AF. This feature, called *autofocusing with manual override*, enables you to set focus initially using autofocusing and then fine-tune focus by turning the manual focusing ring. See your lens manual to find out if your lens offers this option. The kit lenses do, but in a limited way; see the sidebar devoted to the Lens Electronic MF feature for details.

WHAT'S LENS ELECTRONIC MF?

If your lens doesn't offer autofocusing with manual override, you may be able to take advantage of the camera's Lens Electronic MF feature. Simply put, this feature gives you the same autofocusing flexibility as a lens that has the option built in.

However, Lens Electronic MF is available only under the following conditions:

- **Your lens must be compatible with the feature as it's implemented on the 77D.** For a list of lenses compatible with this feature, check the section of the camera manual that covers Lens Electronic MF. The 18–55mm and 18–135mm kit lenses qualify.

- **You're shooting in the P, Tv, Av, or M exposure modes.**

- **You've set the AF Operation mode to One-Shot autofocusing.** This setting tells the camera to lock focus when you press and hold the shutter button halfway. (Later sections show how to adjust the AF Operation mode.)

Although this feature gives you the ability to manually fine-tune the camera's autofocus to a very fine degree, you also need to be somewhat coordinated to make it work correctly. After you press the shutter button halfway to autofocus, you have to keep it pressed halfway while you rotate the manual focusing ring to fine-tune focus. If you mess up and release the shutter button, autofocusing begins anew when you press the shutter button to take the picture.

By default, electronic manual focusing is disabled. If you want to try it out, open Shooting Menu 1 and choose Lens Electronic MF, as shown in the figure on the left. On the next screen, choose Enable After One-Shot AF, as shown in the figure on the right. Again, you see the menu option only when the Mode dial is set to P, Tv, Av, or M.

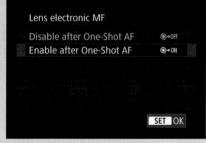

Exploring Viewfinder Focusing Options

Chapters 1 and 3 offer brief primers in focusing, but in case you're not reading the book from beginning to end, here's a quick recap of focusing basics. Again, this information applies when you use the viewfinder to compose your image; details for focusing in Live View and Movie modes come later.

> » **To autofocus:** After setting the lens switch to the autofocusing mode (AF, on the kit lenses), frame your subject so that it appears within the autofocus brackets, highlighted in the left screen in Figure 5-2. Then press and hold the shutter button halfway.

Autofocus brackets   Selected focus points   Focus achieved light

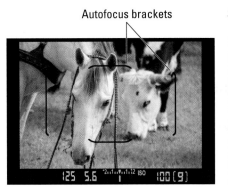 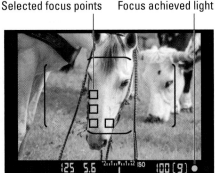

FIGURE 5-2: The viewfinder offers these focusing aids.

What happens next depends on your exposure mode:

- *Scene Intelligent Auto, Flash Off, Creative Auto, and all Creative Filter modes except the four HDR settings:* With stationary subjects, one or more of the focus points appear to indicate the points the camera used to set the focusing distance, as shown on the right in Figure 5-2. (In dim lighting, the focus brackets and focus points first flash red to help you spot them.) You also see the viewfinder focus achieved light, also labeled in the figure, and hear a beep. Focus remains locked as long as you hold down the shutter button.

  If the camera detects subject motion, however, it tracks the movement and adjusts focus continuously until you take the picture. As this focus tracking happens, different focus points may flash on and off to show you what area of the frame the camera considers to be the current focusing target. You don't see the viewfinder's focus-indicator light during continuous autofocusing, but the beep sounds each time the camera re-establishes focus.

For continuous autofocusing to work properly, you must adjust framing as necessary to keep the subject under the area covered by the autofocus area brackets.

- *Sports and Kids modes:* The continuous-autofocusing setup is used.

- *All other Scene modes and P, Tv, Av, and M modes:* The camera assumes that you're shooting a stationary subject, so it locks focus when you press the shutter button halfway. In the P, Tv, Av, and M exposure modes, however, you can switch to continuous autofocusing if you want; see the upcoming section "Changing the AF Operation mode" for details.

You can press and hold the AF ON button instead of the shutter button to initiate autofocus when using the viewfinder, using Live View, or shooting movies.

In all cases, if the viewfinder focus light blinks rapidly, the camera can't find a focusing target. Try focusing manually instead. Also try backing away from your subject a little; you may simply be exceeding the close-focusing capabilities of your lens.

>> **To focus manually:** After setting the lens switch to the manual focusing (MF) position, rotate the focusing ring on the lens.

Even when focusing manually, you can confirm focus by pressing the shutter button halfway. The focus point or points over the area that's in focus flash for a second or two, the viewfinder's focus lamp lights, and you hear the focus-achieved beep.

By the way, if you find the focusing beep annoying, you can disable it via the Beep option on Setup Menu 3. However, if you disable the focusing beep, you also disable the sounds the camera makes when you tap the touchscreen.

Adjusting autofocus performance

By default, your camera's autofocusing system behaves as outlined in the preceding section. But depending on your exposure mode, you may be able to modify autofocus performance through one or both of the following settings:

>> **AF Area Selection mode:** This setting determines which of the 45 autofocus points the camera uses to establish focusing distance. You can leave all 45 in play, giving the camera wide latitude on finding a focus target, or you can require the autofocusing system to lock focus only within a particular portion, or *zone,* of the frame. You also can set focus based on just a single focus point that you select.

>> **AF Operation:** This option determines whether the camera locks focus when you press the shutter button halfway (One-Shot autofocusing), automatically switches from One-Shot to continuous AF when it detects a moving subject (AI Focus autofocusing), or continues to adjust focus from the time you press the shutter button halfway until you press it the rest of the way to take the shot (AI Servo autofocusing).

The next few sections detail both autofocusing options. But a few reminders before you dig in:

>> **You have control over both settings only in the P, Tv, Av, and M exposure modes.** In most other exposure modes, you can adjust the AF Area Selection mode but not the AF Operation mode. A few exposure modes lock you out of both settings.

>> **In the P, Tv, Av, and M exposure modes, symbols representing both options appear in the Quick Control display, as shown in Figure 5-3.** In Basic Zone modes, this information isn't provided in the display.

>> **Information in this chapter assumes that you haven't changed the default settings for Custom Functions related to autofocusing.** Straying from the defaults will definitely confuse your journey as you familiarize yourself with the autofocusing system. But after you have the focusing system down cold, check out the upcoming section "Considering a few other autofocusing tweaks" to read about other ways to customize things.

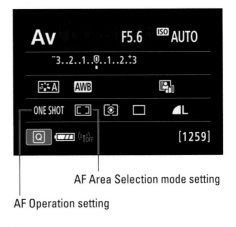

AF Area Selection mode setting

AF Operation setting

FIGURE 5-3:
In P, Tv, Av, and M exposure modes, the Quick Control display shows you which autofocusing options are in force.

AF Area Selection mode: One focus point or many?

One way you can control autofocusing behavior is to specify how you want the camera to select the autofocus point that it uses to set the focusing distance. The option that controls this autofocusing behavior is the AF Area Selection mode.

You have access to this setting in all exposure modes except Candlelight Scene mode and two Creative Filters modes, Fisheye and Miniature. Assuming that you're not shooting in those modes, you can choose from the following options:

>> **Automatic Selection AF:** The camera selects the autofocus point for you, considering all 45 focus points within the autofocus brackets when looking for a focusing target. If the scene contains people, the camera knows to give them priority when making a focusing decision. (This feature, called color-tracking autofocusing, relies on the camera being able to recognize skin tones.) If the frame doesn't contain anyone who's showing any skin, the camera focuses on the closest object.

>> **Large Zone AF:** The camera's 45 focus points are divided into three zones — left, right, and center — with each zone containing 15 points. For example, the left screen in Figure 5-4 shows the points contained in the center zone. You select which of the three zones you want to use, and the camera then selects a point within that zone for you. Again, the camera gives focusing priority to skin tones and then the closest object that falls within the selected zone.

Large Zone AF, center 15 points active Zone AF, center nine points active

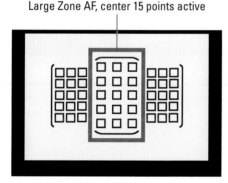
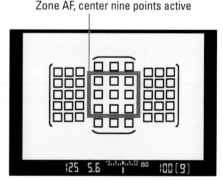

FIGURE 5-4: Zone AF modes limit the camera to choosing a focus point within a specified portion of the frame.

>> **Zone AF:** This mode also uses the zone concept, but with smaller zones of nine points each. In the right screen in Figure 5-4, for example, the nine points at the center of the frame are highlighted.

>> **Single-Point AF:** This mode is the only one that puts you in control over which focus point is used. You can choose any of the 45 focus points, and the camera bases focus only on the object under that point.

Although the AF Area Selection options aren't that hard to understand, the way you lock in the setting you want to use is, shall we say, "less than intuitive." Here's how to get the job done:

TIP

>> **Accessing the AF Area Selection Mode setting:** You can press either of the two buttons labeled in Figure 5-5 to display a screen where you choose the option you want to use. (If nothing happens when you press the buttons, the camera may be in sleep mode; to wake it up, press the shutter button halfway and release it. Then try again.)

However, because the AF Point Selection button has no other function when it comes to this setting than to display the screen, just ignore it and handle everything with the AF Area Selection button. That button is used both to access the setting and to adjust it.

In the P, Tv, Av, and M exposure modes, you also can adjust the setting via the Quick Control screen. See the last point in this list for specifics.

>> **Decoding the settings screen:** The appearance of the AF Area Mode settings screen changes depending on which option is active. Figure 5-6 shows you how things look in Automatic Selection mode (left) and the Large Zone mode (right).

AF Area Selection Mode button

AF Point Selection button

FIGURE 5-5:
These curiously marked buttons both access the settings screen, but only the AF Area Selection Mode button enables you to cycle through the settings with successive presses.

Here's a guide to the various screen elements:

- *A text label at the top of the screen indicates the name of the current mode.* But the label is a little confusing because the Large Zone, Zone, and Single-Point labels begin with the words *Manual select,* which may lead you to believe you've switched to manual focusing somehow. You haven't — the camera is just telling you that in the current mode, you get to select the specific zone or focus point you want to use. So concentrate on the words after *Manual select;* that text tells you the name of the current mode.

AF Area Selection button symbol

Currently selected mode   Mode icon

Large Zone AF symbol

Auto selection AF

Manual select. Large Zone AF

Active focusing area boundaries   Exit arrow

Active zone

FIGURE 5-6: In Auto Area and Large Zone modes, the brackets indicate the current auto-focusing area.

- *The icons below the text label represent the four modes.* An orange highlight box surrounds the currently selected zone.

- *The diagram below the icons show you which focus points are currently active.* In Automatic Selection mode, you see the same brackets that appear in the viewfinder, indicating that anything within that portion of the frame is a potential focusing target. Brackets also appear in the Large Zone AF mode, this time indicating which of the three zones is active — left, center, or right.

Figure 5-7 shows you how the screen appears in Zone mode (nine active points) and Single-Point (one point) modes. On these screens, the currently active points appear in color.

Zone AF, center nine points selected

Single-Point AF, center point selected

FIGURE 5-7: In Zone mode (left) and Single-Point mode (right), the colored points are active.

- *The appearance of the Automatic Selection screen varies depending on the AF Operation setting.* If that option is set to One-Shot, the screen appears as shown on the left in Figure 5-6, with just the focus brackets visible. But if you use continuous autofocusing — AI Servo is the official setting name — the frame shown in Figure 5-8 appears, now showing all 45 focus points, with the center point in color. This altered diagram is designed to remind you that when you use continuous autofocusing, the camera

FIGURE 5-8:
When the AF Operation is set to AI Servo (continuous autofocusing,) the display changes to remind you to initiate focusing with your subject under the center focus point.

sets focus initially on a single point — the center point, by default. (The next section explains more about the AF Operation setting.)

Making things even more confusing, you can't control the AF Operation setting in the Basic Zone shooting modes, and different modes use different settings. Meaning that which version of the screen you see depends on the Basic Zone exposure mode you use. The key thing to remember is that if you see the version shown in Figure 5-8, frame your subject so that it falls under the center focus point before setting focus.

>> **Choosing a different AF Area Selection Mode:** And now for the most perplexing part of adjusting this setting: How the heck do you switch from one mode to the other? The techniques that work on most menu screens — rotating the Quick Control dial, rotating the Main dial, or pressing the left/right Quick Control keys — don't do the trick. Instead, you press the AF Area Selection Mode button to cycle from one mode to the next. See the symbol to the far right of the setting icons? (Refer to Figure 5-6.) It's the same one that appears on the button, and it's there to remind you that the button is the key to changing the mode. It's okay, *no one* figures this one out or remembers what it means the next time they change the setting.

TIP

When you shoot in the P, TV, Av, and M exposure modes, you *can* use the Main dial to change the setting. However, you need to enable that option via Custom Function 6, named AF Area Selection Method. (Access Custom Functions via Setup Menu 4.) If you make this change, you can't use the Main dial for its normal purpose, which is to select the zone or single focus point you want to use, as explained next. In this case, though, the Quick Control dial still works; use it to scroll through the different zones if you prefer.

>> **Selecting a zone or focus point:** In Large Zone, Zone, or Single-Point mode, press the Quick Control keys to select a different zone or focus point. You can also cycle through the available zones by rotating the Quick Control or Main dial. To select a single point, rotate either dial to move left to right through the grid of points and use the up/down Quick Control keys to move up and down. If the touchscreen is enabled, you also can just tap the point or zone you want to use (although tapping a single point can be tricky because the point markers are small).

TIP

In Automatic Selection AF mode, you can choose an initial focusing point only when continuous autofocusing is used. To use a point other than the center one, use the same techniques just described for Single-Point mode.

Press the Set button to quickly select the center zone or focus point.

If you change Custom Function 6 so that you use the Main dial to cycle from one AF Area Selection mode to another, as outlined in the preceding bullet, use the Quick Control keys or the touchscreen to choose a zone or focus point.

>> **Looking at viewfinder symbols:** After you press either of the two buttons that bring the AF Area Selection Mode screen to life, the viewfinder displays the same icons and grid graphics that you see on the monitor. In the readout at the bottom of the screen, you see one of two graphics: AF with a dashed rectangle or SEL with a single rectangle (the AF or SEL indicators and rectangles also appear on the top LCD panel). The AF graphic appears for Auto Selection, Large Zone, and Zone modes. SEL represents the Single-Point mode. However, you're on your own as far as remembering that you press the AF Area Selection button to cycle through the four modes; the icon reminder shown on the monitor screen doesn't appear.

>> **Taking advantage of Quick Control mode:** In the P, Tv, Av, and M exposure modes, you also can adjust the AF Area Selection Mode setting via the Quick Control screen. After selecting the setting, as shown on the left in Figure 5-9, rotate the Quick Control or Main dial to display icons representing each mode, as shown on the right. Keep rotating the dial to select the mode you want to use. To display the zone or point selection screen, press the Set button. After choosing the zone or point you want to use, tap the Menu icon or press the Menu button to exit to the Quick Control screen, which remains active. Press the Q button or tap the Q touchscreen symbol to exit to shooting mode.

FIGURE 5-9:
You also can access the AF Area Selection mode setting via the Quick Control screen.

AF Operation mode: Focus lock or continuous AF?

In the P, Tv, Av, and M exposure modes, you also can adjust autofocus performance by changing the AF Operation mode, which determines how and when focus is set. You have three choices:

>> **One Shot:** This mode, geared to shooting stationary subjects, locks focus when you press and hold the shutter button halfway down.

WARNING

One important point to remember about One Shot mode is that if the camera can't achieve focus, it won't let you take the picture, no matter how hard you press the shutter button. Also be aware that if you pair One Shot autofocusing with one of the Continuous Drive modes, detailed in Chapter 2, focus for all frames in a burst is based on the focus point used for the first shot.

>> **AI Servo:** In this mode (the *AI* stands for *artificial intelligence*), the camera adjusts focus continually as needed from when you press the shutter button halfway to the time you take the picture. This mode is designed to make focusing on moving subjects easier.

WARNING

For AI Servo to work properly, you must reframe as needed to keep your subject under the active autofocus point or zone if you're using the Single-Point or Zone AF Area Selection modes. If the camera is set to Automatic Selection AF, the camera bases focus initially on the center focus point, but you can select a different point if you like. (See the preceding section for how-to's.) If the subject moves away from the chosen point, focus should still be okay as long as you keep the subject within the area covered by one of the other autofocus points.

In either case, the green focus dot in the viewfinder blinks rapidly if the camera isn't tracking focus successfully. If all is going well, the focus dot doesn't light, and you don't hear the beep that normally sounds when focus is achieved. (You can hear the autofocus motor whirring a little when the camera adjusts focus.)

If you use AI Servo with the Continuous Drive mode, focus is adjusted as needed between frames, which may slow the maximum shots-per-second rate. However, it's still the best option for shooting a moving subject.

» **AI Focus:** This mode automatically switches the camera from One Shot to AI Servo as needed. When you first press the shutter button halfway, focus is locked on the active autofocus point (or points), as in One Shot mode. But if the subject moves, the camera shifts into AI Servo mode and adjusts focus as it thinks is warranted.

TIP

Because AI Focus can sometimes misinterpret what it sees and choose the wrong autofocusing setup, it's best to ignore this option. Instead, stick with One Shot for stationary subjects and AI Servo for moving subjects.

Here's one way to remember which mode is which: For still subjects, you need only *one shot* at setting focus. For moving subjects, think of a tennis player *serving* the ball — so use *AI Servo* for action shots.

You can choose the AF Operation setting in two ways:

» **AF button:** Your fastest move is to press the Quick Control button with the AF label, shown in Figure 5-10. The selection screen shown in the figure appears. As always, if pressing the button produces no results, you may need to wake the camera out of sleep mode by pressing the shutter button halfway and releasing it.

FIGURE 5-10: Pressing the AF button is the fastest path to the AF Operation setting.

With the settings screen displayed, select the option you want to use by rotating the Quick Control or Main dial, pressing the right/left Quick Control keys, or tapping the icon for the setting you want to use. Then tap the Set icon or press the Set button to exit the screen.

» **Quick Control method:** After pressing the Q button or tapping the Q touchscreen symbol, select the AF Operation icon, as shown in Figure 5-11. The name of the selected setting appears at the bottom of the screen. Rotate the Quick Control or Main dial to cycle through the three mode options.

If you prefer, you can tap the icon or press Set to display the same screen shown in Figure 5-10, where all three choices appear on a single screen.

AF Operation setting

FIGURE 5-11:
You also can adjust the setting via the Quick Control screen.

Choosing the right autofocus combo

TIP

You'll get the best autofocus results if you pair your chosen AF mode with the most appropriate AF Area Selection mode because the two settings work in tandem. Here are the combinations that we suggest:

» **For still subjects: AF Area Selection mode, Single-Point AF; AF Operation mode, One-Shot.** You select a specific focus point, and the camera locks focus on that point at the time you press the shutter button halfway. Focus remains locked on your subject even if you reframe the shot after you press the button halfway.

» **For moving subjects: AF Area Selection mode, Automatic Selection AF; AF Operation mode, AI Servo.** Begin by selecting an initial focusing point; by default, the center point is selected, but you can select a different point if you prefer. Frame your subject initially so that it's under the selected point and then press the shutter button halfway to set the initial focusing distance. The camera adjusts focus as needed if your subject moves within the frame before you take the shot. All you need to do is keep the shutter button pressed halfway and reframe the shot as needed to keep your subject within the boundaries of the autofocus brackets.

Keeping these two combos in mind should greatly improve your autofocusing accuracy. But in some situations, no combination will enable speedy or correct autofocusing. For example, if you try to focus on a very reflective subject, the camera may hunt for an autofocus point forever. And if you try to focus on a subject behind a fence, the autofocus system may continually insist on focusing on the fence instead of your subject. In such scenarios, don't waste time monkeying around with the autofocus settings — just switch to manual focusing.

Finally, remember that to have control over the AF Operation mode, you must use one of the advanced exposure modes (P, Tv, Av, or M).

Considering a few other autofocus settings

In the P, Tv, Av, or M exposure modes, you have access to the following additional Custom Functions (Setup Menu 4), all of which enable you to make additional tweaks to the autofocusing system. These features relate only to view-finder shooting:

>> **Auto AF Point Selection: Color Tracking (Custom Function 7):** By default, the AF system is programmed to recognize skin tones. It selects AF points on that basis when you set the AF Operation mode to One-Shot or AI Servo and set the AF Area Selection mode to Large Zone, Zone, or Automatic Selection. The idea is to make focusing on people quicker and easier. If the camera doesn't detect any skin tones, the camera focuses on the nearest object.

>> If you prefer the camera not prioritize people during autofocusing, you can turn off the skin-tone priority feature by setting Custom Function 7 to Disable.

>> **AF Point Display During Focus (Custom Function 8):** By default, the selected AF points (or brackets) are displayed in the viewfinder any time the camera is ready to shoot. The markings also appear when you're choosing an AF point, during autofocusing, and when focus is achieved. Through this menu option, you can indicate when you want the focus points to appear or specify that you always want to see all points, all the time. (You're probably going to get tired of that option quickly.)

>> **VF Display Illumination (Custom Function 9):** This setting, too, affects the viewfinder display. At the default setting, Auto, AF points used to achieve focus appear black in normal light and turn bright red in dim light. If you want the points to appear red regardless of the ambient light, change the setting to Enable. To instead have the focus markings always appear black, choose Disable.

If you're new to Custom Functions, check out Chapter 1 for a primer in how to make your way through these menu screens.

PREVENTING SLOW-SHUTTER BLUR

A poorly focused photo isn't always caused by incorrect focusing. A slow shutter speed can also be the culprit.

Chapter 4 explains shutter speed in detail, but here's the short story as it relates to focus: When you photograph moving subjects, a slow shutter speed can make them appear blurry because their motion is recorded the entire time the shutter is open. And when you handhold the camera, a slow shutter speed increases the chances of camera movement — *camera shake* — during the exposure, which can blur the entire photo.

You can avoid camera shake by using a tripod, of course. But when you don't have a tripod or another way to steady the camera, some lenses offer a feature that can compensate for small amounts of camera shake. On Canon lenses, this feature is called Image Stabilization, but other manufacturers use different names, such as Vibration Compensation or Optical Stabilization. The Canon lenses featured in this book offers Image Stabilization; enable and disable it via the Stabilizer switch on the lens.

Focusing in Live View and Movie Modes

You can opt for autofocusing or manual focusing during Live View and movie shooting, assuming that your lens supports autofocusing with the 77D. The actual focusing process is the same as for viewfinder photography: To autofocus, press and hold the shutter button halfway; to focus manually, rotate the focusing ring on the lens. (See the first section of the chapter for help setting the lens to automatic or manual focusing.)

TIP

In Live View and Movie mode, however, you also have the option of tapping your subject on the touchscreen to set focus. When focus is achieved, the focus frame turns green, as shown in Figure 5-12. (The focus frame appearance varies depending on the autofocusing settings you choose.)

WARNING

For still photography, remember that if the Touch Shutter feature is enabled, the camera takes the shot as soon as you lift your finger off the screen. Look for the Touch Shutter status in the

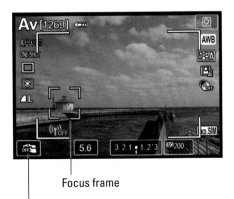

Focus frame

Touch Shutter status

FIGURE 5-12:
When the Touch Shutter is Off, tapping the touchscreen sets focus but doesn't trigger the shutter release.

lower-left corner of the display, as shown in Figure 5-12. (If you don't see the symbol, press the Info button to change the data that's displayed). Toggle the touch shutter on and off by tapping the symbol.

The next several sections offer more details about focusing in Live View and Movie modes.

AF Method: Setting the focusing area

As with viewfinder photography, the camera offers two settings that enable you to tweak autofocus performance. First up is the AF Method, which is the equivalent of the AF Area Selection Mode option provided for viewfinder photography. It enables you to tell the camera which region of the frame to analyze when setting focus. You can control this setting in the same exposure modes that you can during viewfinder photography — that is, any mode but Candlelight, Fisheye, and Miniature.

The settings available for Live View and Movie mode are different than for viewfinder photography, however. You get the following choices:

>> **Face+Tracking AF:** This setting is designed to speed up focusing when you shoot portraits. If the camera detects a face, it automatically places a focus frame over that face, as shown in Figure 5-13. If the person attached to the face moves before you initiate autofocusing, the camera tracks the movement (thus, *face+tracking*), automatically repositioning the focus frame. In a group portrait, you can press the right/left Quick Control keys to move the frame over a different face.

REMEMBER

Note that the face-selection process is only part of the game; you still have to press the shutter button halfway or tap the touchscreen to initiate autofocusing. But with face tracking, autofocusing can happen a little faster because the camera knows exactly where to set focus.

FIGURE 5-13:
In Face+Tracking mode, the camera focuses on a face if one is detected; otherwise, it looks for a focus target within the Auto Area focus frame.

If the camera doesn't detect a face, it looks for a focusing target within the Auto Area focus frame, which is represented by the four corner marks, one of which is labeled in Figure 5-13. You can tap the touchscreen to put a focusing frame over your subject if you want. Otherwise, the camera will choose a focus point when you press the shutter button halfway. The selected point or points will appear green.

» **Smooth Zone AF:** The Auto Area focus frame is replaced by a smaller frame, as shown on the left in Figure 5-14. Before focusing, use the Quick Control keys to move the frame over your subject. Or, if you're a touchscreen fan, tap the screen to place the frame and start the autofocusing process.

AF Method (Smooth Zone symbol)   AF Method (Live 1-point symbol)

Smooth Zone focus frame   Live 1-point focus frame

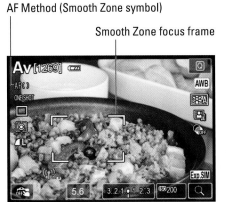
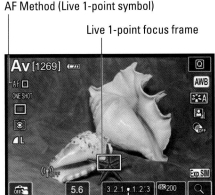

FIGURE 5-14: In Smooth Zone and Live 1-Point modes, use the Quick Control keys to move the focusing frame over your subject.

» **Live 1-point AF:** This mode works just like Smooth Zone AF except that the focusing frame is smaller, enabling you to more precisely indicate the intended focusing target. The right screen in Figure 5-13 offers a look at the Live 1-point focus frame.

A symbol representing the current mode appears in the display; refer to Figures 5-13 and 5-14 for a look. Unfortunately, the Auto Area frame partially obscures the symbol when you use the Face+Tracking mode.

To adjust the setting, the easiest option is to press the Q button or tap the Q touchscreen symbol to put the camera in Quick Control mode. Figure 5-15 shows that screen with the AF Method setting selected. The figure shows where to find the setting during Live View still photography; when the camera is in

Movie mode, the setting appears in the same spot but several other options on the screen relate to movie recording instead of still photography.

You also can adjust the setting via the Shooting Menu. Exactly *which* Shooting Menu varies depending on your exposure mode and whether you're shooting stills or movies. For still photography in the P, Tv, Av, and M exposure modes, the option is found on Shooting Menu 6. In Movie mode (with the Mode dial set to P, Tv, Av, or M exposure modes), look for the option on Shooting Menu 4. In Basic Zone exposure modes (still photos or when in Movie mode), it's found on Shooting Menu 2.

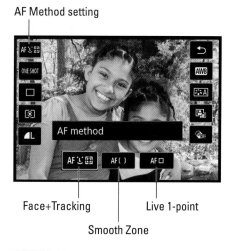

AF Method setting

Face+Tracking   Live 1-point

Smooth Zone

FIGURE 5-15:
The fastest way to change the AF Method setting is via the Quick Control screen.

AF Operation: One-Shot or Servo?

The second autofocusing control, AF Operation, works just like its viewfinder-photography counterpart, determining when the final focusing distance is set. For Live View photography, though, you have only two options:

>> **One Shot:** Focus locks when you press the shutter button halfway. The AF point or points used turn green when focus is achieved.

>> **Servo:** This one is the equivalent of the AI Servo option available for viewfinder photography. The initial focus point is set when you press the shutter button halfway but is continuously adjusted to track a moving subject up to the time you take the picture. When the camera achieves focus, the AF point or points used turn blue when in Live View mode.

There is no AI Focus setting, which is the viewfinder-photography setting that lets the camera decide which of the two options to use.

How you choose the setting you want to use is different depending on whether you're shooting photographs or movies, as follows:

>> **Live View photography:** Your only option for changing the AF Operation setting is to put the camera in Quick Control mode (press the Q button or tap the Q touchscreen symbol). The left screen in Figure 5-16 offers a look at the Quick Control screen as it appears when the AF Operation setting is active.

AF Operation setting

FIGURE 5-16:
For photography,
adjust the AF
Operation
setting via the
Quick Control
screen (left); in
Movie mode,
tap the Servo
AF symbol
to pause
and restart
continuous
autofocusing.

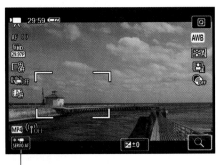

Tap to pause/restart continuous autofocusing

>> **Movie mode:** By default, the camera uses a special continuous autofocus setting called Movie Servo AF. The camera focuses automatically on the object within the focusing frame — you don't have to press the shutter button halfway to set focus as you do for still photography. To interrupt focus adjustment, tap the Servo AF icon in the lower-left corner of the screen, labeled on the right in Figure 5-16. Tap again to resume continuous autofocusing.

During shooting, you can tap the screen to reset focus on a different portion of the screen. Your movie footage may be blurred for a second or two during the time the camera adjusts focus.

The downside to Movie Servo AF is that with some lenses, the sounds made by the autofocusing system can be heard on the movie audio track. Do some tests with your lens to find out whether the focusing noise is disruptive; if it is, you may want to disable continuous autofocusing altogether. To do so, open Shooting Menu 4 and change the Movie Servo AF setting to Disable. Then press the shutter button to set focus, which remains locked even if you release the button. If necessary, reset focus by pressing the shutter button again, keeping in mind the same problems arise when you reset focus when using Movie Servo AF.

Manual focusing in Live View and Movie modes

Manual focusing is the easiest of the Live View focusing options — and in most cases, it's faster, too. The first part of the chapter provides information on manual focusing basics, but also be aware of these points specific to Live View and Movie mode:

TIP

WHY FACE-DETECTION AUTOFOCUSING ISN'T A SURE THING

In the Face+Tracking autofocus mode, the camera searches for faces in the frame. If it finds one, it displays a focus frame over the face. In a group shot, the camera chooses one face to use as the focus point; you can move the focus frame over a different face by pressing the Quick Control keys or tapping the face.

When the conditions are *just right* in terms of lighting, composition, and phase of the moon, the face-detection technology works fairly well. However, it has a number of issues:

- **People must be facing the camera to be detected.** The feature is based on the camera recognizing the pattern created by the eyes, nose, and mouth. So if you're shooting the subject in profile, don't expect face detection to work.

- **The camera may mistakenly focus on an object that has a similar shape, color, and contrast to a face.**

- **Face detection sometimes gets tripped up if the face isn't just the right size with respect to the background, is tilted at an angle, is too bright or dark, or is partly obscured.**

- **Autofocusing isn't possible when a subject is very close to the edge of the frame.** The camera alerts you to this issue by displaying a gray frame instead of a white one over your subject. You can always temporarily reframe to put the subject within the acceptable autofocus area, press and hold the shutter button halfway to lock focus, and then reframe to your desired composition.

If the camera has trouble finding your subject's face, the fix is easy: Just tap the touchscreen to position the focus frame yourself. Alternatively, you can switch to Smooth Zone AF or Live 1-Point AF and move the focus frame over the face by tapping the screen or pressing the Quick Control keys.

WARNING

» **If Servo AF is engaged, exit Live View or Movie mode before changing the lens switch to the MF (manual focus) position.** Moving the switch while continuous autofocusing is engaged can damage your equipment.

» **The Live View and Movie displays don't offer any indication that manual focusing is in force.** The screens continue to show the current AF Method and AF Operation symbols, along with the respective autofocus frames.

TIP

» **You can magnify the display to verify focus.** Most people who shy away from manual focusing do so because they don't trust their eyes to judge focus. But thanks to a feature that enables you to magnify the Live View preview, you can feel more confident in your manual focusing skills. See the next section for details.

Zooming in for a focus check

Here's a cool focusing feature not available during viewfinder photography: You can magnify the Live View or Movie display to ensure that focus is accurate. This trick works during manual focusing or when you autofocus using any AF Method but Face+Tracking.

After setting focus, follow these steps to magnify the display:

1. **Position the focus frame over the area you want to inspect.**

For example, in Figure 5-17, the frame appears over the center of the rose. (The frame appearance depends on whether you set the AF Method to Zone AF or Live 1-point AF.) You can tap the screen or use the Quick Control keys to position the frame.

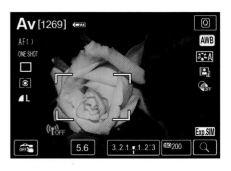

FIGURE 5-17:
When the magnifying glass is displayed, you can tap it to zoom the preview.

2. **Press the AF Point Selection button or tap the magnifying glass on the screen, shown in Figure 5-17.**

You then see a second rectangle, as shown on the left in Figure 5-18, which is the magnification frame. In the lower-right corner of the screen you also see a white thumbnail that represents your image along with a magnification level value. In the left screen of Figure 5-18, the magnification value is 1x — in other words, no magnification has been applied yet.

3. **Press the AF Point Selection button or tap the magnifying glass symbol again to magnify the display.**

Your first press of the button displays a view that's magnified five times, as shown on the right in Figure 5-18. Now the thumbnail icon changes, and the tiny white rectangle indicates the area of the frame you're viewing. Additionally, scroll arrows appear on each side of the frame.

Magnification frame   Magnification level   Scroll arrow   Location of visible area

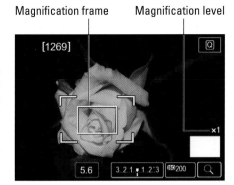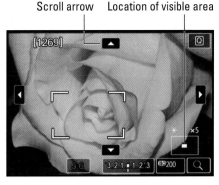

FIGURE 5-18:
Tap the
scroll arrows
or use the
Quick Control
buttons to
scroll the
zoomed
display.

If needed, tap the scroll arrow or press the Quick Control keys to reposition the magnification frame so that you can view a different portion of the scene.

Press the AF Selection Point button or tap the magnifying glass again for a 10x magnification.

4. **To exit magnified view, press the AF Point Selection button or tap the magnifying glass again.**

TIP

Pretty cool, yes? Just a couple of tips on using this feature:

» Press the Set button to quickly shift the magnification frame back to the center of the screen.

» Exit magnified view before you actually take the picture. Otherwise, the exposure may be off. However, if you *do* take the picture in magnified view, the entire frame is captured — not just the area currently displayed on the monitor.

CORRECTING LENS DISTORTION AND DIFFRACTION

Some lenses can cause slight distortion or result in *diffraction,* a phenomenon that causes a loss of sharpness at certain aperture settings. In P, Tv, Av, and M exposure modes, you may be able to deal with these issues by choosing Lens Aberration Correction from Shooting Menu 1. If the text at the top of the next screen shows your lens model, the camera has the information it needs to apply the corrections. By default, Distortion Correction is disabled and Diffraction Correction is turned on. Experiment with these settings to see whether they improve results with your lens. Both features are available only for still photography. See the camera manual for additional details, including how you can download information for additional lenses to the camera.

Manipulating Depth of Field

Getting familiar with the concept of depth of field is one of the biggest steps you can take to becoming a better photographer. Chapter 3 introduces you to depth of field, but here's a quick recap:

» *Depth of field* refers to the distance over which objects in a photograph appear acceptably sharp.

» With a shallow depth of field, the subject is sharp but objects in front of and behind it appear blurry. The farther an object is from the subject, the blurrier it looks.

» With a large depth of field, the zone of sharp focus extends to include objects at a greater distance from your subject.

Which arrangement works best depends on your creative vision and your subject. In portraits, for example, a classic technique is to use a shallow depth of field, as in the example shown in Figure 5-19. But for landscapes, you might choose to use a large depth of field, as shown in Figure 5-20. Because the historical marker, the lighthouse, and the cottage are all sharp, they have equal visual weight in the scene.

Again, though, which part of the scene appears blurry when you use a shallow depth of field depends on the spot at which you establish focus. Consider the lighthouse scene: Suppose you opted for short depth of field and set focus on the lighthouse. In that case, both the historical marker in the foreground and the cottage in the background might be outside the zone of sharp focus.

FIGURE 5-19:
A shallow depth of field blurs the background and draws added attention to the subject.

So, how do you manipulate depth of field? You have three points of control:

>> **Aperture setting (f-stop):** The aperture is one of three main exposure settings, all explained fully in Chapter 4. Depth of field increases as you stop down the aperture (by choosing a higher f-stop number). For shallow depth of field, open the aperture (by choosing a lower f-stop number).

Figure 5-21 offers an example. Notice that the tractor in the background is in much sharper focus in the first shot, taken at f/20, than in the second image, shot at f/2.8.

>> **Lens focal length:** *Focal length,* which is measured in millimeters, determines what the lens "sees." As you increase focal length, the angle of view narrows, objects appear larger in the frame, and — the important point in this discussion — depth of field decreases. Additionally, the spatial relationship of objects changes as you adjust focal length.

FIGURE 5-20:
A large depth of field keeps both near and far subjects in sharp focus.

f/20, 93mm

f/2.8, 93mm

FIGURE 5-21:
Lowering the f-stop value decreases depth of field.

For example, Figure 5-22 compares the same scene shot at focal lengths of 138mm and 255mm. The aperture was set to f/22 for both examples.

138mm, f/22

255mm, f/22

FIGURE 5-22:
Using a longer focal length also reduces depth of field.

Whether you have any focal-length flexibility depends on your lens: If you have a zoom lens, you can adjust the focal length by zooming in or out. If your lens offers only a single focal length — a prime lens in photo-speak — scratch this means of manipulating depth of field (unless you want to change to a different prime lens, of course).

>> **Camera-to-subject distance:** When you move the lens closer to your subject, depth of field decreases. This statement assumes that you don't zoom in or out to reframe the picture, thereby changing the focal length. If you do, depth of field is affected by both the camera position and the focal length.

REMEMBER

Together, these three factors determine the maximum and minimum depth of field that you can achieve, as follows:

>> **To produce the shallowest depth of field:** Open the aperture as wide as possible (select the lowest f-stop number), zoom in to the maximum focal length of your lens, and move as close as possible to your subject.

>> **To produce maximum depth of field:** Stop down the aperture to the highest possible f-stop setting, zoom out to the shortest focal length your lens offers, and move farther from your subject.

Here are a few additional tips and tricks related to depth of field:

>> **Aperture-priority autoexposure mode (Av) enables you to easily control depth of field while enjoying exposure assistance from the camera.** In this mode, you rotate the Main dial to set the f-stop, and the camera selects the appropriate shutter speed to produce a good exposure. The range of available aperture settings depends on your lens.

If you're not up to speed on using Av mode, Creative Auto mode is your next best choice. In that mode, detailed in Chapter 3, use the Background Blur option to adjust depth of field. (The camera accomplishes this by adjusting aperture automatically for you.)

>> **For greater background blurring, move the subject farther from the background.** The extent to which background focus shifts as you adjust depth of field also is affected by the distance between the subject and the background.

TIP

>> **Depth of field preview:** When you look through your viewfinder and press the shutter button halfway, you can see only a partial indication of the depth of field that your current camera settings will produce. You can see the effect of focal length and the camera-to-subject distance, but because the aperture doesn't actually stop down to your selected f-stop until you take the picture, the viewfinder doesn't show you how that setting will affect depth of field.

By using the Depth-of-Field Preview button on your camera, however, you can do just that when you shoot in the advanced exposure modes. Almost hidden away on the front of your camera, the button is labeled in Figure 5-23.

Depth-of-Field Preview button

FIGURE 5-23:
Press this button to see how the aperture setting will affect depth of field.

To use this feature, press and hold the shutter button halfway and then press and hold the Depth-of-Field Preview button with a finger on your other hand. Depending on the selected f-stop, the scene in the viewfinder may get darker. In Live View mode, the same thing happens in the monitor preview. Either way, this effect doesn't mean that your picture will be darker; it's just a function of how the preview works.

Note that the preview doesn't engage in P, Tv, or Av mode if the aperture and shutter speed aren't adequate to expose the image properly. You have to solve the exposure issue before you can use the preview.

Chapter **6**

Mastering Color Controls

C ompared with certain camera settings —resolution, aperture, shutter speed, and so on — your camera's color options are fairly simple to figure out. Most color problems can be easily fixed by adjusting one setting: White Balance. And getting a grip on color requires learning only a couple of new terms, an unusual state of affairs for an endeavor that often seems more like university-level science than art.

Some of the settings screens you use to adjust color options, on the other hand, are more than a little confusing, often presenting symbols or letters that don't offer much of a clue as to their meaning. This chapter helps you make sense of things so that you can more easily control image colors.

Before you dig in, note an important rule of the color road: You can adjust the settings discussed in this chapter only in a Creative Zone exposure mode (P, Tv, Av, or M). Also, settings discussed in this chapter apply to both still photography and movie recording, with one exception: The Color Space option is out of your control in Movie mode.

Understanding White Balance

Every light source emits a particular color cast. The old-fashioned fluorescent lights found in most public restrooms, for example, put out a bluish-green light, which is why our reflections in the mirrors in those restrooms look so sickly. And if you think that your beloved looks especially attractive by candlelight, you aren't imagining things: Candlelight casts a yellow-red glow that's flattering.

Science-y types measure the color of light, or *color temperature*, on the *Kelvin scale.* You can see an illustration of the Kelvin scale in Figure 6-1.

When photographers talk about "warm light" and "cool light," though, they aren't referring to the position on the Kelvin scale — or at least not in the way we usually think of temperatures, with a higher number meaning hotter. Instead, the terms describe the visual appearance of the light. Warm light, produced by candles and incandescent lights, falls in the red-yellow spectrum you see at the bottom of the Kelvin scale; cool light, in the blue-green spectrum, appears at the top of the scale.

At any rate, most of us don't notice these fluctuating colors of light because our brains automatically compensate for them. Except in extreme lighting conditions, a white tablecloth appears white to us no matter whether we view it by candlelight, fluorescent light, or regular house lights. Similarly, a digital camera compensates for different colors of light through a feature known as white balancing. Simply put, white balancing neutralizes light so that whites are always white, which in turn ensures that other colors are rendered accurately. If the camera senses warm light, it shifts colors slightly to the cool side of the color spectrum; in cool light, the camera shifts colors in the opposite direction.

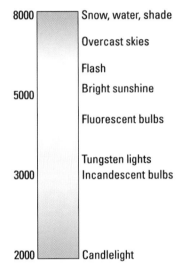

FIGURE 6-1:
Each light source emits a specific color.

Your camera's Automatic White Balance (AWB) setting tackles this process well in most situations. In some lighting conditions, though, it doesn't quite do the trick.

Problems most often occur when your subject is lit by a variety of light sources. For example, Figure 6-2 features an alabaster-colored figurine set against a black velvet background. The scene was lit by both tungsten photo lights and strong daylight coming through a nearby window. In Automatic White Balance mode, hence, the original image, shown on the left in the figure, has a golden color cast. Switching to the Tungsten Light option rendered colors correctly, as shown on the right.

FIGURE 6-2: Multiple light sources can result in a color cast in Auto White Balance mode (left); try switching to manual White Balance control to solve the problem (right).

The next several sections explain how to make a basic white-balance adjustment and discuss some advanced White Balance options. Again, remember that these options are available only for the P, Tv, Av, or M exposure modes.

TIP

If you're not ready to step up to the Creative Zone modes, some Basic Zone modes enable you to make minor adjustments to color. Specifically, you can tweak colors in Creative Auto mode through the Ambience setting. Additionally, some scene modes enable you to make colors warmer or cooler. For help, visit Chapter 3.

Changing the White Balance setting

A symbol representing the current White Balance setting appears in the Quick Control and Live View displays, in the areas labeled in Figure 6-3. (If your Live View screen doesn't show the symbol, press the Info button to cycle through the Live View display variations until you see the one shown in the figure.)

In addition to Auto, you can choose from six prefab settings, each designed for a specific type of lighting. You also get a Custom option, which selects a setting that you create based on the exact lighting conditions in the scene. (The next section explains how to store a custom setting.)

White Balance setting

White Balance setting

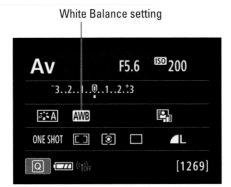

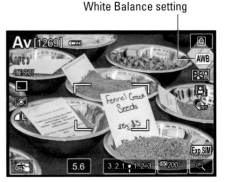

FIGURE 6-3:
AWB stands
for Auto White
Balance.

You can access the White Balance setting in the following ways:

>> **Press the WB button (viewfinder shooting only).** Figure 6-4 points out the
WB button, also known as the top Quick Control key. As soon as you press the
button, the camera displays the selection screen shown in the figure. Rotate
the Quick Control or Main dial, or press the left/right Quick Control keys to
scroll through the White Balance settings. To lock in your choice and exit the
settings screen, tap the option you want to use, or tap the Set symbol, or
press the Set button.

Press to access White Balance setting

Tap to toggle AWB priority option

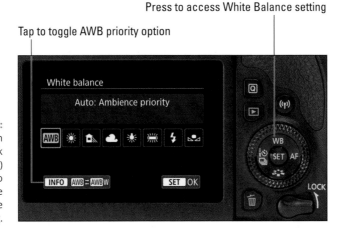

FIGURE 6-4:
The WB button
(top Quick
Control key)
takes you to
the White
Balance
setting.

REMEMBER

Figure 6-5 gives you a close-up look at the symbols used to represent each
setting. Don't feel obligated to memorize them, though, because the camera
always displays a text label telling you the name of the currently selected
option, as shown in Figure 6-4.

FIGURE 6-5:
Here's a guide to the symbols used to represent White Balance settings.

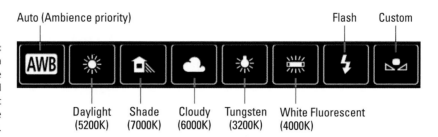

Auto (Ambience priority)

Flash Custom

Daylight (5200K) Shade (7000K) Cloudy (6000K) Tungsten (3200K) White Fluorescent (4000K)

In most cases, the label reports the approximate Kelvin temperature of the light source the setting is designed to handle. The Auto and Custom options don't display this value because they aren't associated with any one color temperature; Auto reacts to the color of the light in the current scene, and the Custom setting value adjusts White Balance according to whatever lighting you use when you create your Custom setting. Nor do you see a Kelvin value for the Flash option, which is geared to the color temperature of whatever flash unit you're using (the built-in flash or an external flash).

» **Use the Quick Control feature.** Press the Q button or tap the Q touchscreen symbol to shift to Quick Control mode, and then highlight the White Balance option. The current setting appears at the bottom of the screen; rotate the Quick Control or Main dial to cycle through the various options. To display all settings on a single screen, as shown in Figure 6-4, tap the White Balance icon or press Set.

The Live View and Movie Quick Control screens provide a benefit that you don't enjoy during viewfinder photography: As you adjust White Balance, the monitor updates to show you the effect of the setting on the subject colors, as shown in Figure 6-6. This feature makes it easy to experiment with different settings to see which one renders colors best.

FIGURE 6-6:
In Live View mode, the preview updates to show how the current White Balance setting affects colors.

Tap to toggle AWB priority setting   Tap to fine-tune or bracket white balance

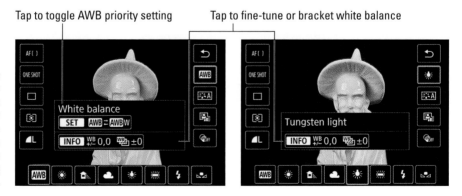

>> **Select the White Balance option from Shooting Menu 3.** Figure 6-7 gives you a look at the menu option. Don't see Shooting Menu 3? Check the Mode dial. Remember, you can adjust White Balance only when the camera is set to the P, Tv, M, or Av exposure modes; if any other mode is selected, you get only a single Shooting menu.

FIGURE 6-7:
You also can adjust the White Balance setting from Shooting Menu 3.

A few final notes about the White Balance setting:

>> **You can choose from two AWB (Auto White Balance) options: Ambience Priority and White Priority.** Your choice is relevant only when you shoot in tungsten lighting (or a light source that has a similar color temperature, such as incandescent household bulbs). At the Ambience setting, the White Balance setting doesn't completely remove the warm cast created by tungsten lighting. For portraits and certain other subjects, that little hint of warmth is lovely. Additionally, the Ambience Priority uses the same color-balance formula as the standard Auto setting on Cameras that don't offer a priority option, so if you're used to those results, you may prefer to stick with Ambience Priority.

But if you want your whites to be white, switch to White Priority. Change the setting as follows:

- *Viewfinder photography:* Tap the Info symbol labeled in Figure 6-4 or press the Info button to toggle between the two settings.

- *Live View and Movie Mode:* Press the Set button or tap the Set icon, labeled in Figure 6-6.

When White Priority is in force, a *W* appears to the right of the AWB symbol. If you don't see the W, Ambience Priority is active. (Ambience Priority is the default setting for all exposure modes except the Food scene mode.)

One final note: When you add flash, the camera always uses Ambience Priority to render colors even when White Priority is selected. Flash light already has a cool color cast, and if the camera added to that light the additional cooling used to neutralize warm light in White Priority mode, your subjects may appear blue — literally.

>> **Your selected White Balance setting remains in force for the P, Tv, Av, and M exposure modes until you change the setting.** To avoid accidentally using an incorrect setting later, get in the habit of resetting the option to the automatic setting (AWB) after you finish shooting whatever subject it was that caused you to switch to manual white balancing.

>> **When shooting in mixed light, choose the White Balance setting based on the most prominent light source.** If none of the preexisting settings produce accurate colors, try the advanced options outlined in the next three sections.

Creating a custom White Balance setting

Through the Custom White Balance option, you can create a white balance setting that's precisely tuned to the color of the light hitting your subject, whether that light comes from one source or many sources. To use this technique, you need a piece of card stock that's either neutral gray or absolute white — not eggshell white, sand white, or any other close-but-not-perfect white. (You can buy reference cards made for this purpose in many camera stores.)

After positioning the reference card in the lighting you plan to use for your subject, follow these steps to create the custom setting:

1. **With the camera in still photography mode (not Movie mode), set the Mode dial to P, Tv, Av, or M.**

You can't use this feature in any of the other exposure modes. In M exposure mode, ensure that the exposure is correct before taking the photo. If the image is greatly under- or overexposed, the resulting white balance will be affected.

Although you can't create a custom setting in Movie mode, you can select one that you created in still photography mode. Just select the Custom setting when you set the White Balance option. (Refer to Figure 6-5 for a look at the symbol that represents the Custom setting.)

2. **Take a picture of the reference card.**

Frame the shot so that the reference card fills the viewfinder (or, if you're using Live View, the monitor). For best results, focus manually. (The autofocus system usually has a hard time focusing on a blank field on color.)

3. **Display Shooting Menu 3 and choose Custom White Balance, as shown on the left in Figure 6-8.**

You then see the screen shown on the right in the figure. The image you just captured should appear in the display, along with a brief message that tells you that the camera will only display that image and others that are compatible with the custom white-balancing option. If your picture doesn't appear on the screen, press the right or left Quick Control key or rotate the Quick Control dial to scroll to it. (Note that you may see additional data on the screen depending on the current playback display mode; press the Info button to cycle through the various displays.)

Custom White Balance symbol

FIGURE 6-8: Choose this option from Shooting Menu 3 to create a White Balance setting precisely tailored to the current lighting.

REMEMBER

Again, notice the Custom White Balance symbol appearing in red in the upper-left corner of the screen and inside the Set label at the bottom of the screen.

4. **Tap the Set icon (or press the Set button) to select the displayed image as the basis for your custom white balance reference.**

    You're asked to confirm that you want to use the image to create the Custom White Balance.

5. **Tap OK or highlight it and press the Set button.**

    A message tells you that the custom setting is stored.

6. **Tap OK (or highlight it and press Set) to finish.**

Your custom setting remains stored until the next time you replace it by working your way through these steps again. Any time you want to base white balancing on this custom setting, just look for the Custom setting in the White Balance selection screens.

Fine-tuning color with White Balance Shift

In addition to creating a custom White Balance setting, you can use White Balance Shift to recalibrate the White Balance system so that no matter which White Balance setting you choose, colors are shifted to toward a particular part of the color spectrum. (In the instruction manual, this feature is named White Balance Correction, but it goes by the Shift moniker on camera screens and menus.)

As with other White Balance features, this one is available only in P, Tv, Av, or M exposure modes. However, you can set up White Balance Shift in Movie mode, as well as during still photography.

After setting the Mode dial to P, Tv, Av, or M, follow these steps:

1. **Display the White Balance Shift screen.**

You can get to the screen in two ways:

- *Use the Quick Control feature.* During viewfinder photography, the White Balance Shift option appears after you put the camera in Quick Control mode, as shown on the left in Figure 6-9. Tap the option or highlight it and press Set to display the screen shown on the right.

White Balance Shift/Bracketing setting   Scroll arrows   Shift marker   Shift amount

FIGURE 6-9:
After putting
the camera in
Quick Control
mode, select
the White
Balance Shift/
Bracketing
option (left)
to display the
adjustment
screen (right).

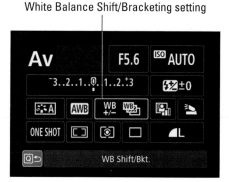
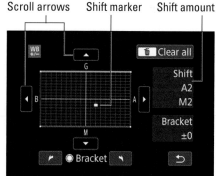

In Live View or Movie mode, the Quick Control screen displays an Info label when the White Balance option is active, as shown on the left in Figure 6-10. Tap that label or press the Info button to get to the adjustment screen shown on the right.

- *Open Shooting Menu 3 and select White Balance Shift/Bkt.* The camera displays the same adjustment screen shown on the right in Figure 6-9.

Both versions of the adjustment screen contain a grid that's oriented around two color pairs: green and magenta (represented by the G and M labels) and blue and amber (represented by B and A).

White Balance Shift/Bracketing setting | Quick Control keys symbol | Shift amount

2. **Move the shift marker (the white square) in the grid to set the amount and direction of the adjustment.**

When using the adjustment screen shown in Figure 6-9, move the marker by tapping the grid, tapping the scroll arrows around the grid, or using the Quick Control keys. In Live View or Movie mode, tap the grid or use the Quick Control keys to move the marker. (The symbol labeled Quick Control keys in Figure 6-10 reminds you that those keys move the marker.)

As you move the marker, the Shift area of the display tells the amount of color bias you've selected. For example, in Figures 6-9 and 6-10, the shift is two levels toward amber and two toward magenta.

TECHNICAL STUFF

If you're familiar with traditional lens filters, you may know that the density of a filter, which determines the degree of color correction it provides, is measured in mireds (pronounced "*my*-reds"). The White Balance grid is designed around this system: Moving the marker one level is the equivalent of adding a filter with a density of 5 mireds.

WARNING

The White Balance Shift screen also contains controls for enabling White Balance Bracketing, explained in the next section. Be careful not to accidentally use the controls that set up bracketing: the Quick Control dial and the touch-screen symbols that appear on either side of the word *Bracket*.

3. **Press the Set button to apply the change and return to the initial menu or Quick Control screen.**

You also can tap the exit arrow (in the lower-right corner of the viewfinder or menu version of the adjustment screen; in the upper-right corner of the Live View and Movie screen).

4. **Press the menu button to exit the menu or the Q button to exit the Quick Control display. (You can also press the shutter button halfway and release it.)**

As a reminder that White Balance Shift is in force, the symbol labeled on the left in Figure 6-11 appears in the Quick Control display. A +/- sign appears under the White Balance symbol on the Live View and Movie screens, as shown on the right.

White Balance Shift enabled

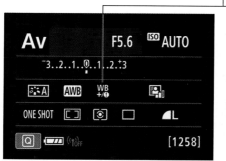
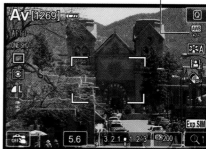

FIGURE 6-11:
These symbols remind you that White Balance Shift is being applied.

By default, you also see an exclamation point in the viewfinder, at the left end of the data display. However, the exclamation point also appears if you set the Picture Style option to Monochrome, as covered later in this chapter, and when you set the Hi ISO Speed Noise Reduction feature to the Multi Shot setting. (Chapter 4 covers that option.) You can specify which of these features results in the alert through Custom Function 11. Access the Custom Functions through Setup Menu 4.

WARNING

TIP

5. **To cancel White Balance Shift, repeat Steps 1 and 2 and then set the marker back to the center of the grid.**

Be sure that both values in the Shift area of the display are set to 0.

For a fast way to move the marker to the center of the grid, press the Erase button or tap its onscreen symbol. However, doing so also cancels White Balance Bracketing, explained in the next section.

Bracketing White Balance

Chapter 4 introduces you to Automatic Exposure Bracketing, which makes it easy to *bracket exposures* — capture the same scene at three different exposure settings. Similarly, the camera offers White Balance Bracketing, which accomplishes the same thing but varying white balance instead of exposure between frames.

Before you explore the steps involved in bracketing white balance, here are some preliminary points to understand:

>> **You can take advantage of White Balance Bracketing only in the P, Tv, Av, and M exposure modes.** Also, the feature isn't available for movie recording, for obvious reasons.

>> **White Balance Bracketing is based on the same color grid you use to set up White Balance Shift.** In fact, you adjust both settings on the same screen. If you want, you can enable both white-balance shift and bracketing.

ELIMINATING COLOR FRINGING (CHROMATIC ABERRATION)

Pictures taken with some lenses may reveal chromatic aberration, a defect that creates weird color halos along the edges of objects. This phenomenon is also known as color fringing.

When you shoot in P, Tv, Av, or M exposure modes, your camera offers a Chromatic Aberration filter to address this problem. Access it by selecting Lens Aberration Correction from Shooting Menu 1, as shown in the first figure here. You then see the second screen in the figure. If the label at the top of the screen indicates that correction data is available for your lens, the feature is enabled by default. If you object, just change the setting to Off. (Canon recommends that you keep the option off when using a non-Canon lens even if the correction data is available.)

Note these other important aspects of the Chromatic Aberration filter:

- The correction is applied only to JPEG images. You can manually apply the correction to Raw images in Canon Digital Photo Professional 4. See Chapter 10 for help with Raw processing.

- You can register additional lenses with the camera by using another free program, Canon EOS Utility. Download both the program and its user manual from the Canon support site.

- Because the filter is applied after you take the shot, it reduces the number of frames you can record per second in the Continuous Drive modes, covered in Chapter 2.

 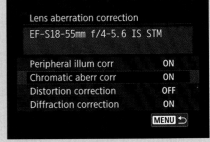

>> **You can bracket white balance along one axis of the color grid only.** That is, you can shift colors along the blue/amber axis between frames or along the green/magenta axis.

>> **White balance bracketing is most helpful when you're shooting JPEGs only.** If you shoot Raw images, you can perform non-destructive White Balance adjustments in software later. This is one of the great advantages of shooting Raw.

REMEMBER

>> **You take just one picture to create a bracketed series.** In this regard, bracketing white balance is different from bracketing exposure, which requires you to snap three shots. With White Balance Bracketing, the camera records one shot when you press the shutter button and records that image using the current White Balance setting. From that original frame, the camera then creates two variations, recorded using the specified shift along the green/magenta or the blue/amber axis.

Because the camera needs time to process the second and third images, your shot-to-shot frame rate may slow a little when you enable White Balance Bracketing.

Figure 6-12 offers an example of the kind of results you can expect from White Balance Bracketing. For this series, frames were bracketed along the blue/amber axis, using the maximum amount of color shift between the neutral, blue, and amber frames. As you can see, the difference is subtle, although your mileage may vary depending on the subject of the photo.

+3 Blue bias   Neutral   +3 Amber bias

FIGURE 6-12: With White Balance Bracketing, the camera automatically creates three frames that vary in color.

To enable White Balance Bracketing, follow these steps:

1. **Set the Mode dial to P, Tv, Av, or M.**

2. **Display the setup grid shown in Figure 6-13 by using Quick Control mode or by selecting WB/Shift Bkt. from Shooting Menu 3.**

   The steps in the earlier section "Fine-tuning color with White Balance Shift" provide specifics; refer to Figures 6-9 and 6-10 for a visual reminder of how the Quick Control screens appear.

Bracketing indicators | Type and amount of adjustment between frames

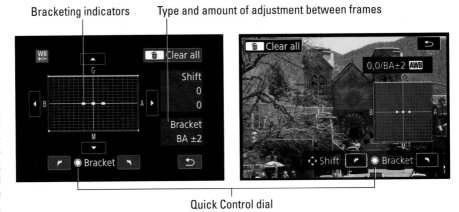

Quick Control dial

3. **Rotate the Quick Control dial to set the amount and direction of the bracketing shift.**

   Rotate the dial to the right to apply bracketing along the blue to amber axis; rotate left to bracket along the green to magenta axis.

   As you rotate the dial, three markers appear on the grid, indicating the amount of shift that will be applied. The Bracket area of the screen also shows bracketing type and amount. For example, in Figure 6-13, the bracketing is set to plus and minus two levels on the blue/amber axis.

   You also can adjust the settings by tapping the markers on either side of the word *Bracket,* at the bottom of the screen.

TIP

4. **Tap the exit arrow or press the Set button to exit the adjustment screen.**

   Verify the bracketing value by checking the White Balance Shift/Bkt. setting on Shooting Menu 3; the value after the slash shows the bracketing setting. The two values to the left of the slash indicate the White Balance Shift direction and amount.

The Quick Control display contains a White Balance Bracketing symbol, as shown on the left in Figure 6-14. In the Live View display, the White Balance setting symbol appears smaller than usual, as shown on the right in the figure, and blinks to indicate that the bracketing is enabled. Neither display shows you the specifics of the bracketing setting.

Appears when bracketing enabled

Blinks when bracketing enabled

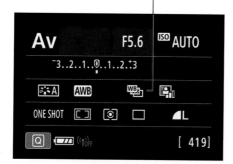
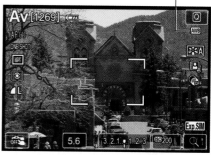

WARNING

Bracketing remains in effect until you turn off the camera. You can also cancel bracketing by revisiting the adjustment screen (refer to Figure 6-13) and resetting the Bracketing value to 0. You can do this quickly by tapping the Clear All symbol or pressing the Erase button.

Taking a Quick Look at Picture Styles

Picture Styles give you an additional way to tweak image colors. But the Picture Style setting also affects color saturation, contrast, and image sharpening.

TECHNICAL STUFF

Sharpening is a software process that adjusts contrast in a way that creates the illusion of slightly sharper focus. Emphasis on the word *slightly:* Sharpening cannot remedy poor focus; instead, it produces a subtle improvement to this aspect of your pictures.

The camera offers the following Picture Styles, which are indicted in the displays by the initials shown in the list:

>> **Auto (A):** The camera analyzes the scene and determines which Picture Style is the most appropriate. (This setting is the default.)

>> **Standard (S):** Produces the image characteristics that Canon considers as suitable for the majority of subjects.

>> **Portrait (P):** Reduces sharpening slightly to keep skin texture soft. Color saturation, on the other hand, is slightly increased. You can adjust skin coloring along a magenta-to-yellow tonal range.

>> **Landscape (L):** Emphasizes greens and blues and amps up color saturation and sharpness.

>> **Fine Detail (FD):** Use this setting for extra sharpening and slightly more intense colors.

>> **Neutral (N):** Reduces saturation and contrast slightly compared to how the camera renders images at the Standard setting.

>> **Faithful:** Renders colors as closely as possible to how the human eye perceives them.

>> **Monochrome:** Produces black-and-white photos.

If you set the Quality option to Raw (or Raw+Large/Fine), the camera displays your image on the monitor in black and white during playback. But during the Raw converter process, you can either choose to go with your black-and-white version or view and save a full-color version. Even better, using the Raw file enables you to process and save the image once as a grayscale photo and again as a color photo.

If you *don't* capture the image in the Raw format, you can't access the original image colors later. In other words, you're stuck with *only* a black-and-white image. For this reason, shooting in the Monochrome Picture style in JPEG only isn't a great idea.

>> **User Defined (1, 2, and 3):** You can create and store three of your own Picture Styles. More on that possibility a little later.

The extent to which Picture Styles affect your image depends on the subject, the exposure settings you choose, and the lighting conditions. Figure 6-15 shows the Auto version of an image; Figure 6-16 shows the six variations produced by the other full-color Picture Styles. As you can see, the difference between the styles is sometimes pretty subtle. Feel free to experiment to find which style best suits the effect you're after.

You have control over the Picture Style setting only in the P, Tv, Av, M, and Movie modes. In the Quick Control screen and Live View displays, the symbol labeled in Figure 6-17 represents the current stetting. (In Movie mode, the symbol appears in the same spot as in Live View still-photography mode.)

FIGURE 6-15:
Here's how the Auto Picture Style rendered the example image.

Standard	Portrait	Landscape

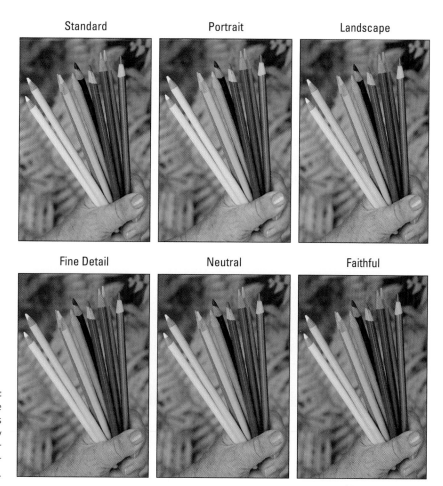

Fine Detail	Neutral	Faithful

FIGURE 6-16: Here are the variations produced by the six other full-color Picture Styles.

Picture Style setting

FIGURE 6-17: This symbol represents the Picture Style.

Picture Style setting

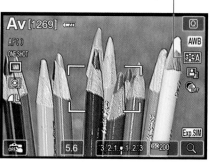

To change the Picture Style setting, use one of these methods:

» **Quick Control method:** After shifting to Quick Control mode, highlight the Picture Style icon and then rotate the Quick Control or Main dial to cycle through the available styles. To see all styles on a single screen, press Set or tap the Picture Style icon. On that second screen, highlight the style you want to use and press Set to finish up. Or just give the setting a quick tap on the touchscreen.

Figure 6-18 shows the Quick Control screens as they appear during viewfinder photography. In Live View and Movie mode, the screens vary in appearance but the process of selecting and adjusting the setting is the same.

FIGURE 6-18:
You can select
a Picture Style
via the Quick
Control screen.

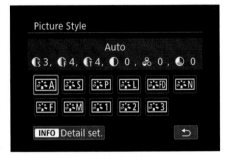

» **Shooting Menu 3:** Select Picture Style from the menu to display a variation of the selection screen shown on the right in Figure 6-18.

» **Bottom Quick Control key (viewfinder shooting only):** When you're not in Live View or Movie mode, you have an even faster option for getting to the Picture Style setting: Just press the bottom Quick Control key — the one that's labeled with the same symbol that decorates the Picture Style setting in the displays. Figure 6-19 offers a look.

Now for the question on everyone's mind: What the heck is the deal with all the crazy numbers and symbols that appear in the Picture Control settings screens? Well, in their very Canon-like cryptic style, the symbols represent specific picture characteristics, such as sharpness, color saturation, and contrast. The number values indicate the strength at which those characteristics are applied to the picture when the camera processes the image data. But the different characteristics are based on different number ranges, so those values aren't a big help unless you spend time researching and understanding them.

Press to display Picture Style setting screen

TIP

So, why does Canon go to the trouble of including these details? Because you can modify a Picture Style by adjusting the values for the various picture characteristics.

Unless you're tickled pink by the prospect of experimenting with Picture Styles, however, just stick with the default setting (Auto) and ignore the fine-tuning options. Why add one more setting to the list of options you have to remember, especially when the impact of changing it is minimal?

Plus, if you want to play with the characteristics that the Picture Style options affect, you're better off shooting in the Raw format and then making those adjustments on a picture-by-picture basis in your Raw converter. (See Chapter 10 for help processing Raw files in Digital Photo Professional 4.)

For these reasons, this book presents just this brief introduction to Picture Styles, making room for functions that make a bigger difference to your photographic success

For details on Picture Style features not covered here, consult your camera manual.

Changing the Color Space

By default, your camera captures JPEG images using the *sRGB color mode,* which refers to an industry-standard spectrum of colors. (The *s* is for *standard,* and the *RGB* is for *red, green,* and *blue,* which are the primary colors in the digital color world.)

Because the sRGB color spectrum leaves out some colors that *can* be reproduced in print and onscreen, at least by some devices, your camera also offers the Adobe

RGB, which includes a larger spectrum of colors. Know that some colors in the Adobe RGB spectrum *can't* be reproduced in print; the printer just substitutes the closest color, if necessary.

If you plan to print and share your photos without making any adjustments in your photo editor, stick with sRGB; most printers and web browsers are designed around that color space. Also, your editing software must support Adobe RGB — not all programs do.

REMEMBER

You can't use Adobe RGB when recording movies or when shooting in any exposure mode except P, Tv, Av, and M. Change the setting via the Color Space option on Shooting Menu 3.

Filenames of pictures captured in the Adobe RGB color space start with an underscore, as in _MG_0627.jpg. Pictures captured in the sRGB color space start with the letter *I*, as in IMG_0627.jpg.

Chapter **7**

Putting It All Together

arlier chapters break down critical picture-taking features, explaining controls that affect exposure, picture quality, focus, color, and more. This chapter pulls all that information together to help you set up your camera for specific types of photography. Keep in mind, though, that there's no one "right way" to shoot a portrait, a landscape, or whatever. So feel free to wander off on your own, tweaking this exposure setting or adjusting that focus control, to discover your own creative vision. Experimentation is part of the fun of photography!

Recapping Basic Picture Settings

For some camera options, such as exposure mode, aperture, and shutter speed, the best settings depend on your subject, lighting conditions, and creative goals. But for certain basic options, the same settings work well for almost every scenario.

Table 7-1 offers recommendations for these settings and lists the chapter where you can find more information about each option.

TABLE 7-1   **All-Purpose Picture-Taking Settings**

Option	Recommended Setting	See This Chapter
Image Quality	Large/Fine (JPEG) or Raw (CR2)	2
Drive mode	Action photos, Continuous Low or High; all others, Single	2
ISO	100	4
Metering mode	Evaluative	4
Exposure Compensation (P, Tv, and Av modes only)	Set as needed; raise value for brighter exposure, lower for darker exposure	4
AF Operation mode	Moving subjects, AI Servo; stationary subjects, One Shot	5
AF Point Selection Mode	Moving subjects, Auto Selection; stationary subjects, Single Point	5
White Balance	Auto (AWB), Ambient Priority	6
Auto Lighting Optimizer	Standard for P, Tv, and Av modes; Disable for M mode	4
Picture Style	Auto	6

Figure 7-1 shows the information display, where you can see the current status of many of these settings. (You may need to press the shutter button halfway or press the Info button to view the screen.) Don't forget that by pressing the Q button or tapping the Q touchscreen symbol, you activate Quick Control mode, which enables you to adjust settings right from the screen. Chapter 1 explains the process.

REMEMBER

One key point: Instructions in this chapter assume that you're using one of the advanced exposure modes: P, Tv, Av, or M. Other modes prevent you from accessing settings that can be critical for capturing certain subjects, especially in difficult lighting. Also, this chapter discusses viewfinder photography. However, most things work the same way during Live View photography, with the exception of focusing options, which are quite different.

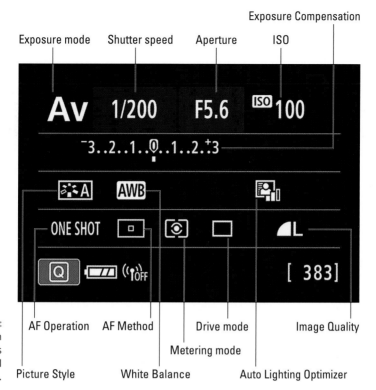

Exposure Compensation

Exposure mode   Shutter speed   Aperture   ISO

Av   1/200   F5.6   ISO 100

⁻3..2..1..0..1..2.⁺3

FIGURE 7-1:
The information
display shows
the most critical
picture settings.

AF Operation   AF Method   Drive mode   Image Quality

ONE SHOT

Metering mode

Picture Style   White Balance   Auto Lighting Optimizer

[383]

Shooting Still Portraits

By *still portrait,* we mean that your subject isn't moving. For subjects who aren't keen on sitting still, use the techniques given for action photography instead.

Assuming that you do have a subject willing to pose, the classic portraiture approach is to keep the subject sharply focused while throwing the background into soft focus, as shown in Figure 7-2. The blurred background emphasizes the subject and diminishes the impact of any distracting background objects.

The following steps show you how to achieve this look:

1. **Set the Mode dial to Av and rotate the Main dial to select the lowest f-stop value possible.**

   A low f-stop setting opens the aperture, which not only allows more light to enter the camera but also shortens *depth of field,* or the distance over which focus appears acceptably sharp. So dialing in a low f-stop value is the first step in softening your portrait background.

WARNING

For a group portrait, you typically need a higher f-stop than for a single portrait. At a very low f-stop, depth of field may not be large enough to keep everyone in the sharp-focus zone. Take test shots and inspect the results at different f-stops to find the right setting.

Also remember that when you use aperture-priority autoexposure mode (Av), the camera selects the shutter speed that will properly expose the image at your chosen f-stop. But you still need to pay attention to shutter speed to make sure that it's not so slow that any movement of the subject or camera will blur the image.

2. **Check the lens focal length.**

A focal length between 85mm and 120mm is ideal for a classic head-and-shoulders portrait. Avoid using a short focal length (wide-angle lens) for portraits. It can cause features to appear distorted — sort of like how people look when you view them through a security peephole in a door. On the flip side, a very long focal length can flatten and widen a face.

FIGURE 7-2:
To diminish a distracting background and draw more attention to your subject, use camera settings that produce a short depth of field.

Keep in mind that focal lengths are stated in terms of 35mm equivalency. The 18–55mm kit lens produces an equivalent focal length of 29–88mm, so it's fine for portrait work as long as you zoom to its longest focal length. The 18–135mm kit lens is even better. Zoom from about 55mm to 75mm to operate in the best portrait focal length range. Chapter 1 explains this issue.

3. **To further soften the background, increase the lens focal length, get closer to your subject, and put more distance between subject and background.**

A good rule is to put your subject as least an arm's distance from the background.

4. **Check composition.**

Two quick pointers on this topic:

- *Consider the background.* Scan the entire frame, looking for distracting background objects. If necessary and possible, reposition the subject against a more flattering backdrop.

- *Frame the subject loosely to allow for later cropping to a variety of frame sizes.* Your camera produces images that have an aspect ratio of 3:2. That means your portrait perfectly fits a 4-x-6 print size but will require cropping to print at any other proportion, such as 5 x 7 or 8 x 10.

5. **For indoor portraits, shoot flash-free if possible.**

Shooting by available light rather than flash produces softer illumination and avoids the problem of red-eye. During daytime hours, pose your subject near a large window to get results similar to what you see in Figure 7-3.

In Av mode, keeping the flash closed disables the flash. If flash is unavoidable, see the tips at the end of the steps to get better results.

6. **For outdoor portraits in daylight, using flash may help.**

Even in daylight, a flash can add a beneficial pop of light to subjects' faces, as illustrated in Figure 7-4. A flash is especially important when the background is brighter than the subjects; when the subject is wearing a hat; or when the sun is directly overhead, creating harsh shadows under the eyes, nose, and chin. In Av mode, press the Flash button to enable flash.

Courtesy of Mandy Holmes

FIGURE 7-3:
For soft, even lighting, forego flash and instead expose your subject using daylight coming through a nearby window.

No Flash

With Flash

FIGURE 7-4:
To better illuminate faces in outdoor portraits, use flash.

WARNING

One caveat about using flash outdoors: The fastest shutter speed you can use with the built-in flash is 1/200 second, and in extremely bright conditions, that speed may be too slow to avoid overexposing the image even if you use the lowest ISO (light sensitivity) setting. If necessary, move your subject into the shade.

If you use an external flash, you may be able to select a faster shutter speed than 1/200 second; see your flash manual for details. Your other option is to stop down the aperture (use a higher f-stop setting), but that brings more of the background into sharp focus.

7. **Press and hold the shutter button halfway to engage exposure metering and, if using autofocusing, to establish focus.**

REMEMBER

Setting the AF Operation mode to One-Shot and the AF Method to Single-Point works best for portrait autofocusing. After selecting a focus point, position that point over one of your subject's eyes (the closest one to the camera if you have a choice) and then press and hold the shutter button halfway to lock focus.

8. **Press the shutter button the rest of the way to capture the image.**

When flash is unavoidable, try these tricks for best results:

>> **Pay attention to white balance if your subject is lit by flash and ambient light.** When you mix light sources, photo colors may appear slightly warmer or cooler (more blue) than neutral. A warming effect typically looks nice in portraits, giving the skin a subtle glow. If you aren't happy with the result, see Chapter 6 to find out how to fine-tune white balance. Don't forget that your camera offers two Auto settings, one that holds onto a slight warm cast when you shoot in incandescent light (Ambient Priority mode) and one that eliminates that color cast (White Priority mode).

>> **Indoors, turn on as many room lights as possible.** With more ambient light, you reduce the flash power needed to expose the picture. Adding light also causes the pupils to constrict, further reducing the chances of red-eye. (Pay heed to the preceding white-balance warning, however.) As an added benefit, the smaller pupil allows more of the iris to be visible, so you see more eye color in the portrait.

>> **In dim lighting, try enabling Red-Eye Reduction (Shooting Menu 2).** Warn your subject to expect both a light coming from the Red-Eye Reduction lamp, which constricts pupils, and the actual flash. See Chapter 2 for details about this flash option.

>> **For nighttime pictures, try switching to Tv exposure mode and using a slow shutter speed.** The longer exposure time enables the camera to soak up more ambient light, producing a brighter background and reducing the flash power needed to light the subject. Just remember that the slower the

shutter speed, the greater the possibility that subject movement or camera shake will blur the image. So use a tripod and ask your subject to remain as still as possible.

» **For professional results, use an external flash with a rotating flash head.** Then aim the flash head up so that the flash light bounces off the ceiling and falls softly down on the subject. (This is called *bounced light.*) An external flash isn't cheap, but the results make the purchase worthwhile if you shoot lots of portraits. Compare the portraits in Figure 7-5 for an illustration. In the first example, the built-in flash resulted in strong shadowing behind the subject and harsh, concentrated light. Bounced lighting produced the better result on the right.

Direct flash | Bounced flash

FIGURE 7-5: To eliminate harsh lighting and strong shadows (left), use bounce flash and move the subject farther from the background (right).

Make sure that the surface you use to bounce the light is white; otherwise the flash's light will pick up the color of the surface and influence the color of your subject.

» **Invest in a flash diffuser to further soften the light.** A *diffuser* is simply a piece of translucent plastic or fabric that you place over the flash to soften and spread the light — much like sheer curtains diffuse window light. Diffusers come in lots of different designs, including small, fold-flat models that fit over the built-in flash.

>> **To reduce shadowing from the flash, move your subject farther from the background.** Moving the subject away from the wall helped eliminate the background shadow in the second example in Figure 7-5. The increased distance also softened the focus of the wall a bit (because of the short depth of field resulting from the f-stop and focal length). You may also want to light the background separately.

TIP

If you can't move the subject farther from the background, try going the other direction: If the person's head is smack against the background, any shadow will be smaller and less noticeable.

Capturing Action

A fast shutter speed is the key to capturing a blur-free shot of any moving subject, whether it's a spinning Ferris wheel, a butterfly flitting from flower to flower, or in the case of Figures 7-6 and 7-7, a hockey-playing teen.

In Figure 7-6, a shutter speed of 1/125 second was too slow to catch the subject without blur. A shutter speed of 1/1000 second froze the action cleanly, as shown in Figure 7-7. (The backgrounds are blurry in both shots because the images were taken using a lens with a long focal length, which decreases depth of field. Also, in the first image, the skater is farther from the background, blurring the background more than in the second image.)

FIGURE 7-6:
A too-slow shutter speed (1/125 second) causes the skater to appear blurry.

FIGURE 7-7:
Raising the
shutter speed
to 1/1000
second freezes
the action.

Along with the basic capture settings outlined earlier (refer to Table 7-1), try the techniques in the following steps to photograph a subject in motion:

1. **Set the Mode dial to Tv (shutter-priority autoexposure).**

In this mode, you control shutter speed, and the camera chooses the aperture setting that will produce a good exposure at the current ISO setting.

2. **Rotate the Main dial to select the shutter speed.**

The shutter speed you need depends on how fast your subject is moving, so you have to experiment. Another factor that affects your ability to stop action is the *direction* of subject motion. A car moving toward you can be stopped with a lower shutter speed than one moving across your field of view, for example. Generally speaking, 1/500 second should be plenty for all but the fastest subjects — speeding hockey players, race cars, or boats, for example. For slower subjects, you can even go as low as 1/250 or 1/125 second.

Remember, though, that when you increase shutter speed in Tv exposure mode, the camera opens the aperture to maintain the same exposure. At low f-stop numbers, depth of field becomes shorter, so you have to be more careful to keep your subject within the sharp-focus zone as you compose and focus the shot, especially if the subject is moving toward or away from your camera.

TIP

You also can take an entirely different approach to capturing action: Instead of choosing a fast shutter speed, select a speed slow enough to blur the moving objects, which can create a heightened sense of motion and, in scenes that feature very colorful subjects, cool abstract images such as the carnival ride images in Figure 7-8. For the left image, the shutter speed was 1/30 second; for the right version, 1/5 second. In both cases, Julie used a tripod, but because nearly everything in the frame was moving, the entirety of both photos is blurry — the 1/5 second version is simply blurrier because of the slower shutter.

FIGURE 7-8:
Using a shutter speed slow enough to blur moving objects can be a fun creative choice, too.

For an alternative effect, try panning (rotating the camera horizontally or vertically) with the movement. The subject you track during the pan will remain relatively sharp, even with a slower shutter speed. (Lots of practice and experimentation are required to get it right.)

WARNING

If the aperture value blinks after you set the shutter speed, the camera can't select an f-stop that will properly expose the photo at that shutter speed and the current ISO setting.

3. **Raise the ISO setting to produce a brighter exposure, if needed.**

In dim lighting, you may not be able to create a good exposure at your chosen shutter speed without taking this step. Raising the ISO increases the possibility of noise, but a noisy shot is better than a blurry shot. You can access this setting quickly by pressing the ISO button on top of the camera.

If Auto ISO is in force, ISO may go up automatically when you increase shutter speed. Auto ISO can be a big help when you're shooting fast-paced action; just be sure to limit the camera to choosing an ISO setting that doesn't produce an objectionable level of noise. Chapter 4 provides details on Auto ISO.

TIP

Why not just add flash to throw some extra light on the scene? That solution has a number of drawbacks:

- The flash needs time to recycle between shots, which slows down your shooting pace.

- The fastest possible shutter speed when you enable the built-in flash is 1/200 second, which may not be fast enough to capture a quickly moving subject without blur. (You can use a faster shutter speed with certain Canon external flash units, however.)

- The built-in flash has a limited range, so unless your subject is pretty close to the camera, you're just wasting battery power with flash, anyway.

 4. For rapid-fire shooting, set the Drive mode to one of the Continuous options.

The camera then shoots a burst of images as long as the shutter button is pressed. In High-speed Continuous mode, the camera can capture as many as six frames per second; in Low-speed Continuous mode, three frames per second.

You can access the Drive mode setting quickly by pressing the Drive button (left Quick Control key).

5. If possible, use manual focusing; otherwise, select the AF Operation mode to AI Servo (continuous autofocus) and the AF Method to Automatic Selection.

With manual focusing, you eliminate the time the camera needs to lock focus during autofocusing. Of course, focusing manually gets a little tricky if your subject is moving in a way that requires you to change the focusing distance quickly from shot to shot. In that case, try the AI Servo and Automatic Selection autofocusing options.

When you use these autofocus settings, the camera initially sets focus on the center focus point. So frame your subject under that point, press the shutter button halfway to set the initial focusing distance, and then reframe as necessary to keep the subject within the area covered by the focus points. As long as you keep the shutter button pressed halfway, the camera continues to adjust focus up to the time you actually take the shot. Chapter 5 details these autofocus options.

6. Compose the subject to allow for movement across the frame.

Don't zoom in so far that your subject might zip out of the frame before you take the shot — frame a little wider than usual. You can always crop the photo later to a tighter composition. (Many examples in this book were cropped to eliminate distracting elements.)

One other key to shooting sports, wildlife, or any moving subject: Before you even put your eye to the viewfinder, spend time studying your subject so that you get an idea of when it will move, where it will move, and how it will move. The more you can anticipate the action, the better your chances of capturing it.

Capturing Scenic Vistas

Providing specific camera settings for landscape photography is tricky because there's no single best approach to capturing a beautiful stretch of countryside, a city skyline, or another vast subject. Depth of field is an example: One person's idea of a super cityscape might be to keep all buildings in the scene sharply focused. Another photographer might prefer to shoot the same scene so that a foreground building is sharply focused while the others are less so, thus drawing the eye to that first building.

That said, here are a few tips to help you photograph a landscape the way *you* see it:

>> **Shoot in aperture-priority autoexposure mode (Av) so that you can control depth of field.** If you want extreme depth of field so that both near and distant objects are sharply focused, select a high f-stop value. Keep in mind that f-stop is just one factor that determines depth of field, though: To extend depth of field, use a wide-angle lens (short focal length) and increase the distance between the camera and your subject.

WARNING

The downside to using a high f-stop to achieve greater depth of field is that you need a slower shutter speed to produce a good exposure. If the shutter speed is slower than you can comfortably handhold, use a tripod to avoid picture-blurring camera shake. You also can increase the ISO setting to increase light sensitivity, which in turn allows a faster shutter speed, but that option brings with it the chance of increased image noise. See Chapter 4 for details.

>> **In large landscapes, include a foreground subject to provide a sense of scale.** The bench in Figure 7-9 serves this purpose. Because viewers are familiar with the approximate size of a typical wooden bench, they can get a better idea of the size of the vast mountain landscape beyond.

>> **For dramatic waterfall and fountain shots, consider using a slow shutter to create that "misty" look.** The slow shutter blurs the water, giving it a soft, romantic appearance, as shown in Figure 7-10. Shutter speed for this shot was 1/15 second. Again, use a tripod to ensure that camera shake doesn't blur the rest of the scene.

TIP

In bright light, using a slow shutter speed may overexpose the image even if you stop the aperture all the way down and select the camera's lowest ISO setting. As a solution, consider investing in a *neutral-density filter* for your lens. This type of filter works something like sunglasses for your camera: It simply reduces the amount of light that passes through the lens, without affecting image colors, so that you can use a slower shutter than would otherwise be possible.

FIGURE 7-9:
The bench in the foreground helps provide a sense of the vastness of the landscape beyond.

Courtesy of Kristen E. Holmes

>> **At sunrise or sunset, base exposure on the sky.** The foreground will be dark, but you can usually brighten it in a photo editor, if needed. If you base exposure on the foreground, on the other hand, the sky will become so bright that all the color will be washed out — a problem you usually can't easily fix after the fact.

You can also invest in a graduated neutral-density filter, which is a filter that's dark on top and clear on the bottom. You orient the filter so that the dark half falls over the sky and the clear side over the dimly lit portion of the scene. This setup enables you to better expose the foreground without blowing out the sky colors.

FIGURE 7-10:
For misty water movement, use a slow shutter speed (and tripod).

Enabling Highlight Tone Priority can also improve your results, so take some test shots using that option, too. Chapter 4 offers more information.

>> **For cool nighttime city pics, experiment with a slow shutter.** Assuming that cars or other vehicles are moving through the scene, the result is neon trails of light, like those you see in Figure 7-11. Shutter speed for this image was 10 seconds. The longer your shutter speed, the blurrier the motion trails.

TIP

Rather than change the shutter speed manually between each shot, try Bulb mode. Available only in M (manual) exposure mode, access this option by increasing the length of the shutter speed until you see Bulb displayed where the shutter speed should be. Bulb mode records an image for as long as you hold down the shutter button. So just take a series of images, holding down the button for different lengths of time for each shot. In Bulb mode, you can exceed the camera's normal slow-shutter limit of 30 seconds.

FIGURE 7-11:
A slow shutter also creates neon light trails in city-street scenes.

>> **For more dramatic lighting, wait for the "golden hour" or "blue hour."** *Golden hour* is the term photographers use for early morning and late afternoon, when the light cast by the sun gives everything a soft, warmed glow. By contrast, *blue hour,* which occurs just after sunset and just before sunrise, infuses the scene with a cool, bluish light.

>> **In tricky light, bracket shots.** *Bracketing* simply means to take the same picture at several different exposures to increase the odds that at least one captures the scene the way you envision. Bracketing is especially a good idea in difficult lighting situations such as sunrise and sunset.

REMEMBER

Your camera offers automatic exposure bracketing (AEB). See Chapter 4 to find out how to take advantage of this feature.

Also experiment with the Auto Lighting Optimizer and Highlight Tone Priority options; capture some images with the features enabled and then take the same shots with the features turned off. See Chapter 4 for help. Remember, though, that you can't use both these tonality-enhancing features concurrently; turning on Highlight Tone Priority disables Auto Lighting Optimizer.

Capturing Dynamic Close-Ups

For great close-up shots, start with the basic capture settings outlined earlier, in Table 7-1. Then try the following additional settings and techniques:

» **Check your owner's manual to find out the minimum close-focusing distance of your lens.** How "up close and personal" you can be to your subject depends on your lens, not on the camera body.

» **Take control of depth of field by setting the camera mode to Av (aperture-priority autoexposure) mode.** Whether you want a shallow, medium, or extreme depth of field depends on the point of your photo. For the "romantic" scene shown in Figure 7-12, for example, setting the 18–55mm kit lens' aperture to f/5.6 blurred the background, helping the subjects stand out more from the similarly colored background. But if you want the viewer to clearly see all details throughout the frame — for example, if you're shooting a product shot for your company's sales catalog — go in the other direction, stopping down the aperture as far as possible.

FIGURE 7-12:
Using a shallow depth-of-field helped the subjects stand apart from the similarly colored background.

» **Remember that both zooming in and getting close to your subject decrease depth of field.** Back to that product shot: If you need depth of field beyond what you can achieve with the aperture setting, you may need to back away or zoom out, or both. (You can always crop your image to show just the parts of the subject that you want to feature.)

» **When shooting flowers and other nature scenes outdoors, pay attention to shutter speed, too.** Even a slight breeze may cause your subject to move, causing blurring at slow shutter speeds.

» **Experiment with adding flash for better outdoor lighting.** Just as with portraits, a tiny bit of flash typically improves close-ups when the sun is your primary light source. You may need to reduce the flash output slightly, via the camera's Flash Exposure Compensation control. Chapter 2 offers details. Also remember that turning on the built-in flash limits the maximum shutter speed to 1/200 second and may affect image colors. When using flash outside, you may need to tweak the White Balance setting.

>> **When shooting indoors, try not to use flash as your primary light source.** Because you're shooting at close range, the light from your flash may be too harsh even at a low Flash Exposure Compensation setting. If flash is inevitable, turn on as many room lights as possible to reduce the flash power that's needed. Remember that if you have multiple light sources, though, you may need to tweak the White Balance setting.

>> **To get *very* close to your subject, invest in a macro lens or a set of diopters.** A true macro lens is an expensive proposition; expect to pay at least several hundred dollars. If you enjoy capturing the tiny details in life, it's worth the investment.

For a less expensive way to go, you can spend about $40 for a set of *diopters,* which are sort of like reading glasses you screw onto your existing lens. Diopters come in several strengths: +1, +2, +4, and so on, with a higher number indicating a greater magnifying power. In fact, a diopter was used to capture the rose in Figure 7-13. The left image shows the closest shot possible with the regular lens; to produce the right image, a +6 diopter was attached. The downfall of diopters, sadly, is that they typically produce images that are very soft around the edges, as in Figure 7-13 — a problem that doesn't occur with a good macro lens.

No diopter

+6 diopter

FIGURE 7-13:
To extend the close-focus ability of a lens, add magnifying diopters.

IN THIS CHAPTER

» **Recording your first movie using the default settings**

» **Understanding the frame rate, frame size, and movie quality options**

» **Adjusting audio-recording options**

» **Controlling exposure during movie recording**

» **Playing movies**

Chapter **8**

Shooting and Viewing Movies

I n addition to being a stellar still-photography camera, your 77D can record high-definition (HD) digital movies. This chapter gets you started on your cinematic path by providing step-by-step instructions for recording movies the easy way — that is, using Scene Intelligent Auto exposure mode, autofocusing, and auto just-about-everything else. After that, you can find details on how to adjust recording settings such as movie frame size and audio-recording volume.

However, note that some camera settings, such as those that affect focusing, exposure, and color, work the same way for movie recording as they do for still photography. Instead of repeating all that information here, this chapter concentrates on movie-specific features.

For help with two specialty video functions — Video Snapshot and Time-Lapse Movies — see Chapter 12. That chapter also shows you how to use the Creative Filters feature to apply special effects to a movie during recording.

Recording Movies Using Default Settings

Recording a movie using the camera's default settings is a cinch. The following steps show you how:

1. **To use an external microphone, plug the mic into the jack on the side of the camera, labeled in Figure 8-1.**

   Otherwise, sound is recorded via the internal microphone, which picks up its audio signal via two clusters of tiny holes, one of which is labeled in Figure 8-1 and the other of which (not shown) is tucked away on the opposite side of the flash, to the left of the AF Assist Lamp. Be careful not to cover up the microphone holes with your finger, and remember that anything you say during the recording likely will be picked up by the internal mic. Also don't confuse the camera's speaker, labeled in the figure, with the microphone openings.

2. **Set the On/Off/Movie switch to the Movie mode position, as shown in Figure 8-2.**

   The viewfinder shuts off, and the live preview appears on the monitor. By default, you see limited data onscreen, as shown on the left in Figure 8-3. (Press the Info button to cycle through the available Movie displays.) The most critical value to note is the available recording time — 29 minutes and 59 seconds, in the figure. This value represents the maximum possible recording time at the default movie settings, but it may be less depending on your memory card capacity.

Internal microphone   Speaker

Microphone jack

FIGURE 8-1:
You can attach an external microphone or rely on the built-in mic.

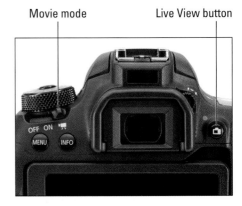

Movie mode   Live View button

FIGURE 8-2:
Set the On/Off switch to Movie mode and then press the Live View button to start and stop recording.

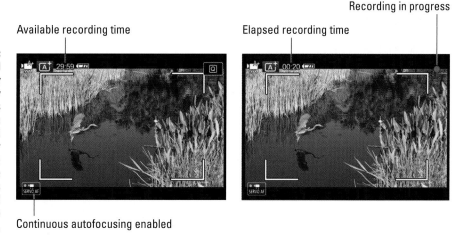

Available recording time   Elapsed recording time   Recording in progress

FIGURE 8-3:
The initial
movie display
shows how
many minutes
of video you
can record
(left); after
you begin
recording, the
value shows
the elapsed
recording time
(right).

Continuous autofocusing enabled

3. **Set the Mode dial to Scene Intelligent Auto (the green A+).**

   In this mode, the camera handles all critical recording settings for you.

4. **Frame your initial shot and set focus.**

   By default, the camera uses continuous autofocusing (Movie Servo AF) and the Face+Tracking AF Method setting. Chapter 5 has details, but here's the short story: If the camera detects a face, it automatically focuses on that face; otherwise, it looks for a focusing target within the area bordered by the four corner marks, shown in Figure 8-3.

REMEMBER

   In Movie mode, continuous focusing begins automatically when you use the default autofocusing settings. You don't have to press the shutter button halfway to focus as you do for still photography. In fact, when you do press the shutter button halfway, you interrupt continuous autofocusing, and the camera resets the focus point and locks it at that distance. Continuous autofocusing begins again when you lift your finger off the button.

   If your subject doesn't come into focus automatically, try tapping it on the touchscreen. A white box appears to mark the spot you tapped, and the camera tries to focus on that area.

5. **To start recording, press the Live View button (refer to Figure 8-2).**

   You then see a screen like the one shown on the right in Figure 8-3. The red dot indicates that recording is in progress. (The red dot near the Live View button is meant to remind you to press that button to start and stop recording.)

6. **To stop recording, press the Live View button again.**

But of course, you didn't buy this book so that you could remain trapped in the camera's default behaviors. So the next several pages explain all your recording options, which range from fairly simply to fairly not.

If you haven't yet done so, also check out the Chapter 1 section that lists precautions to take while Live View is engaged for photography or movie recording. To answer your question: No, you can't use the viewfinder for movie recording; Live View is your only option.

Choosing between NTSC and PAL

Before you dig into movie-recording settings, open Setup Menu 3 and check the Video System option, shown in Figure 8-4. This setting tells the camera which of two television standards to use when recording your movie: NTSC or PAL. Your camera was set at the factory to the standard used by the country in which it was meant for sale. The United States, Canada, and Japan are among countries that use NTSC. Australia and many European countries adhere to the PAL standard.

FIGURE 8-4:
Set the Video System option to the television broadcast standard used by the country in which the movie will be shown.

The selected Video System option determines the frame-rate options you're given when you set the movie recording size, as outlined in the next section. More important, you can't play an NTSC movie on a TV or other device that uses the PAL standard, and vice versa.

Customizing Recording Settings

As is the case with still photography, how many movie-recording settings you can adjust depends on which exposure mode is dialed in when you flip the On/Off switch to the Movie position. You get the most control in the Creative Zone modes (P, Tv, Av, and M). But even in Scene Intelligent Auto and other Basic Zone modes, you get access to the settings labeled in Figure 8-5 (press the

Info button to cycle through display options until you see those shown). You can find information about all these options in upcoming sections, with one exception: Video Snapshot. Chapter 12 explains how to use this specialty video feature.

Note: When you use the detailed data display shown in Figure 8-5, the focus frame used for the default AF Method setting (Face+Tracking) partially obscures some data — including, ironically, the symbol used to represent Face+Tracking autofocusing. So Figure 8-5 and other figures from this point forward show the focus frame as it appears when you use Smooth Zone AF or Live 1-Point AF, both of which display less intrusive focus frames.

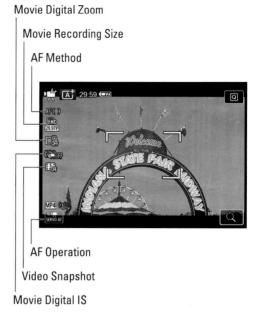

Movie Digital Zoom

Movie Recording Size

AF Method

AF Operation

Video Snapshot

Movie Digital IS

FIGURE 8-5:
These symbols represent the major recording options.

Choosing a Movie Recording Size setting

One of the most important recording options to consider is Movie Recording Size, which determines movie resolution (frame size), frames per second (fps), and how much file compression is applied.

A symbol representing the current setting appears in the area labeled in Figure 8-5. You can adjust the option by using the Quick Control screen, as shown in Figure 8-6, or via Shooting Menu 1, as shown in Figure 8-7.

If you use the Quick Control method (press the Q button to get started), the initial text on the screen shows the name of the selected option, as shown on the left in Figure 8-6; rotate the Quick Control or Main dial, or press the left/right Quick Control keys to move the orange selection box at the bottom of the screen. As you do, information about the currently selected setting appears, as shown on the right in the figure. The menu version of the settings screen displays the same information, but at the top of the screen (see the right side of Figure 8-7).

Movie Recording Size

Frame size   Frame rate

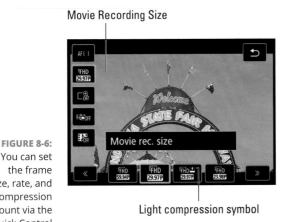

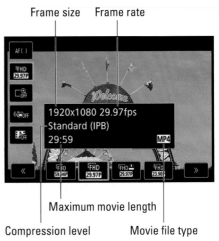

FIGURE 8-6:
You can set the frame size, rate, and compression amount via the Quick Control screen.

Light compression symbol

Compression level

Maximum movie length

Movie file type

FIGURE 8-7:
The Movie Recording Size setting is also adjustable through Shooting Menu 1.

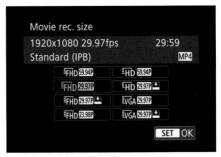

Unless you're an experienced digital videographer, the recording characteristics resulting from your each Movie Recording Setting option probably need some explanation. So the following list offers those basics, along with information about a few symbols and letters that may confuse even those who already understand frame size, frame rate, and compression.

» **Frame size (FHD, HD, or VGA):** Like still photos, digital movies are made out of pixels. In this case, the pixel count — or resolution — determines the size of each movie frame. In the video world, a resolution of 1920 x 1080 pixels is considered *Full HD* (*High Definition,* as in HDTV). A resolution of 1280 x 720 is *Standard HD* and produces slightly lesser quality than Full HD when both are displayed at the same size. Both options result in a frame with a 16:9 aspect ratio.

You also can record at a resolution of 640 x 480, known as *VGA* resolution or, more commonly, *standard resolution.* Frames shot at this setting have a 4:3 aspect ratio.

On the camera displays, the frame size settings are abbreviated as FHD, HD, and VGA.

» **Frame rate (frames per second):** This value determines how many frames are used to record one second of footage — thus, *fps,* or *frames per second.* When the camera is set to the NTSC Video System, you can choose from three frame rates: 24, 30, and 60. For PAL, you're limited to 25 and 50 fps.

TECHNICAL STUFF

Technically, NTSC frame rates are 23.98 fps, 29.97 fps, and 59.94 fps, so those are values the camera screens display for each frame rate option. But in the everyday world, people who debate this kind of thing round the values up to 24, 30, and 60, as do future discussions in this book.

Whether you go with the common lingo or remain a stickler for accuracy, a higher frame rate transfers to smoother playback, especially for fast-moving subjects. But frame rate also influences the crispness of the picture. It's hard to explain the difference in words, but to give you some reference, 30 fps is the NTSC standard for TV-quality video and 25 is the PAL broadcast standard. In both worlds, 24 fps is the motion-picture standard and delivers a slightly softer appearance. Recordings at 50 and 60 fps appear very sharp and detailed.

TIP

The uber-high frame rate is good for maintaining video quality if you edit your video to create slow-motion effects. Additionally, if you want to "grab" a still frame from a video to use as a photograph, 60 fps gives you more frames from which to choose.

As for the letter *P* that appears at the end of the frame rate value, it stands for *progressive video,* which refers to the technology used to build each frame of the movie. Your camera doesn't offer the other technology, *interlaced video,* but not to worry — progressive is the newest and latest standard.

» **Compression (IPB Standard or Light):** To keep the size of movie files reasonable, the camera applies *IPB file compression.* With this form of video compression, the camera looks for stretches of video that contain multiple frames that are the same. In that way, it can reuse the data from a single frame instead of storing the same data over and over for each frame. Don't worry about what IPB means — really, it will tangle your brain cells. Just know that you can choose from two compression levels: Standard and Light. Despite what the names may lead you to think, the Standard setting applies less compression than Light, so Light files are smaller.

» **File Type (MP4):** You also see a symbol representing the movie file type, MP4, on the settings screens and on the Live View display. You can't shoot regular movies in any other format on the 77D, so that bit of information is really irrelevant. However, if you create a time-lapse movie — which is really a long series of still shots that are stitched into a movie file — the camera creates that file a different video format, MOV. You can read more about time-lapse movies in Chapter 12.

Both formats, by the way, are very common digital video formats, so you can open the movie files in just about any movie-editing or playback software or app.

REMEMBER

Together, the frame size, frame rate, and compression level determine the movie file size and image quality. Lots of pixels, a high frame rate, and the Standard compression setting result in the largest files; the VGA/30 fps/Light setting produces the smallest files. As for quality, the goal is to choose the setting that produces the quality you need at the smallest possible file size. To figure out that answer, do some test recordings and play them on the device that you plan to use to screen the movie. That will give you a better idea about which setting is right for your project. For simple online tutorials, for example, one of the VGA settings may work well, while you obviously want the maximum quality if you're recording an important event that will be shown on a large screen.

REMEMBER

It's also important to know that movie file size determines the maximum length of a single recording. Here's the deal:

>> **The maximum file size for a single movie clip is 4GB.** Obviously, you reach that limit faster when you record a movie using a large frame size, frame rate, or Standard compression than when you reduce the frame size or frame rate or set the compression option to Light.

At the default setting (Full HD, 30 fps, and Standard compression), you hit 4GB at about 17 minutes. But if you up the frame rate to 60 fps, you can fit only 8 minutes in that same 4GB. Choose VGA (640 x 480), 30 fps, and Light compression, and your movie can be up to 2 hours and 43 minutes long.

>> **Your memory card determines what happens when you continue recording beyond the 4GB limit.** Although the maximum file size for a single clip is 4GB, you can continue recording after you reach that limit, as long as your memory card has room for more frames. But whether you wind up with a series of individual, 4GB clips or a single file that includes all the clips combined into one movie depends on your memory card.

To figure out how things will work with your card, check the card label to see whether it bears the initials SD, SDHC, or SDXC. An SD card tops out at 4GB of storage space; an SDHC card contains up to 32GB of space; an SDXC card, more than 32GB.

Obviously, recording stops automatically at 4GB on an SD card (before that, if the card has a lower capacity). But there's more to the memory card story than mere capacity. When you format the card using the Format Card option (Setup Menu 1), the camera performs the formatting differently for SDHC cards than it does for SDXC cards. That formatting determines what the camera does when you keep recording past the 4GB file limit.

REMEMBER

With an SDHC card, the camera creates a new movie file each time you reach the 4GB limit. You can keep recording as many 4GB movies as card space allows, but they exist as separate files, which means you have to play each clip one at a time. ("Okay, this movie is the first half of Johnny's awesome violin performance . . . now here's the second half . . . and here's the final clip, where he gets a standing ovation from the entire third grade.")

With an SDXC card, the camera still creates a new file for each 4GB movie clip, but the files are collected into a single movie file so that you enjoy seamless playback.

TIP

Long story short (too late, you say?): If you do a lot of movie shooting, invest in SDXC cards and format them in the camera before use.

Setting audio options

In Scene Intelligent Auto, Creative Auto, and all the other Basic Zone modes, you have very limited control over the audio portion of your movie: You can choose to record sound or disable audio recording. Make your preferences known through the Sound Recording option on Shooting Menu 1 as shown in Figure 8-8.

FIGURE 8-8:
In Scene Intelligent Auto and other Basic Zone exposure modes, your only control over audio is to enable or disable sound recording.

When you set the camera to P, Tv, Av, or M exposure mode, you get a slightly larger set of audio recording options. To explore them, choose Sound Recording from Shooting Menu 1, as shown on the left in Figure 8-9, to display the screen shown on the right.

The options on the Sound Recording settings screen work as follows:

>> **Sound Rec.:** At the default setting, Auto, the camera adjusts sound volume automatically. Select Manual if you want to take control over sound levels; choose Disable to record a silent movie. When audio is disabled, you see a microphone and the word Off near the bottom of the screen.

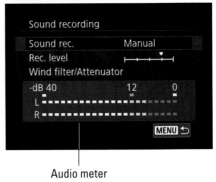

FIGURE 8-9:
In P, Tv, Av, and M exposure modes, you have a few more audio options.

Audio meter

If you choose the Manual Sound Recording option, a microphone with the letter M appears near the lower edge of the live preview after you exit the menus. The symbol reminds you that you're in charge of this setting.

WARNING

Unfortunately, the camera doesn't display any volume meters on the live preview to let you know when audio levels may need adjusting. Nor can you attach a headset to the camera in order to monitor audio with your own ears.

» **Rec. Level:** This option, highlighted on the left in Figure 8-10, enables you to adjust the audio level after you switch to manual volume control. The volume scale to the right of the option name shows the current setting; to change it, either tap the option name or highlight it and press Set. You then see the adjustment screen, shown on the right in Figure 8-10.

Current level

New level   Original level

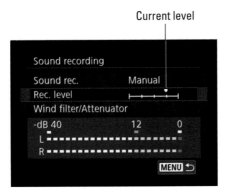

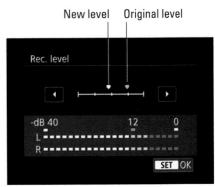

FIGURE 8-10:
Select Rec. Level (left) to open the screen where you can adjust the audio recording level (right.)

At the bottom of the screen, volume meters indicate the sound level being picked up by the microphone. Stereo audio contains two channels, left and right, so you see a volume meter for each channel. Note that although the built-in mic is a stereo mic, you can't control the channels individually, so both meters always reflect the same data.

TECHNICAL STUFF

Audio levels are measured in decibels (dB). Levels on the volume meter range from –40 (very, very soft) to 0 (as loud as can be measured digitally; think of 0dB as a full bucket that can't be filled anymore without overflowing). The general goal is to set the audio level so that sound peaks consistently in the –12 range. The indicators on the meter turn yellow in this range. (The extra space beyond that level, called *headroom,* gives you both a good signal and a comfortable margin of error.) If the sound is too loud, the volume indicators peak at 0, with the last notch on the meter turning red — a warning that the audio may be distorted.

» **Wind Filter/Attenuator:** This option is located on the Sound Recording settings screen, shown on the right in Figure 8-9. To access it, tap Wind filter/ Attenuator or highlight it and press the Set button. Here are the options that you can choose from:

- *Wind Filter:* Ever seen a newscaster out in the field, carrying a microphone that looks like it's covered with a big piece of foam? That foam thing is a wind filter. It's designed to lessen the sounds that the wind makes when it hits the microphone. You can enable a digital version of the same thing via the Wind Filter menu option. Essentially, the filter works by reducing the volume of noises that are similar to those made by wind. The problem is that some noises *not* made by wind can also be muffled when the filter is enabled. So when you're indoors or shooting on a still day, keep this option set to Disable. Also note that when you use an external microphone, the Wind Filter feature has no effect.

  By default, the Wind Filter is set to Auto, and the camera decides whether to apply it and at what strength. If you change the setting to Off, a microphone symbol decorated on one side with wavy lines (representing wind) and on the other with the letters Off. Don't let the Off label mislead you into thinking that the microphone itself is turned off.

- *Attenuator:* This feature is designed to eliminate distortion that can occur with sudden loud noises. Experiment with enabling this feature if you're shooting in a location where this audio issue is possible. When the attenuator is turned on, the letters ATT appear near the bottom edge of the monitor.

WARNING

The internal microphone may pick up sounds made by the camera's autofocusing system, especially if you use an older lens. (Newer Canon lenses offer quieter autofocusing operation.) Using an external microphone or locking in autofocusing before beginning recording are the two best solutions.

Using Movie Digital Zoom

Digital zoom enables you to capture a movie using a smaller area of the image sensor than normal. The frames are then enlarged so that you wind up with the frame size called for by your chosen Movie Recording Size setting. The result is a movie that gives you a smaller angle of view, as if you zoomed to a longer focal length to record the scene — or, to put it another way, as if you shot the movie using the whole sensor and then cropped away the perimeter of each frame.

The best way to understand the feature is to try it:

1. **Choose any exposure mode except SCN or Creative Filters.**

2. **Set the Movie Recording Size to one of the following three options:**

   - *FHD, 29.97P, Standard compression*

   - *FHD, 29.97P, Light compression*

   - *FHD, 23.98 fps, Standard compression*

   When any other setting is selected, Movie Digital Zoom is disabled. Adjust the Movie Recording Size setting via the Quick Control screen or Shooting Menu 1.

3. **Enable Movie Digital Zoom from via the Quick Control screen, as shown in Figure 8-11.**

Digital IS (Image Stabilization)

Movie Digital Zoom

Live 1-Point AF Method

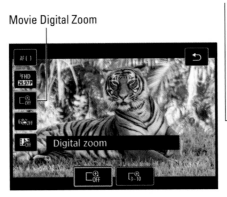

FIGURE 8-11: Enable Movie Digital Zoom via the Quick Control screen.

The preview shows your subject at the initial 3x zoom level, as shown on the right in Figure 8-11.

You also can turn on the feature via Shooting Menu 1.

4. **Return to shooting mode by pressing the Q button or tapping the exit arrow in the upper-right corner of the screen.**

Or, if you selected the setting from the menu, press the shutter button halfway and release it. Either way, the live preview now looks something like what you see on the left in Figure 8-12. (The screen shows how the display appears in Scene Intelligent Auto mode, using the detailed display mode. Press the Info button as needed to get to that display.) The zoom level is initially set at x3 magnification, with that value appearing in the area labeled in Figure 8-12.

When you enable Movie Digital Zoom, the camera automatically changes the AF Method setting to Live 1-Point AF, which results in the square focus frame you see in the figure. During normal photography or movie shooting, you can reposition the frame so that it falls over the subject, but when Movie Digital Zoom is engaged, the frame is locked at the center of the screen. So reframe as needed to move your subject under the frame instead.

Note that the AF Method option is dimmed in the display, indicating that you can't change the selected setting. Also off limits is the Movie Digital IS function, whose symbol also appears dimmed in the display.

5. **To change the zoom level, press the up/down Quick Control keys or tap the Zoom symbol on the touchscreen.**

FIGURE 8-12:
From the initial zoomed view (left), tap the Zoom icon or press the up/down Quick Control keys to display a screen where you can adjust the zoom level (right).

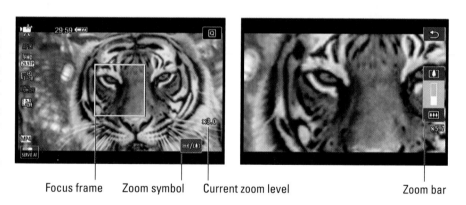

Focus frame   Zoom symbol   Current zoom level   Zoom bar

You then see the adjustment screen shown on the right in the figure. Press the up/down Quick Control keys to adjust the zoom level. You also can tap the top of the zoom bar to increase the zoom level and tap the bottom to decrease the level.

6. **Return to shooting mode by tapping the exit arrow or pressing the shutter button halfway and releasing it.**

7. **Ensure that focus is set.**

   If Movie Servo AF is in force (as it is by default), the area under the focus frame should already by in focus. When you turn off Movie Servo AF, press the shutter button halfway to set focus. You can then lift your finger off the shutter button.

8. **Press the Live View button to start and stop recording.**

   You can zoom in and out using Digital Zoom while recording. Although we don't recommend doing so in most circumstances, experiment to see what shots you can come up.

REMEMBER

Although Movie Digital Zoom is a fun tool, keep these limitations in mind:

>> **Movie quality may be reduced.** Again, digital zoom records the scene on a reduced area of the image sensor and then fills out the remaining frame area by adding pixels during the processing stage. Any time you add pixels to an existing image or, in this case, a movie frame, picture quality is reduced. So movie quality may not appear as finely rendered as a movie shot without digital zoom.

   In digital imaging lingo, adding pixels is known as *upsampling*.

>> **The maximum ISO speed when using digital zoom is ISO 6400.** In very dim lighting, that may not be adequate to produce a good exposure. (See Chapter 4 for an explanation of ISO.)

>> **Autofocusing may be slower than usual.** The slowdown occurs because the camera has to use a different type of autofocusing than when digital zoom is turned off.

Reviewing Other Movie Options

Depending on your exposure mode, you can access some or all of the additional recording features labeled in Figure 8-13. The next sections provide the details on these options along with a few others that you control via the menu system. If you want to access all the options shown in the figure, you must set the Mode dial to P, Tv, Av, or M. Also, if your display doesn't contain all the data shown in the figure, press the Info button to cycle through the various Movie display styles until you get to the detailed version.

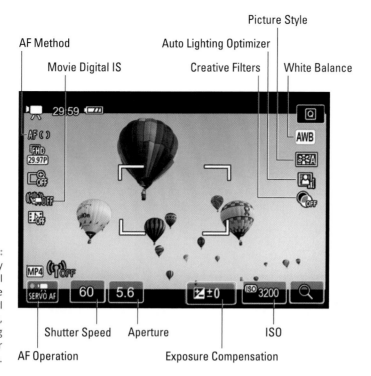

FIGURE 8-13: You may have control over these additional options, depending on your exposure mode.

AF Method

Movie Digital IS

Picture Style

Auto Lighting Optimizer

Creative Filters

White Balance

AF Operation

Shutter Speed

Aperture

Exposure Compensation

ISO

Autofocusing options

REMEMBER

In Movie mode, you can control both of the autofocusing options, AF Method and AF Operation. You're not locked out of the AF Operation setting when you use Basic Zone exposure modes as you are for still photography.

For AF Method, you get the same three settings as for Live View photography: Face+Tracking, Zone, and Live 1-Point. If you turn on Movie Digital Zoom, however, the camera insists on using Live 1-Point autofocusing.

As for AF Operation, you get just two choices: You can enable or disable continuous autofocusing, called Movie Servo AF. Tap the icon labeled in Figure 8-13 to toggle that feature on or off. (The symbol in the figure shows Movie Servo AF enabled.) If you turn off continuous autofocusing, press the shutter button halfway to set focus. You can then lift your finger off the shutter button and focus will remain set at the current focusing distance.

When Movie Servo AF is enabled, pressing the shutter button halfway interrupts continuous autofocusing and resets the focus point. Continuous focusing resumes when you lift your finger off the button.

For more focusing details, see Chapter 5.

Movie Digital IS

Some lenses, including the 18–55mm and 18–135mm kit lenses featured in this book, offer *image stabilization,* which helps reduce blurring caused by camera shake (minor movement of the camera during the exposure). When you shoot movies, you can turn on an additional level of shake compensation, called Movie Digital IS. You can take advantage of this feature in an exposure mode except SCN and Creative Filters.

An icon representing the current setting Movie Digital IS setting appears in the detailed movie display, as shown in Figure 8-13. By default, the feature is disabled. Turn it on via the Quick Control method or, in the P, Tv, Av, and M exposure modes, via Shooting Menu 5, as shown in Figure 8-14. In Basic Zone modes, the option lives on Shooting Menu 3.

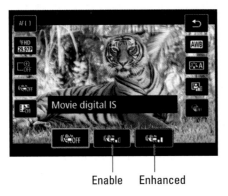 

Enable   Enhanced

FIGURE 8-14:
Movie Digital IS may help reduce the impact of camera shake in a movie.

Choose the Enable setting for the least amount of anti-shake correction; select Enhanced for a stronger effect. If your lens has its own stabilization system, be sure to enable it as well — otherwise, Movie Digital IS won't work. On the kit lenses, move the Stabilizer switch to the On position.

TIP

The neat thing about Movie Digital IS is that it works even with lenses that don't offer their own stabilization systems. However, because this stabilization is digital in nature, it does present one complication: Because of how the technology works, your subject is magnified by 10 percent at the Enable setting and 30 percent at the Enhanced setting. To put it another way, the normal angle of view is reduced to 90 percent or 70 percent, respectively. Thankfully, the monitor accurately displays the subject area that will be recorded.

Here are a few other pointers to keep in mind:

» **Movie quality may be lower.** Because of the magnification factor, your movie may appear grainier than normal. In some cases, your subject may briefly go out of focus as the digital stabilization does its thing.

» **Your lens makes a difference.** First off, not all lenses can deal with Movie Digital IS. The Canon website has information on compatible lenses; just do a search on the term "Canon Movie Digital IS" to find the details. If your lens isn't listed, turn the feature off.

Lens focal length also has an impact. Movie Digital IS works best with wide-angle lenses (short focal length), and it doesn't work at all with lenses that have a focal length exceeding 800mm.

» **Turn the feature off when using a tripod.** Otherwise, the system may actually increase blurring by trying to compensate for camera movement that isn't occurring.

Playing with exposure and color

In the Basic Zone modes, you don't have any control over these aspects of your movie. The one exception is SCN mode, which offers an HDR option that captures a larger spectrum of darks to lights than can normally be recorded. (See the side-bar "What's an HDR movie?" for more information.)

Set the Mode dial to P, Tv, Av, or M, and you gain a bit more control, as follows:

» **M mode gives you full control over exposure, just as for still photography.** However, determining the correct shutter speed involves slightly different considerations than for still photography. This option is best left to experts and involves more details than can fit in this book, so see the camera instruction manual for the full story.

» **You can control ISO only in the M exposure mode, but you can limit the maximum ISO in P, Tv, and Av modes.** In M mode, set the ISO value by pressing the ISO button, tapping the ISO symbol on the touchscreen, or through the ISO Speed option on Shooting Menu 2.

In P, Tv, and Av modes, you're locked into using Auto ISO. However, you still have the option to limit the maximum ISO the camera can choose. Look for this setting, ISO Auto, on Shooting Menu 2 as well.

>> **In P, Tv, and Av modes, you can adjust exposure via Exposure Compensation.** The symbol labeled in Figure 8-13 indicates how much compensation is applied — none, in the figure. To adjust the setting, rotate the Quick Control dial. You also can access the setting by tapping the Exposure Compensation symbol on the screen or by choosing the option from Shooting Menu 2, as shown in Figure 8-15. A higher value produces a brighter recording; a lower value reduces brightness.

FIGURE 8-15: The camera forces you to use Auto ISO in the P, Tv, and Av exposure modes, but you can limit the maximum ISO value that it can select.

>> **In P, Tv, and Av exposure modes, you can press the AE Lock button to interrupt continuous exposure adjustment.** When you shoot in these exposure modes, the camera adjusts exposure during the recording as needed. If you prefer to use the same settings throughout the recording — or to lock in the current settings during the recording — you can use AE (autoexposure) Lock. Just press the AE Lock button. A little asterisk appears in the lower left of the screen.

To cancel AE Lock during recording, press the AF Point Selection button. When recording is stopped, AE Lock is canceled automatically after 8 seconds by default. This shutoff timing is determined by the Metering Timer option on Shooting Menu 4.

>> **You also can adjust exposure through the Auto Lighting Optimizer setting, labeled in Figure 8-13.** The Highlight Tone Priority option, activated through Custom Function 4, is also available. As with still photography, you can enable only one of these features at a time. See Chapter 4 for details on both.

>> **The White Balance and Picture Control options work the same way as they do for still photography.** Figure 8-13 shows you where to find the icons that represent the current settings. You can adjust both through the Quick Control screen or Shooting Menu 3. On the menu, you also can create a custom White Balance setting or apply White Balance Shift (choose WB Correction). See Chapter 6 for help with these and other color features.

WHAT'S AN HDR MOVIE?

By setting the Mode dial to SCN and putting the camera in Movie mode, you automatically set the camera to a special recording mode: HDR Movie. HDR stands for *high dynamic range,* which refers to a spectrum of brightness values that is larger than what your camera can normally capture in a single shot — or movie frame, in this case.

When you're shooting a high-contrast subject (one that includes both very bright highlights and very deep shadows), give this feature a whirl to see whether it improves the look of your movie. If things go well, the movie will retain more details in the brightest areas of the scene.

Understand, though, that you've very limited as to other recording options when creating an HDR movie. You can turn audio recording on or off (Shooting Menu 1) and adjust autofocusing settings (Quick Control screen or Shooting Menu 2), but that's it. You can't even change the Movie Recording Size; it's locked in at Full HD (FHD), 30 fps, and Standard IPB compression for NTSC video mode and FHD, 25fps, Standard IPB compression for PAL. Nor can you use Movie Digital Zoom or Movie Digital IS (image stabilization).

In order to produce the greater brightness range of an HDR movie, the camera exposes frames at multiple settings and then merges them together to create the final movie file. Because of that processing, you may notice a loss of movie quality, with some portions appearing distorted or noisy (grainy). Camera shake also may become more noticeable, so for best results, use a tripod.

Note that when the camera is in Movie mode, HDR Movie is the only SCN option you can select. You don't have access to the other special scene modes, which Chapter 3 covers.

Checking out a few final features

To wrap up movie-recording coverage, the following list offers a look at few miscellaneous settings not already covered in this chapter:

>> **Metering Timer:** By default, exposure information such as f-stop and shutter speed disappears from the display after 8 seconds if you don't press any camera buttons. If you want the exposure data to remain visible for a longer period, you can adjust the shutdown time through this option, found on Shooting Menu 4, shown on the left in Figure 8-16. This option is accessible only in the P, Tv, Av, or M exposure modes.

>> **Grid Display:** You can display three different grid styles on the monitor to help ensure alignment of vertical and horizontal structures when you're framing the scene. In the Creative Zone modes, enable the grid via Shooting Menu 4; in other exposure modes, the option lives on Shooting Menu 2.

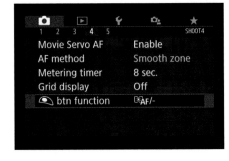

FIGURE 8-16:
In P, Tv, Av, and M exposure modes, open Shooting Menu 4 to access a few additional movie settings.

>> **Shutter Button Function:** This option, highlighted in Figure 8-16, enables you to change what happens when you press the shutter button halfway and what happens when you press it all the way. (Yeah, that graphic doesn't look much like a shutter button to us, either.)

For now, leave this option at the default setting, shown in the figure. A half-press then kickstarts exposure metering and autofocusing; a full press does nothing (because you can't take a still photo in Movie mode). Again, you access the setting from Shooting Menu 4 in the Creative Zone modes and Shooting Menu 2 in Basic Zone modes. For a look at all button customization possibilities, check out Chapter 11.

>> **Lens Aberration Correction:** This option appears on Shooting Menu 1 when the mode dial is set to P, Tv, Av, or M. It provides access to tools that try to automatically correct image defects that can occur with some lenses. In Movie mode, you can apply only two of the four settings that are available for still photography: Peripheral Illumination Correction and Chromatic Aberration Correction. The first one attempts to brighten image corners that appear unnaturally dark, as detailed in Chapter 4. Chromatic Aberration Correction tackles a color defect that you can read about in Chapter 6.

>> **Lens Electronic MF:** Also found on Shooting Menu 1 in the P, Tv, Av, and M modes only, this option enables you to fine-tune autofocusing by using the lens manual focus ring without officially switching the lens to manual-focusing mode. See Chapter 1 for details.

>> **Remote Control Shooting:** Found on Shooting Menu 5 in the Creative Zone exposure modes (Shooting Menu 3 in the Basic Zone modes) this option applies only if you use the camera with certain Canon remote control units (BR-E1 and RC-6). Set the option to Enable if you want to use the remote control to start and stop movie recording. See the camera manual for specifics on how to use the remote unit for that purpose. You can also perform remote shooting and control the camera from a mobile device or your computer, as explained in Appendix A.

Playing Movies

 To play a movie, press the Playback button to put the camera in Playback mode. When a movie file is displayed, the touchscreen contains two items, as shown on the left in Figure 8-17: a playback arrow and a Set symbol.

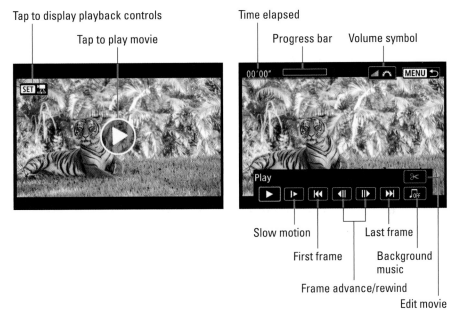

If you see thumbnails instead of a full movie frame, tap the movie thumbnail or use the Quick Control keys to highlight it. Then tap the thumbnail again or press the Set button to display the file in the full-frame view. Or just tap the thumbnail. (You can't play movies in thumbnail view.)

Use these techniques to start, stop, and control playback:

» **Start playback.** You can start playback in two ways:

- *Tap the playback arrow, labeled in Figure 8-17.* Your movie begins playing, with a progress bar and time-elapsed value provided at the top of the screen. (Press the Info button if you don't see the progress bar during playback.)

- *Press the Set button or tap the Set icon.* Now you see the first frame of your movie plus a slew of control icons, as shown on the right in Figure 8-17. To start playback, tap the Play icon or use the Quick Control dial or Quick Control keys to highlight it and then press the Set button.

>> **Adjust volume.** Rotate the Main dial or tap the Volume symbol, labeled in Figure 8-17. (The notched half-circle represents the Main dial in this and other onscreen graphics.)

>> **Pause playback.** Tap anywhere on the screen or press the Set button to pause playback and redisplay the movie-control symbols. To resume playback, tap the Play symbol or press Set again.

>> **Play in slow motion.** Tap the slow-motion icon, labeled in Figure 8-17, or select it and press Set. Press the right Quick Control key or turn the Quick Control dial to the right to increase playback speed; press the left Quick Control key or rotate the Quick Control dial to the left to decrease it. You also can adjust the speed by dragging your finger along the little scale that appears in the upper-right corner of the monitor during slo-mo playback.

>> **Go forward/back one frame while paused.** Use the symbols labeled Frame advance/rewind in Figure 8-17. Tap or highlight the symbol representing the direction you want to go. Then press the Set button once. Each time you press the button, you go forward or backward one frame.

>> **Fast forward/fast rewind.** Use the same process just described, but keep holding down the Set button until you reach the frame you want to view.

>> **Skip to the first or last frame of the movie.** Tap the symbols labeled First frame or Last frame in Figure 8-17. Or use the Quick Control dial or Quick Control keys to highlight the icon and press the Set button.

>> **Enable Background Music.** If you recorded a movie without sound, you can enable the Background Music option to play a sound file. In order to use this feature, you must install Canon EOS Utility, a program that you can download from the Canon website. Use that program to copy music files to your camera memory card. The EOS Utility program's user guide, also available for download, offers the details you need to know to copy music files to the card.

>> **Edit the movie.** After you begin playing the movie, the Scissors symbol, labeled Edit movie in Figure 8-17, becomes available. Tap the icon or highlight it and press set to trim frames from the start or end of the movie. Chapter 12 steps you through this process.

>> **Exit playback.** Tap the Menu icon or press the Menu button.

3

After the Shot

IN THIS CHAPTER

» **Exploring picture playback functions**

» **Magnifying your picture to check details**

» **Deciphering the picture information displays**

» **Understanding histograms**

» **Connecting your camera to a TV for big-screen playback**

Chapter **9**

Picture Playback

Without question, one of the best things about digital photography is being able to view pictures right after you shoot them. No more guessing whether you got the shot you want or need to try again; no more wasting money on developing and printing pictures that stink.

Displaying your pictures is just the start of the things your camera can do in Playback mode, though. You also can see which settings you used to take the picture, view graphics that alert you to exposure problems, and magnify a photo to check details. This chapter introduces you to these playback features and more.

Note: Although some playback features discussed in this chapter work for movies as well as still photos, some functions do not. The sections describing each feature spell out whether it's available for movies. For help with movie-only playback steps, see the end of Chapter 8.

Adjusting Automatic Image Review

After you take a picture, it automatically appears on the monitor for two seconds. You can adjust the post-capture display time via the Image Review option on Shooting Menu 1, shown in Figure 9-1. (The figure shows the menu as it appears in P, Tv, Av, and M exposure modes; the Basic Zone version contains a few different options, but both menus contain the Image Review setting.)

FIGURE 9-1:
Control the timing of instant-picture review.

You can select from the following Image Review options:

TIP

>> **A specific review period:** Pick 2, 4, or 8 seconds.

>> **Off:** Disables image review. Turning off the monitor saves battery power, so keep this option in mind if your battery is running low. You can still view pictures by pressing the Playback button.

>> **Hold:** Displays the current image indefinitely or until the camera automatically shuts off to save power. Camera shutdown timing is controlled through the Auto Power Off option on Setup Menu 2.

Viewing Pictures in Playback Mode

To switch to Playback mode, press the Playback button, labeled in Figure 9-2. Then scroll through your picture or movie files one by one by rotating the Quick Control dial, pressing the right or left Quick Control keys, or swiping your fingertip horizontally across the touchscreen.

Here are a few other playback fundamentals to note:

>> **Data display options:** You may see your photo only, as in Figure 9-2, or see shooting data along with the image. Press the Info button, highlighted in the figure, to change how much data appears. The upcoming section "Viewing Picture Data" explains how to interpret the data.

Magnify display

Display thumbnails/zoom out

Press to change data display

Quick Control button

FIGURE 9-2: The default Playback mode displays one picture at a time, with basic picture data.

Playback button   Erase button

>> **Single-image view versus Index (thumbnails) view:** If you see multiple thumbnails of your photos and movies rather than a single image or movie frame, the camera is in the Index display mode. To return to single-image view, just press the Set button. See the next section for more information on Index mode.

>> **Quick Control functions:** You can access several playback features via the Quick Control screen. However, to get to the screen, you must press the Q button. There's no Q touchscreen symbol to tap as there is when the camera is in shooting mode.

Figure 9-3 offers a map to the various tools accessible via the Quick Control screen. Details on each feature are provided throughout this chapter and the next. If you need help understanding how to operate the Quick Control screen, Chapter 1 provides a tutorial.

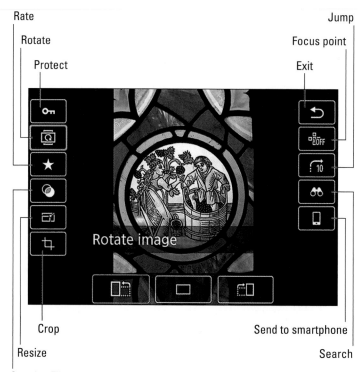

Rate

Rotate

Protect

Jump

Focus point

Exit

Rotate image

FIGURE 9-3:
Press the
Quick Control
button for
fast access to
these playback
features.

Crop

Resize

Creative Filter

Send to smartphone

Search

>> **Touchscreen operations:** In addition to swiping across the screen to scroll through your images and movies, a number of other features can be activated via the touchscreen. For example, you can pinch out to magnify an image and pinch in to reduce the magnification, just as you can on most smartphones and tablets. Again, details on how and where to tap, pinch, or swipe appear in the discussions related to these playback features.

>> **Exit Playback mode:** To return to shooting, press the Playback button or give the shutter button a quick half-press and release.

Viewing thumbnails (Index mode)

In Index mode, you can view 4, 9, 36, or 100 thumbnails, each representing a photo or the first frame of a movie. Figure 9-4 shows the 9- and 36-thumbnail views.

Movie file   Selected thumbnail   Scroll bar

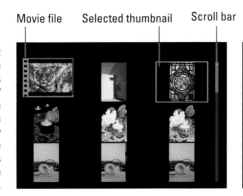
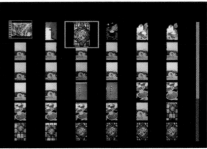

Here's your guide to viewing images and performing other tasks in Index mode:

>> **Shifting from single-image view to Index mode:** You have two options:

- *Pinch inward on the touchscreen.* In other words, put one finger on one edge of the monitor and your thumb on the opposite edge. Then drag toward the center of the screen. Each time you pinch, you display more thumbnails.

- *Press the Index/Reduce button.* That's the button shown in the margin here and labeled "Display thumbnails/zoom out" in Figure 9-2. Officially, the button has the lengthy name *AE Lock/FE Lock/Index/Reduce* because it performs all those functions. But for playback purposes, only the Index/ Reduce part of the name applies, so that's the name used in sections that discuss playback features.

Whatever you call the button, your first press puts the camera in Index mode. Each subsequent press displays more thumbnails at a time.

TIP

Note the blue checkerboard and magnifying glass under the button. Blue labels indicate that a button serves a playback function. In this case, the checkerboard indicates the Index function, and the minus sign in the magnifying glass is visual shorthand for "reduce size." (Many people refer to this button as the *zoom-out button,* which is perfectly fine, too.)

>> **Reducing the number of thumbnails:** Press the button shown in the margin and labeled "Magnify display" in Figure 9-2. This button also has a blue magnifying glass icon, this time with a plus sign in the center to indicate that pressing it enlarges the thumbnail size. It's officially called the AF Point Selection/Magnify button, but for purposes of discussions relating to playback, let's agree to call it the Magnify button, okay?

Press the button once to switch from 100 thumbnails to 36; again to go from 36 to 9; once more to switch from 9 thumbnails to 4; and one last time to switch from 4 thumbnails to single-image view. You also can pinch outward on the touchscreen to reduce the number of thumbnails.

» **Distinguishing picture files from movie files:** Movie files are decorated with a border like the one that appears on the top-left thumbnail in Figure 9-4. The design is supposed to evoke the sprocket holes in traditional movie film.

» **Scrolling to the next screen of thumbnails:** If a scroll bar appears on the right side of the screen, additional pages of thumbnails are just out of sight. To scroll to the next page, swipe your finger up or down the screen, rotate the Main dial, or press the up or down Quick Control keys.

» **Selecting a photo or movie file:** You can perform many file operations, such as deleting images, while in Index mode. But you first have to select the file — or, more accurately, the thumbnail that represents it. A highlight box surrounds the selected file, as shown in Figure 9-4. To select a different file, tap its thumbnail or either rotate the Quick Control dial or press the Quick Control keys to move the highlight box over it.

TIP

When the display shows 36 or 100 thumbnails, the currently selected photo is slightly enlarged compared to the rest, as shown in the right screen in Figure 9-4. This makes it a little easier to spot amid all the other thumbnails.

If you want to select multiple files at a time, check out the Chapter 10 section that explains the Image Search feature. That option enables you to select all files that meet a specific criteria, such as being taken during a particular date range.

TIP

» **Returning to single-image view:** You can keep pinching outward or pressing the Magnify view until you shift from four thumbnails to single-frame view. But assuming that you're viewing more than four thumbnails, it's quicker to just tap a thumbnail or to select the thumbnail and press the Set button. That image or movie then appears all by its lonesome on the monitor.

Jumping through images

If your memory card contains scads of images, here's a trick you'll love: By using the Jump feature, you can leapfrog through images instead of scrolling the display a bazillion times to get to the picture you want to see. To initiate a jump, you rotate the Main dial or swipe two fingers from left to right across the screen.

Even better, you get a number of options for specifying where you want the camera to land when it jumps. You can choose from these settings:

TIP

» **Display Images One by One:** This option, in effect, disables jumping, restricting you to browsing pictures one at a time. So, what's the point? Not much of one, actually. The 77D already enables you to quickly scroll through photos and movies one at a time using the Quick Control dial. This is easier than swiping across the touchscreen or pressing the right/left Quick Control keys. However, this option enables you to use the Main dial to scroll through files — which you may prefer.

Note that both movie files and still photos are displayed when you use this option.

» **Jump 10 Images:** This setting, which is the default, advances the display ten files at a time. Again, although the name indicates that the setting jumps only through images, movies are included in the ten-file grouping.

» **Jump a specified number of files:** Choose any value between 1 and 100. The camera sets this to 30 initially.

» **Display by Date:** If your card contains pictures and movies shot on different dates, you can jump from a picture taken on one date to the first file created on the next date. For example, if you're viewing the third of 30 pictures taken on June 1, you can jump past all others from that day to the first image taken on, say, June 5.

» **Display by Folder:** If you create custom folders on your memory card — an option outlined in Chapter 11 — choose this setting to jump from the current folder to the first photo in a different folder.

» **Display Movies Only:** Does your memory card contain both still photos and movies? If you want to view only the movie files, select this option. Then rotate the Main dial or do the two-finger touchscreen swipe to jump from one movie to the next without seeing any still photos.

» **Display Stills Only:** This one is the opposite of the Movies option: Movie files are hidden, and the camera displays one photo at a time, just as when you use the Display Images One by One option.

» **Display Protected Images Only:** By using the Protect feature covered in Chapter 10, you can tag your best images in a way that prevents them from being erased by the camera's normal file-deletion options (choosing Erase from the Playback menu or pressing the Erase button). Selecting this Jump option limits playback to Protected files only.

A little side note here: The Protect option does *not* safeguard files from being deleted when you format the memory card, an operation discussed in the Chapter 1 section that covers memory cards.

» **Display by Image Rating:** If you rate photos, another Chapter 10 topic, you can use this Jump method to view all rated photos or only those with a specific rating.

Use one of these methods to specify which type of jumping you want to do:

>> **Quick Control screen:** In Figure 9-5, the Jump option is set to Number of Images. (The *C* in the icon for this setting presumably stands for *custom.*)

REMEMBER

When you select the Number of Images setting or the Rating setting, an Info symbol appears, as shown in Figure 9-5. Tap the symbol or press the Info button to display a screen where you can specify the number of images to jump at a time or the rating you want the Jump function to use.

>> **Playback Menu 2:** Select the last option on the menu, as shown in Figure 9-6. (The *w/* followed by a notched semicircle is shorthand for *with the Main dial.*) After you select the menu option, you see the selection screen shown on the right. This figure features the By Rating setting. Change the rating level for the Jump function by rotating the Quick Control or Main dial, or tapping the arrows on either side of the displayed rating symbol (five stars, in the figure). Tap Set or press the Set button to lock in your choice.

Press the Playback button to exit the menus and return to Playback mode.

FIGURE 9-6:
You can also select the Jump method via Playback Menu 2.

After selecting a Jump method, take the following steps to jump through your photos during playback:

REMEMBER

1. Set the camera to display a single photo.

If the camera is in Index mode, you can switch to single-photo view by tapping a thumbnail or selecting a thumbnail and pressing the Set button.

2. **Rotate the Main dial or swipe two fingers across the screen.**

   The camera jumps to the next image or movie according to the Jump setting you selected. A *jump bar* appears for a few seconds at the bottom of the monitor, indicating the current Jump setting.

3. **To exit Jump mode, rotate the Quick Control dial, press the right or left Quick Control key, or swipe a single finger across the touchscreen.**

Rotating pictures

When you take a picture, the camera can tag the image file with the *camera orientation* (that is, whether you held the camera horizontally or vertically). When you view the picture, the camera can read the data and rotate the image so that it appears upright in the monitor, as shown on the left in Figure 9-7, instead of on its side, as shown on the right. The image is also rotated automatically when you view it in the Canon photo software that ships with your camera (as well as in some other programs that can read the rotation data). For obvious reasons, you can rotate only still photos; movies are always displayed in their original landscape orientation.

FIGURE 9-7: Display vertically oriented pictures upright (left) or sideways (right).

Photographers use the term *portrait orientation* to refer to vertically oriented pictures and *landscape orientation* to refer to horizontally oriented pictures. The terms stem from the traditional way that people and places are photographed — portraits, vertically; landscapes, horizontally.

By default, the camera tags the photo with the orientation data and rotates the image automatically both on the camera and on your computer screen. But you have other choices, as follows:

» **Disabling or adjusting automatic rotation:** Open Setup Menu 1 and select Auto Rotate to display the three options shown in Figure 9-8. From top to bottom, the settings are

- *On (Camera and Computer):* This option is the default; rotation happens both on the computer and on the camera.

- *On (Computer Only):* Pictures are rotated only on a computer monitor.

- *Off:* New pictures aren't tagged with the orientation data, and existing photos aren't rotated during playback on the camera, even if they're already tagged.

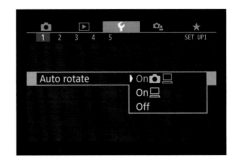

FIGURE 9-8:
Go to Setup Menu 1 to disable or adjust automatic image rotation.

» **Rotating pictures during playback:** If you stick with the default Auto Rotate setting, you can rotate pictures to a different orientation during playback when needed. You might do so to get a larger view of a picture shot in vertical orientation, for example (refer to Figure 9-7).

You can rotate a picture in two ways:

- *Use the Quick Control screen.* Figure 9-9 shows the Rotate option and its three settings.

- *Select Rotate Image from Playback Menu 1,* as shown on the left in Figure 9-10. In single-image view, you then see a screen similar to the one shown on the right in the figure. Tap the Set icon at the bottom of the screen or press the Set button to rotate the image 90 degrees. Press or tap again to rotate 180 additional degrees; press or tap once more to return to the picture's original orienta-

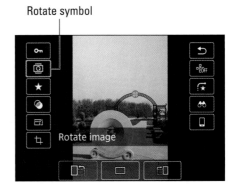

FIGURE 9-9:
During playback, the fastest way to rotate an image is to use the Quick Control screen.

tion (0 degrees of rotation). If you were displaying pictures in Index view before choosing the Rotate Image option, select the image you want to rotate and then tap the Set icon or press the Set button. Tap the Menu symbol or press the Menu button to return to the menu system. Or press the Playback button to return to viewing pictures.

REMEMBER

After you exit the Quick Control or menu screen, the photo remains rotated only if the Setup Menu's Auto Rotate option is set to the default — On (Camera and Computer).

Also be aware of this bit of weirdness: If the Auto Rotate option is set to one of the other two settings, the images don't appear rotated when you select the Rotate option from the Quick Control screen or Playback Menu 1 option. But the file is tagged with the rotation directions you apply nonetheless. So, if you later turn Auto Rotate back on or view the photo in compatible software, the image does appear rotated.

Rotate symbol

 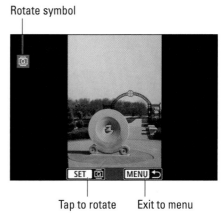

FIGURE 9-10:
You can also rotate photos from Playback Menu 1.

Tap to rotate   Exit to menu

Zooming in for a closer view

During playback, you can magnify a photo to inspect details, as shown in Figure 9-11. Zooming works only for photos and only in single-image view. So, if the camera is currently displaying thumbnails, shift to single-image view by tapping the thumbnail of the picture you want to inspect (or by selecting it and pressing Set).

FIGURE 9-11:
After displaying your photo in single-image view (left), you can magnify the display to check details (right).

Magnified area

Here's a rundown of how to use the magnification feature:

>> **Zooming in:** Pinch outward from the center of the touchscreen or press the Magnify button. Each pinch or press increases the magnification level; you can enlarge the image up to ten times its normal display size.

>> **Viewing another part of the magnified picture:** When the image is magnified, a thumbnail representing the entire image appears in the lower-right corner of the monitor, as shown on the right in Figure 9-11. The solid white box indicates the area of the image that is shown on the monitor. To scroll the display so that you can see a hidden portion of the image, drag your finger on the touchscreen or press the Quick Control keys.

>> **Viewing more images at the same magnification:** While the display is zoomed, rotate the Quick Control dial to display the same area of the next photo at the same magnification. For example, if you shot a group portrait several times, you can easily check each one for shut-eye problems.

>> **Zooming out:** To reduce the magnification level, pinch in toward the center of the touchscreen or press the Index/Reduce button. Each pinch or press decreases the zoom level another step.

>> **Returning to full-frame view when zoomed in:** To exit magnified view in one quick step, tap the exit arrow near the upper-right corner of the screen or press the Playback button.

Showing focus points during playback

You also have the option of seeing the focus point(s) that the camera used to establish focus during playback, as shown in Figure 9-12. To turn focus-point display on and off, use the Quick Control screen, as shown on the left in Figure 9-13, or the AF Point Display option on Playback Menu 3, as shown on the right.

This feature is very helpful for trouble-shooting focus problems. If the focus point is correctly placed over the subject, you can eliminate one cause of poor focus. You then know that the problem

Focus point

FIGURE 9-12:
You can display the focus point(s) the camera used to establish focus.

is a result of some other factor: camera shake during the exposure; exceeding the lens's minimum focusing distance; or using a shutter speed that's too slow to capture a moving subject without blur. (See Chapter 4 for details on focusing.)

AF Display setting

FIGURE 9-13: You can turn the feature on and off via the Quick Control screen (left) or Playback Menu 3 (right).

Viewing Picture Data

REMEMBER

During playback, you have a choice of the following three information display modes:

>> **No Information:** This display hides all shooting information, giving you an uncluttered view of your image or movie. All figures up to this point in the chapter use this display mode.

>> **Basic Information:** Okay, so "basic" is a relative term here. This screen, shown on the left in Figure 9-14, does contain basic shooting settings, such as the shutter speed and the Image Quality setting. But in terms of understanding how the camera presents the data, you may need a little assistance. See the next section for help.

Basic Information display   Shooting Information display

FIGURE 9-14: Press the Info button to change the amount of data displayed with your photo.

>> **Shooting Information:** This display mode presents the smorgasbord of data shown on the right in Figure 9-14. As if the initial screen shown in the figure isn't intimidating enough, you can scroll the display to uncover several more pages of data. But don't worry, the upcoming section "Shooting Information display mode" helps sort things out.

To cycle from one display mode to the next, just press the Info button. However, be aware that the Shooting Information mode isn't available when you're viewing thumbnails (Index playback mode). To return to single-image view, tap the thumbnail or select it and press Set.

For all three display modes, you have the option of displaying the autofocus point(s) used when you took the shot. See the preceding section for details. Also, you can choose any display mode for movies, but after you begin playing the movie, most or all of the data shown on the initial display disappears.

Basic Information display mode

Figure 9-15 labels the data presented in Basic Information playback display mode. Note that the figure shows every possible data item that may appear — if you don't see a particular value on your screen, it just means that you didn't take advantage of the associated feature when you took the picture. For example, you see an Exposure Compensation value only if you enabled that tool, explained in Chapter 4. (The figure doesn't show the actual settings used to photograph the stained-glass window, by the way, in case you're wondering.)

Here's a quick overview of each bit of data on the screen:

>> **Playback number/total images:** These values show the current file number and the total number of files on the memory card. So the numbers in the figure show that you're looking at file 36 out of 39 total files.

>> **Wi-Fi/Bluetooth indicators:** Which of these indicators appears depends on the Wireless Communication settings available through Setup Menu 1. The Appendix provides more detail about these features and what each symbol means.

>> **Rating:** If you rated the photo, a topic covered in Chapter 10, you can see how many stars you assigned it.

>> **Protected:** The key icon appears if you used the Protect feature to prevent your photo from being erased when you use the normal picture-deleting feature. You can find out how to protect photos in the next chapter.

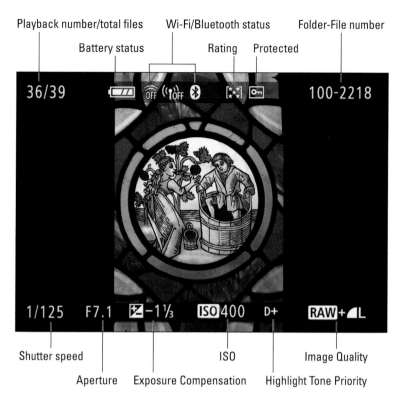

Playback number/total files   Wi-Fi/Bluetooth status   Folder-File number

Battery status   Rating   Protected

36/39   100-2218

1/125   F7.1   ⊞−1⅓   ISO400   D+   RAW+◢L

FIGURE 9-15:
You can view basic exposure and file data in this display mode.

Shutter speed   ISO   Image Quality

Aperture   Exposure Compensation   Highlight Tone Priority

>> **Folder number and last four digits of file number:** See Chapter 1 for information about how the camera assigns folder and file numbers. And visit Chapter 11 for details on how you can create custom folders.

>> **Exposure settings:** Along the bottom of the screen, you see the shutter speed, f-stop (aperture), and ISO setting. If you applied Exposure Compensation, the amount of the adjustment is displayed; if you enabled Highlight Tone Priority, a D+ symbol appears. You can read about all these exposure features in Chapter 4.

>> **Image Quality:** Chapter 2 explains this setting, which determines the file type and resolution of the picture. In the figure, the symbols indicate that the Raw+JPEG Large/Fine setting was selected. (The *L* stands for *Large;* the smooth arc before it represents the Fine JPEG compression setting.)

Shooting Information display mode

From Basic Information display, press the Info button to shift to Shooting Information display mode, featured in Figure 9-16. This display provides detailed shooting data plus charts called *histograms,* which are graphics related to image exposure and color. You can get schooled in the art of reading histograms in the next section.

How much data you see depends on the exposure mode you used to take the picture. Figure 9-16 shows the data dump that occurs when you shoot in the advanced exposure modes (P, Tv, Av, and M), which enable you to control all the settings indicated on the playback screen. When you shoot in the other exposure modes, you get a less detailed playback screen.

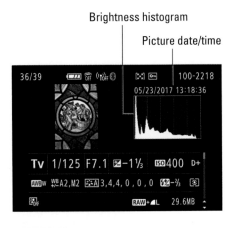

FIGURE 9-16:
The first screen of the Shooting Information display offers this feedback.

We're going to go out on a limb here and assume that if you're interested in the level of detail provided by the Shooting Information display, you *are* shooting in the advanced exposure modes. So, the rest of this section concentrates on the data screens related to shots taken in those modes.

REMEMBER

The first thing to know is that what you see in Figure 9-16 is just the tip of the iceberg. Notice the scroll bar near the lower-right edge of the screen? If you press the up or down Quick Control keys or drag up or down on the touchscreen, the lower half of the display scrolls to reveal several additional pages of information. Well, okay, half pages of information. The top half of the display remains constant when you scroll.

The following list explains what each part of the display reveals. Again, the figures show all possible settings for illustration purposes only. They don't show the settings used to capture the example image, and you're not likely to take a picture that takes advantage of all the features indicated in the figure, either. Again, some values appear only if you enabled a particular feature; otherwise, that area of the screen is empty.

>> **Top half of the display (appears on all pages):**

- *Basic Information*: The top row of the screen contains the same information as the top of the Basic Information display, shown in Figure 9-15.

- *Thumbnail highlight alerts (blinkies):* If you look closely at the thumbnail for images that contain very bright areas, you may notice that those areas blink on and off. Known in the biz as "the blinkies," those flickering spots indicate pixels that are absolute white. A large area of blinkies may indicate a loss of detail in the brightest portions of the scene, which happens when areas that should include a range of very light to white pixels instead contain only full-on white.

However, if your subject is exposed properly and the blinkies exist only in the background or some other insignificant area, don't give the issue too much thought. The important thing is whether you're happy with the subject's exposure.

- *Date and time:* This information indicates when you took the picture or recorded the movie. If the information isn't accurate, head for Setup Menu 2 and adjust the camera's clock via the Date/Time setting. (This change affects only new pictures you shoot; your existing photos still bear the old date/time information.)

- *Brightness histogram:* This chart provides another exposure-evaluation tool. If you're new to histograms, upcoming sections explain how to interpret what you see.

>> **Detail pages:** Again, the bottom half of the display is a scrollable list of picture data. Figures 9-17 through 9-19 break up the pages for easier digestion.

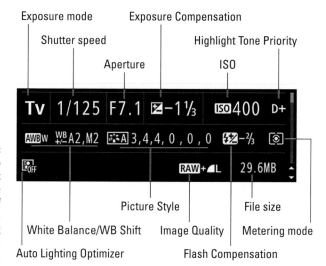

FIGURE 9-17:
Here's a map to the data that appears on the bottom half of the first screen of the Shooting Information display.

Here's a bit of information to help you interpret the data shown in the figures:

>> **Exposure settings:** Check out Chapter 4 for help with the exposure-related data that fills the first row of the readout shown in Figure 9-17. The same chapter also covers the metering mode setting, which got shoved down one floor, to the right end of the second row.

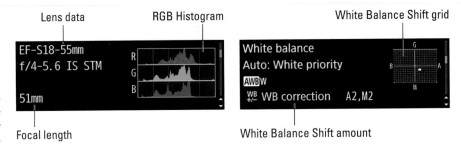

FIGURE 9-18:
The second page has lens details and an RGB histogram (left); the third page concentrates on White Balance settings (right).

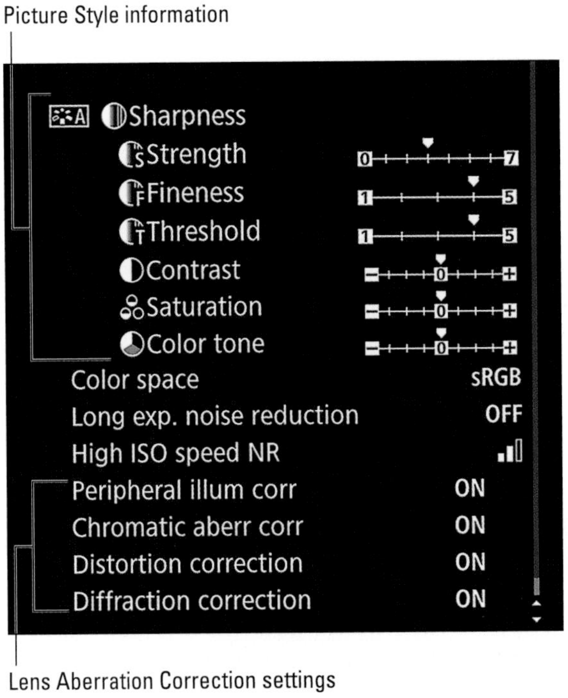

Lens data   RGB Histogram   White Balance Shift grid

Focal length   White Balance Shift amount

Picture Style information

FIGURE 9-19:
Keep scrolling to see these additional settings, which are spread over multiple pages in real life.

Lens Aberration Correction settings

>> **Flash information:** The Flash Compensation value shown in Figure 9-17 appears only if you adjusted the flash power, as discussed in Chapter 2. Otherwise, a lightning bolt appears to show that you used flash. But wait, there's more: If you set the High ISO Speed NR (Noise Reduction) option to Multi Shot, the flash slot in the display is replaced by an NR symbol. (In Julie's classes, nine out of ten students vote this setup the most ridiculously complex of all the Canon data displays. Student number 10 sleeps through this part of the lecture.)

>> **White Balance information:** For whatever reason, information about the White Balance setting appears both on the first page of data (refer to Figure 9-17) and on the third page (shown on the right in Figure 9-18). The only difference is that

the second of the two includes a color grid that makes it easier to see how much and what type of White Balance Shift is in force, if any. In both cases, you see a small *W* next to the AWB (Auto White Balance) symbol if you change the AWB Priority setting from the default, Ambience Priority, to White Priority.

Chapter 6 explains White Balance, as well as other color-related settings.

» **Picture Style data:** This feature, too, gets double billing in the display. The first page (Figure 9-17) shows you the symbol representing the Picture Style (*A*, for *Auto,* in the figure) and numbers indicating the strength at which various characteristics applied by the style are added to the image. Scroll to the page shown in Figure 9-19 to get a detailed look at those characteristics. Chapter 6 also covers Picture Styles.

» **Lens data and focal length:** The left side of the first screen shown in Figure 9-18 provides some specifications about the lens used to take the picture. In the figure, *EF-S* stands for the type of Canon lens, and 18–55mm is the lens focal-length range. On the next row, the values tell you the maximum aperture of the lens at its shortest and longest focal lengths; you see both values only for zoom lenses. (Otherwise, you see just a single maximum aperture value.) The letters *IS* indicate that the lens offers Image Stabilization; and *STM* stands for Canon's Stepping Motor autofocusing technology. You can read about these lens issues in Chapter 1.

REMEMBER

A more important number to note than the lens specifications, though, is the focal length used to take the picture — 51mm, in the figure. As Chapter 5 explains, focal length contributes to *depth of field,* or the distance over which focus appears acceptably sharp. Don't forget that focal lengths are presented in terms of 35mm equivalents; see Chapter 1 for help understanding that issue.

» **RGB histogram:** By default, the Brightness histogram remains displayed at the top of the screen at all times and you must scroll to the screen shown on the left in Figure 9-18 to view the RGB histogram. If you prefer things the other way around, open Playback Menu 3 and set the Histogram Disp option to RGB. The next sections explain what you can learn from both types of histograms.

» **Color Space:** You can record pictures in either of two color spaces, sRGB or Adobe RGB. Stick with the default, sRGB, until you consider the issues involved with making the change to Adobe RGB, which are covered with other color issues in Chapter 6.

» **Long Exposure Noise Reduction and High ISO Speed NR:** These options, also shown in Figure 9-19, indicate whether the camera applied tools designed to deal with *noise,* a defect that gives your image a grainy look. See Chapter 4 for details.

>> **Lens Aberration Correction settings:** The final four lines of information in Figure 9-19 relate to corrections the camera can apply to compensate for specific defects that can occur with some lenses. You access all four options through the Lens Aberration Correction option on Shooting Menu 1. However, that option is available only when the camera is set to the P, Tv, Av, or M exposure mode. See Chapter 4 for help with Peripheral Illumination and Chapter 5 for information on Diffraction correction; visit Chapter 6 for details about Chromatic Aberration and Distortion correction.

Understanding histograms

In Shooting Information display mode, you can view two types of histograms — a brightness histogram and an RGB histogram. The next sections explain how to understand what each reveals about your image.

Interpreting a brightness histogram

REMEMBER

One of the most difficult problems to correct in a photo editing program is known as *blown highlights* or *clipped highlights.* Both terms mean that the brightest areas of the image are so overexposed that they appear as a blob of solid white, with none of the details that you'd see if the area were rendered using a range of brightness values.

In Shooting Information display mode, areas that fall into this category blink in the image thumbnail. The *Brightness histogram,* shown at the top of the Shooting Information display by default, offers another analysis of image exposure. This graph, featured in Figure 9-20, indicates the distribution of shadows, highlights, and *midtones* (areas of medium brightness) in an image. Photographers use the term *tonal range* to describe this aspect of their pictures.

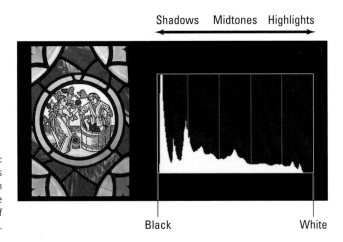

FIGURE 9-20:
A Brightness histogram indicates the tonal range of an image.

The horizontal axis of the graph represents the range of 256 possible brightness values, from black (a brightness value of 0) to white (255). And the vertical axis shows you how many pixels fall at a particular brightness value. A spike indicates a heavy concentration of pixels. For example, in Figure 9-20, which shows the histogram for the stained-glass image, the histogram indicates a broad range of brightness values but with very few at the very brightest end of the spectrum.

Keep in mind that there is no "perfect" histogram that you should try to duplicate. Instead, interpret the histogram with respect to the amount of shadows, highlights, and midtones that make up your subject.

TIP

Also, when you're shooting a subject that contains important highlight details, such as the light grays in the center of the stained-glass window, a histogram that shows a thin population of pixels at the bright end of the scale, as in the figure, is actually a good thing. If you increase exposure to shift more pixels to the right, you can very easily lose those subtle highlight details.

Reading an RGB histogram

Along with a Brightness histogram, the Shooting Information display provides an RGB histogram like the one shown in Figure 9-21. You need to scroll the display to get to the page that contains this graphic, shown in its entirety on the left in Figure 9-18.

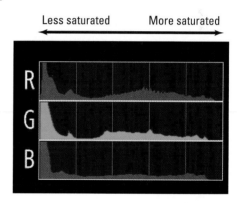

FIGURE 9-21:
The RGB histogram can indicate problems with color saturation.

To make sense of an RGB histogram, you need to know that digital images are known as *RGB images* because they're created from three primary colors of light: red, green, and blue. In the image file, the brightness values for those colors are contained in three separate vats of color data, known as *color channels*. Whereas the Brightness histogram reflects the brightness of all three color channels rolled into one, RGB histograms let you view the value for each individual channel.

When you look at the brightness data for a single channel, though, you glean information about color saturation rather than image brightness. This book doesn't have enough pages to provide a full lesson in RGB color theory, but the short story is that when you mix red, green, and blue light, and each component is at maximum brightness, you create white. Zero brightness in all three channels creates black. If you have maximum red and no blue or green, though, you have fully saturated red. If you mix two channels at maximum brightness, you also create full saturation; for example, maximum red and maximum blue produce fully saturated magenta. And, wherever colors are fully saturated, you can lose picture detail: Imagine a rose petal that should have a range of tones from medium to dark red appearing instead as an expanse of solid, fully saturated red.

The upshot is that if all the pixels for one or two channels are slammed to the right end of the histogram, you may be losing picture detail because of overly saturated colors. If all three channels show a heavy pixel population at the right end of the histograms, you may have blown highlights — again, because the maximum levels of red, green, and blue create white. Either way, you may want to adjust the exposure settings and try again.

A savvy RGB-histogram reader can also spot color balance issues by looking at the pixel values. But frankly, color balance problems are fairly easy to notice just by looking at the image on the camera monitor.

TIP

If you're a fan of RGB histograms, remember that you can swap the standard Brightness histogram that always appears near the top of the Shooting Information playback display with the RGB histogram. Just set the Histogram option on Playback Menu 3 to RGB instead of Brightness.

Taking Advantage of Image Search

TIP

Your camera's Image Search function enables you to quickly find pictures and movies that fall into certain categories, such as all files recorded on a particular date. After you set the search criteria, only files that meet the search conditions appear during playback. You also can use the search function to easily select a group of photos prior to performing certain file operations, such as assigning a rating or including the files in a slide show.

To set the search criteria, open Playback Menu 2 and select Set Image Search Conditions, as shown on the left in Figure 9-22. Or, when the camera is in Playback mode, press the Q button to display the Quick Control screen and then select the binoculars symbol — representing the search function — as shown on the right in the figure. After the symbol is selected, press the Set button or tap the Set icon at the bottom of the Quick Control screen.

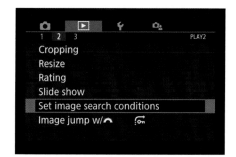

FIGURE 9-22:
You can set up a search from Playback Menu 2 (left) or, during playback, from the Quick Control screen (right).

Whichever route you go, you see the setup screen shown in Figure 9-23. Here, you specify what criteria images or movies need to meet to be included in the search results. The following list offers details:

Name of currently selected search option

Selected setting

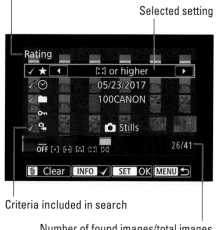

Criteria included in search

Number of found images/total images

» **You get a choice of five search conditions.** The five options work as follows:

- *Rating:* After you assign ratings (see Chapter 10), you can tell the camera to search for files that carry a particular rating, all files that carry any rating, or files that have not been rated.

- *Date:* Use this filter to search for all movies or photos taken on a specific day.

FIGURE 9-23:
You can turn on as many as five search criteria; be sure to press or tap Set before exiting the setup screen.

- *Folder:* If your memory card contains multiple image folders, choose this option to limit the search to a specific folder. By default, the camera sets up just one folder, named 100Canon.

- *Protected:* Choose this option to narrow the search to files that you protected by using the Protect Images feature (see Chapter 10).

- *Type of file:* Using this option, you can search for all stills, all movies, or stills that were taken using a specific Image Quality setting, such as Raw. Chapter 2 explains Image Quality settings.

When you highlight an option, its name appears in the upper-left corner of the screen. It's easy to miss amid all the other stuff on the screen.

>> **To enable a search condition, highlight it and then tap the Info icon or press the Info button.** A check mark appears next to the search condition, as shown in Figure 9-23. Press or tap Info again to toggle the check mark off and remove the condition from the search.

Use the Quick Control dial or press the up/down Quick Control keys to highlight a search option. You can also tap the option to highlight it.

>> **After selecting a search option, press the left/right Quick Control keys or tap the left/right arrows to cycle through the option settings.** For example, in Figure 9-23, the Rating option is set up to include only pictures that have a rating of four stars or above. At the bottom of the screen, symbols appear to represent the various settings. The symbol for the selected setting is shown in blue.

>> **Each time you turn on or change a search filter, the camera indicates how many files meet the current criteria.** Look for this value in the lower-right corner of the display. The number of files that meet the criteria is shown in blue; the total number of files on the card (or in the current image folder) appears in white. So, in Figure 9-23, 26 out of 41 files meet the search criteria. (The camera also displays thumbnails of the images that made the cut, but the thumbnails are so faint in the display that they're not much help.)

>> **You can enable as many search filters as you want.** However, in some cases, selecting one condition automatically disables another. Suppose that you select the Protected option and then set the Type of File to Movies only. If you haven't protected any movies, the camera clears the check mark from the Protected filter.

>> **After setting up the search parameters, press the Set button or tap the Set icon at the bottom of the screen.** You then see a confirmation screen; select OK. If the OK option is dimmed or nothing happens when you press Set, the camera didn't find any files that met all the search criteria.

>> **To view files that met the search criteria, put the camera in Playback mode.** In the display, a bright yellow frame appears around the perimeter of the monitor screen to tell you that the search function is active. In Index view, one thumbnail is also selected, which is indicated by an orange box, as shown in Figure 9-24. You see the yellow search box even in single-image view, however.

>> **Until you cancel the search, certain file operations affect all "found images" — the ones that met your search criteria.** For example, suppose that you ask the camera to find all images with a rating of four or five stars.

After the search is completed, you can protect all of them by selecting Protect Images from Playback Menu 1 or by choosing the Protect icon on the Quick Control screen.

Along with protecting files, you can perform the following *batch processes* (that's geek speak for doing something to a group of selected files): rating files, erasing files, adding files to a photobook setup or print order, and including files in a slide show.

When an operation presents a screen asking you which files you want to affect, choose the setting named All Found Images.

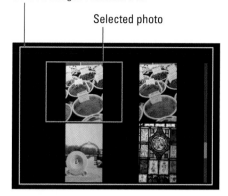

Search Images reminder box

Selected photo

FIGURE 9-24:
The yellow frame reminds you that you're viewing photos turned up by a search; in Index view, the orange box surrounds the selected photo.

>> **The search is cancelled when you turn off the camera or it goes to sleep at the time specified by the Auto Power Off setting.** If the Auto Power Off setting (Setup Menu 2) is 4 minutes or less, however, the camera tacks on extra time, giving you six minutes before putting the camera to sleep. You may want to extend the Auto Power Off delay to give yourself a little more time to get things done before the search is cancelled.

>> **Several other actions also cancel the search.** Taking a picture or recording a movie cancels the search, as does formatting the memory card or creating an edited copy of a photo.

>> **To manually exit the search, reopen the Search setup box and then tap the Clear icon or press the Erase button.** You can see the icon at the bottom of the screen in Figure 9-23 (look in the lower-left corner).

REMEMBER

You then need to press the Set button or tap the Set icon to officially call off the search. A message "Image search cancelled" appears briefly to let you know that the camera did as you asked.

For details on erasing, rating, and protecting photos, see the next chapter. Chapter 11 explains how to set up a slide show and also covers the photo book and print order options.

Viewing Photos and Movies on a TV

Your camera is equipped with a feature that allows you to play your pictures and movies on an HDTV screen. However, you need to purchase an HDMI cable to connect the camera and TV; the Canon part number is HTC-100.

REMEMBER

Before connecting the two devices, make sure that the Video System option on Setup Menu 3 is set to the video standard used in the region in which you're screening your work. In the United States, NTSC is the standard; in many European countries, PAL is required. (The correct setting should've been set at the factory, but if you purchased your camera in another country, you may need to change the setting.)

HDMI port

FIGURE 9-25:
Plug the small end of the cable into the HDMI-out port.

With that bit of business out of the way, turn the camera off and connect the smaller end of the HDMI cable to the HDMI port, found under the cover on the left side of the camera. You can see the port in Figure 9-25. Then check your TV instruction guide to locate the HDMI terminal on the TV where you should connect your camera. You also need to consult the instructions to find out which channel or input source to select for playback of signals from auxiliary devices. After you sort out those issues, turn on your camera to send the signal to the TV.

Here are a few TV-playback pointers to close out this chapter:

TIP

» **Using the touchscreen:** When you plug your camera into a TV, the camera monitor goes dark, but some touchscreen operations are still operational. It's a little weird because you have to use the TV screen as a visual reference, but you can scroll the display from one picture to the next or, in Index mode, from one page of thumbnails to the next. In single-image view, you also can pinch in and out on the monitor to change the image magnification.

» **Controlling playback with the TV remote control:** If your TV offers HDMI CEC technology and you have a CEC-enabled remote control for that set, you may be able to use the remote to perform certain playback operations.

This feature, too, requires a little pre-connection camera setup. Open Playback Menu 3 and set the Ctrl over HDMI option to Enable. Turn the camera off, connect it to the TV, and turn the camera on again. Then press the Playback button on the camera to display your first image or movie on the TV. Press the left and right directional buttons on the remote to scroll to a different picture or movie. With some remote controls, pressing the Enter button displays a menu of playback options.

» **Controlling playback using camera buttons:** Even some CEC-enabled sets and remotes balk at performing camera-playback functions. If you can't get it to work or your TV doesn't offer CEC functions, control playback using the same camera buttons you normally do to view pictures and movies on the camera monitor.

There's one exception: If you're playing a movie or slide show with background music, you can adjust the volume only via your TV's audio controls.

Chapter **10**

Working with Picture and Movie Files

E very creative pursuit involves its share of cleanup and organizational tasks. Painters have to wash brushes, embroiderers have to separate strands of floss, and woodcrafters have to haul out the wet/dry vac to suck up sawdust. Digital photography is no different: At some point, you have to stop shooting so that you can download and process your files.

This chapter focuses on these after-the-shot tasks. First up is a review of several in-camera file-management operations: deleting unwanted files, protecting your best work from accidental erasure, rating files, and cropping photos. Following that, you can get help with transferring files to your computer, processing files that you shot in the Raw (CR2) format, and preparing images for online sharing.

For help with transferring pictures wirelessly to a smartphone or tablet, see the appendix. This chapter deals only with sending pictures to a computer.

REMEMBER

Deleting Files

When you spot clunkers during your picture and movie review, use the Erase button or Erase Images function on Playback Menu 1 to get rid of them.

REMEMBER

Be aware, though, that you can't use either option to delete files that you protected by using the feature discussed in the next section. Follow the steps laid out there to unlock any files you want to erase.

The following list explains options for erasing a single file, a group of files, or all files — again, with the exception of protected files.

>> **Erasing images one at a time:** Display the photo in single-image view or select it in Index view. Then press the Erase button, labeled in Figure 10-1. The words *Cancel* and *Erase* appear at the bottom of the screen. To zap that file into digital oblivion, tap Erase or press the right Quick Control key to highlight Erase and then press the Set button.

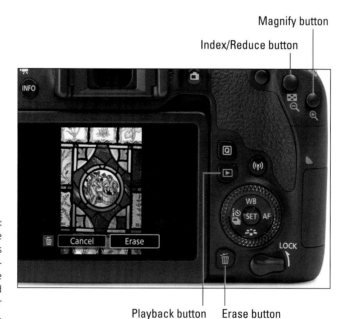

FIGURE 10-1:
During picture playback, press the Erase button to delete the displayed image or movie.

Magnify button

Index/Reduce button

Playback button   Erase button

>> **Erasing all images:** To erase all files, head for Playback Menu 1. Choose Erase Images, as shown on the left in Figure 10-2, and then choose All Images on Card, as shown on the right. On the confirmation screen that appears, choose OK.

FIGURE 10-2:
Choose these
Playback Menu
1 options to
quickly delete
all unprotected
files.

TIP

>> **Erasing all images in a selected folder:** If your card contains more than one folder, you can limit the image dump to a specific folder. Instead of selecting All Images on Card from the screen shown on the right in Figure 10-2, choose All Images in Folder. Choose the folder you want to empty and then tap the Set symbol or press the Set button.

>> **Erasing a batch of selected files:** After choosing Erase Images from Playback Menu 1, choose Select and Erase Images, as shown on the left in Figure 10-3. If the camera is set to single-image Playback mode, you see the current image in the monitor. At the top of the screen, a check box appears, as shown on the right.

Selected for erasing

Number of selected images

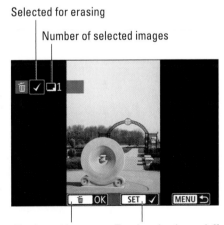

FIGURE 10-3:
Tag a file as
ready for
the trash by
tapping the
Set symbol or
pressing the
Set button.

Erase all selected images   Toggle selection on/off

To the right of the check box is a number showing you how many files are currently tagged for erasure. To tag the current file, tap the check box, tap the Set icon at the bottom of the screen, or press the Set button. A check mark then appears in the box, and the picture is officially marked for erasure. If you change your mind, use the same techniques to remove the check mark.

To tag more files, use the normal playback techniques to scroll through your pictures, adding the check mark to all the files you want to trash.

A couple of tips on using this option:

- To take a closer look at the current image, press the Magnify button or pinch outward on the touchscreen. The display zooms just as it does when you perform those actions during regular playback.

  To exit the magnified view, tap the exit arrow (near the upper-right corner of the screen) or press the Index/Reduce button (refer to Figure 10-1).

- If you don't need to inspect each image closely, you can display up to three thumbnails per screen. Just press the Index/Reduce button to shift the three-thumbnail display. Use the same methods to tag images for erasure and to scroll through files as you do when viewing them one at a time. To return to full-frame view, press the Magnify button or pinch outward on the touchscreen.

When you finish selecting images, press the Erase button or tap the Erase symbol on the touchscreen (refer to the right screen in Figure 10-3). You see a confirmation screen asking whether you really want to get rid of the selected images; if you're ready to take the leap, choose OK.

>> **Selecting a range of files:** Here's an even faster way to select a group of consecutive files: After selecting Erase Images from Playback Menu 1, choose Select Range to display the screen shown on the left in Figure 10-4. Then move the blue box over the first image you want to delete (tap the thumbnail or highlight it with the Quick Control dial or Quick Control keys) and either tap the Set First Img symbol or press the Set button. The symbol then changes to read Set Last Img (not shown in the figure).

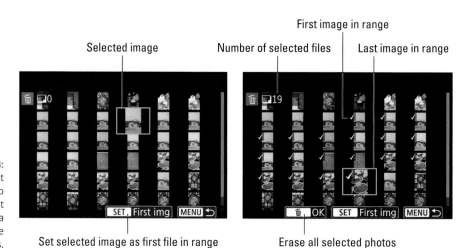

FIGURE 10-4: Use Select Range to quickly select and delete a consecutive series of files.

First image in range

Selected image   Number of selected files   Last image in range

Set selected image as first file in range   Erase all selected photos

Next, move the blue box over the last file in the group using the Quick Control dial or Quick Control keys (you can also tap the last image) and tap Set Last Img or press the Set button. The camera immediately selects the first and last files and all files in between, as shown on the right in the figure. If you're satisfied that all the files you want to delete are selected, tap the trash can symbol in the lower-left corner of the screen or press the Erase button. A confirmation screen appears; choose OK.

>> **Erasing files found by the Image Search function.** By using the Image Search function explained near the end of Chapter 9, you can tell the camera to locate all files that meet certain parameters — date shot, type of file, assigned rating, and so on. After completing the search, choose Erase Images from Playback Menu 1, as shown on the left in Figure 10-5, which displays a different set of options than normal, as shown on the right in the figure. Choose All Found Images to delete just the files turned up by the search.

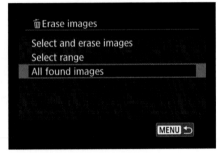

FIGURE 10-5: When the Image Search function is active, choose All Found Images to erase files that met the search criteria.

Protecting Photos and Movies

You can protect pictures and movies from accidental erasure by giving them protected status. After you take this step, the camera doesn't allow you to delete the file from your memory card by using the erase options outlined in the preceding section. (The only way to wipe a protected file off a memory card is to use the Format Card command, found on Setup Menu 1.)

Additionally, when you download protected files to your computer, they show up as *read-only* files, which means that you can't overwrite the originals. If you edit a protected photo using Digital Photo Professional 4, things proceed normally until you try to save the file. When this happens, you're warned that it's read-only and told that you can't overwrite the original. Simply save the file with a new name or unprotect the file using your operating system. This practice ensures that your original remains intact.

When you're ready to protect a file or group of files, use these techniques:

>> **Quick Control screen:** Put the camera in Playback mode, display the photo in single-image view, and then press the Q button to display the Quick Control screen, as shown in Figure 10-6. Select the Protect Images symbol, labeled in the figure, and choose Enable. A key symbol appears at the top of the frame, as shown in the figure, indicating that the file is now locked (protected). To remove the protected status, choose Disable.

Protect Images option   Protected symbol

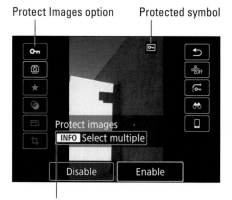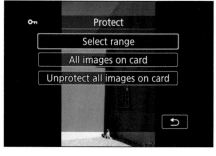

Tap to display menu options

FIGURE 10-6: During play-back, use the Quick Control screen to protect the current file.

To protect a batch of images, tap the Info symbol or press the Info button. The screen shown on the right in the figure appears, enabling you to select a range of files, protect all files on the memory card, or remove protection from all locked files. (See the preceding section for help selecting a range of files.)

>> **Playback Menu 1:** The Protect Images option on Playback Menu 1, shown on the left in Figure 10-7, provides a bit more flexibility in selecting the files you want to protect. You get the options shown on the right in the figure, which work as follows:

FIGURE 10-7: You can access a few additional options for selecting files to protect if you choose Protect Images from Playback Menu 1.

- *Select Images:* Choose this option to protect specific photos or movies. Select a thumbnail and then tap the Set icon or press the Set button to lock the file. A key appears to indicate the locked status. To remove protection, tap the Set icon or press Set to make the key disappear. Scroll the display in the usual playback fashion to reach the next file you want to protect and then lather, rinse, and repeat.

- *Select Range:* Choose this option to protect a range of photos or movies. You select the range of shots just as if you were deleting or rating them.

- *All Images in Folder:* If your memory card contains multiple folders, choose this option to select all images in a specific folder.

- *Unprotect All Images in Folder:* Use this option to unlock all protected images in the folder you select.

- *All Images on Card:* This option does just what it says: locks all images on the card.

- *Unprotect All Images on Card:* Select this option to unlock all pictures and movies on the card.

Whichever option you choose, the last step is to tap the Menu symbol or press the Menu button to exit the protection screens.

REMEMBER

If the Image Search function is in force, only files that met the search criteria — also known as *found images* in Canon lingo — show up during playback, and you get a different selection of protection options. Instead of the Quick Control options shown on the right in Figure 10-6, your options are Select Range, All Found Images, or Unprotect All Found Images. Go through Playback Menu 1, and you get Select Images, Select Range, All Found Images, and Unprotect All Found. Select Range and Select Images enable you to lock specific files turned up by the search function; the last two protect or unprotect all those files. See Chapter 9 for help setting up a search. (Remember that a yellow box around the perimeter of the screen indicates that only files turned up by the most recent search are accessible.)

Rating Photos and Movies

TIP

Using your camera's Rating feature, you can assign a rating to a picture or movie file: five stars for your best work, one star for those you really dislike, and so on.

What's the point, you ask? Well, rating pictures has several benefits. First, when you create a slide show, as outlined in Chapter 11, you can tell the camera to display only photos or movies that have a certain rating. Using the Image Search function, introduced in Chapter 9, you can enjoy the same ratings-based filtering to limit the files that are displayed during regular playback and, thus, are available for such playback functions as protecting and deleting.

Some photo programs, including Canon Digital Photo Professional 4, covered later in this chapter, can read the ratings as well. So, after you download files to your computer, you can sort files by rating, making it easier to cull your photo and movie collection and gather your best work for printing and sharing.

Assign a rating as follows:

» **Quick Control screen:** Put the camera in Playback mode and then press the Q button to display the playback version of the Quick Control screen. Select the Rating option, as shown on the left in Figure 10-8, and then select the rating you want to use from the bottom of the screen.

Tap to assign same rating to multiple files

Rating option   Current rating

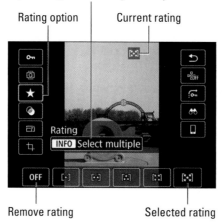

FIGURE 10-8:
You can rate
photos via the
Quick Control
screen.

Remove rating   Selected rating

To assign the same rating to a batch of files, first choose the number of stars you want to award. Then press the Info button or tap the Info symbol. You then see the options shown on the right in the figure. You have the choice of selecting a range of continuous pictures (the process works the same way as outlined in the first section of the chapter) or applying the rating to all files on the card.

» **Playback Menu 2:** After choosing Rating, as shown on the left in Figure 10-9, select one of the four options shown on the right. These all work the same as for the Erase Images option, explained at the beginning of the chapter, except that you're assigning a particular rating instead of tagging pictures for erasing.

FIGURE 10-9:
The Rating
feature on
Playback Menu
2 offers a few
more options
for selecting
the photos to
rate.

TIP

The one thing that may trip you up is the Select Images option, which initially shows the screen shown on the left in Figure 10-10. The symbols seem to indicate that you press the up or down Quick Control keys to change the rating, but that doesn't produce any results. Instead, you must tap the Set icon or press the Set button to get to the screen shown on the right in the figure. Now you can set the rating by tapping the up/down symbols at the bottom of the screen, pressing the up/down Quick Control keys, or using the Quick Control dial.

Number of existing files with this rating

Selected rating

FIGURE 10-10:
After choos-
ing Select
Images, tap Set
(left), tap the
up or down
arrows (right)
to change the
rating, and
then tap the
Menu symbol
or press the
Menu button.

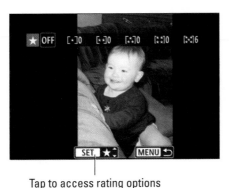
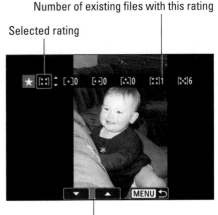

Tap to access rating options

Tap to raise/lower rating

Notice that at the top of both screens in Figure 10-10, a value appears to the right of each rating. The number indicates how many files on the memory card have been assigned that rating. For example, the right screen of Figure 10-10 shows a four-star rating being assigned. The number 1 next to the four-star icon shows that the image is the first to be awarded that grade level. Six other pictures on the card have a five-star rating; no pictures have been assigned any of the other ratings.

After you set the rating, tap the Menu symbol or press the Menu button.

CHAPTER 10 **Working with Picture and Movie Files**   279

REMEMBER

Whether you rate photos from the Quick Control screen or Playback Menu 2, your choices for selecting files to rate change if an Image Search filter is in effect. The All Images in Folder and All Images on Card options disappear, and instead you get the option to rate found images — again, that's the term for images that met the criteria of your search. Chapter 9 offers the complete story on the search feature, if it's new to you.

Cropping Photos

When a picture includes extraneous background, you can eliminate the excess by using the in-camera crop tool. This feature saves your cropped photo as a new file, leaving the original intact.

A few points to consider before you try out the crop tool:

» **Cropping is off limits for Raw files.** Only JPEG photo files can be cropped. See Chapter 2 for help understanding the difference between Raw and JPEG.

» **You can't apply the crop tool to an already cropped copy.** You can, however, start with the original and create a second cropped copy using different crop settings.

» **Your cropped image is saved as a JPEG file.** The cropped copy uses that same JPEG compression setting (Fine or Normal) as the original.

» **You can't perform certain other file operations on a cropped image.** You can't use the Resize option, which eliminates pixels throughout the image to reduce file size. Nor can you apply a Creative Filter to a cropped photo. In other words, crop *after* you do those things.

» **Some file information is stripped from the cropped copy.** Any focus-point information stored with the original file doesn't carry over to the cropped copy, so you can't display the point during playback. (Chapter 9 explains that option.) If you take advantage of the Dust Delete Data function, which provides a map for Canon Digital Photo Professional 4 to use when trying to remove sensor dust from an image, that data isn't included in the cropped file, either. See Chapter 11 for help with this dust-buster feature.

As with the other file operations discussed so far, you can get to the Crop feature in two ways:

» **Quick Control screen:** After putting the camera in Playback mode, display the picture you want to crop, press the Q button to display the Quick Control screen, and highlight the Crop option, as shown on the left in Figure 10-11. Tap the Crop Image option at the bottom of the screen or press the Set button to get to the cropping tools, detailed momentarily.

FIGURE 10-11: You can get to the cropping tool through the Quick Control screen (left) or Playback Menu 2 (right).

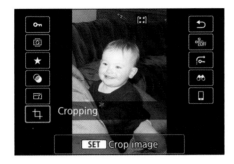

>> **Playback Menu 2:** Choose Cropping, as shown on the right in Figure 10-11. On the next screen, which shows a single image, use the standard methods to scroll to the photo that you want to crop. Then tap the Set symbol at the bottom of the screen or press the Set button.

Either way, your photo appears in a window that contains the controls labeled in Figure 10-12. If you took the photo in landscape orientation, the screen displays the photo normally. If you took the photo holding the camera vertically, the photo isn't rotated and instead appears sideways, as shown in the figure. (This issue isn't affected by the auto-rotation options discussed in Chapter 9.)

Your next step is to adjust the crop frame so that it contains the area of the photo that you want to retain. Here's how:

>> **Set the aspect ratio and frame orientation (vertical or horizontal).** Rotate the Quick Control dial.

Change aspect ratio/orientation

Crop and save as new file

Correct tilt | Display preview

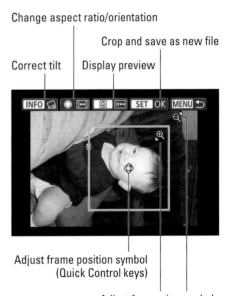

Adjust frame position symbol (Quick Control keys)

Adjust frame size symbols (Magnify and Index/Reduce buttons)

FIGURE 10-12:
Use these controls to set the size, angle, orientation, and aspect ratio of the cropped photo. Vertical photos are not rotated; they're displayed sideways.

You can choose an aspect ratio of 3:2, 16:9, 4:3, or 1:1, and you can set the frame to a landscape or portrait orientation.

>> **Reposition the crop frame.** Use the Quick Control keys or drag on the touchscreen.

>> **Change the size of the frame.** To shrink the frame, press the Index/Reduce button or, if the touchscreen is enabled, pinch inward on the display. Remember that the smaller the frame, the more original image pixels you're trimming away, and the remaining pixel count will determine how large you can print the cropped photo. See Chapter 2 to understand more about how the pixel count, or resolution, affects your print possibilities.

To enlarge the frame, press the Magnify button or pinch outward on the touchscreen.

>> **Correct a tilting horizon line.** This part of the cropping feature really should have its own menu slot because it does more than just trim off excess background: It rotates the image within the crop frame, which enables you to straighten a tilting horizon line. Figure 10-13 offers an illustration.

TIP

To get started, press the Info button or tap the Info symbol found in the upper-left corner of the initial cropping screen. An alignment grid appears over your photo, and the Info symbol is replaced by the symbols shown in Figure 10-13. All other crop-adjustment tools are hidden.

Tap arrows or use Quick Control dial to rotate image within frame

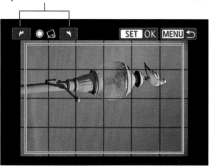
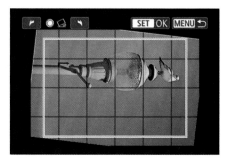

FIGURE 10-13:
Hidden among the cropping features is an option that enables you to correct a tilting horizon line.

Use the Quick Control dial to rotate the image by a tenth of a degree (this is nice, but a smidgen of rotation can be hard to spot); tap the arrow symbols in the upper-left corner of the screen to rotate the image in half-degree increments. You can adjust the angle up to 10 degrees in either direction. The preview updates to show you the rotated image.

Because the correction rotates part of your image off the invisible "canvas" on which it rests, you wind up with empty, black areas around the edges of the scene, as shown on the right in the figure. The camera automatically resizes the crop frame to exclude those areas. (After finishing the rotation, you can further adjust the frame size, position, and aspect ratio.) To apply the correction, tap the Set icon or press the Set button. You're returned to the initial crop screen, and all the other crop tools reappear.

>> **Preview the cropped image.** Tap the Q icon or press the Q button. You see the photo as it would look if cropped using the current settings. Press or tap Q again to return to the cropping screen.

>> **Create the cropped copy.** Tap the Set icon or press the Set button. The camera asks permission to save the cropped photo as a new file; answer in the affirmative to go forward. When the new file is created, the camera displays the filename and then redisplays the original photo.

In Playback mode, the symbols labeled in Figure 10-14 appear with the cropped image if you set the display to include either basic or detailed information. (Press the Info button to change the display.) The first symbol is a general "this image is an edited copy of an original" notation; the second symbol represents the crop function. (That symbol looks like the mechanical crop tools used for trimming photos in a traditional darkroom.)

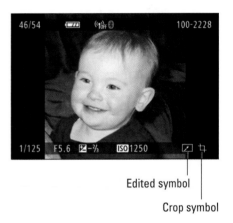

Edited symbol

Crop symbol

FIGURE 10-14:
You see these symbols during playback when you display a cropped photo.

Installing the Canon Software

For certain tasks covered in the rest of the chapter, including downloading photos and processing Raw photos, you can use the free software that Canon provides with your camera purchase. To download the latest versions of the software, head online to www.canon.com/icpd. You also can simply pull up the support pages for your camera. (In the United States, start at www.canonusa.com.) Either way, you must enter your camera's serial number, which appears on the label on the bottom of the camera, before the download will begin.

To perform file functions discussed in this chapter, you need the following programs:

>> **Canon Digital Photo Professional 4:** Enables you to view and organize photos, process Raw files, and create a low-resolution copy of a photo for online sharing

>> **Canon EOS Utility:** Required for downloading pictures directly from the camera to your computer, whether you connect the camera via a USB cable or through a Wi-Fi network

You can download and install the programs separately or download EOS Software Digital Solution Disk, which includes both programs plus the following:

>> **EOS Lens Registration Tool,** for adding lens data used by the camera's Lens Aberration Correction feature (available from Shooting Menu 1 when the camera is in the P, Tv, Av, or M exposure modes)

>> **EOS Web Service Registration Tool,** to create a free Canon Image Gateway account, which provides access to other web services like Facebook, Twitter, Flickr, and more

>> **EOS Sample Music,** for adding background music to a video snapshot or other recording

>> **Picture Style Editor,** which enables you to create custom Picture Styles (see Chapter 6)

WARNING

If you have older versions of the programs installed, update them to the latest releases. Otherwise, some functions may not work with your camera.

In addition to these computer-based programs, Canon also makes available a couple of apps for iOS and Android-based smartphones and tablets. Through the apps, you can connect your camera to your smart device in order to view photos, upload images to the web, and use your camera as a wireless remote control. Check the appendix of this book for information about these tools.

Sending Pictures to the Computer

When you're ready to download photos and movies to your computer, you have two options:

>> **Connect the camera to the computer via a USB cable or Wi-Fi network.**
For USB connection, you need to buy the necessary cable: Canon Interface Cable IFC-400PCU (about $12 from the Canon website). For Wi-Fi transfer, you must have access to the same wireless network that your computer uses.

>> **Use a memory-card reader.** With a card reader, you pop the memory card out of your camera and into the card reader instead of hooking the camera to the computer. Many computers and printers now have built-in card readers; you can also buy standalone readers for under $30.

The next two sections provide information about both options.

Downloading via Wi-Fi or USB

Before you can send files from the camera to the computer, whether over your computer's wireless network or by using a USB cable, you must first install Canon EOS Utility software. It's the only tool that enables the two devices to communicate.

Also make sure that your camera battery is fully charged before you begin the file-download process. If the battery runs out of power during the transfer, you can lose a photo or movie or two (or three or more). You may want to invest in the optional AC adapter to power the camera during transfers if you plan to use this download method frequently.

With those preliminaries out of the way, the next step is to connect the camera to the computer. How you accomplish that depends on whether you're going the wired or wireless route:

>> **USB connection:** Turn the camera off and then insert the small end of the cable into the port on the left side of the camera, shown in Figure 10-15. Then turn the camera on.

USB port

FIGURE 10-15:
Connect the USB cable to this port.

>> **Wi-Fi connection:** If you haven't yet set up your camera for wireless functions, flip to the appendix of this book to find out how to do so. For the purposes of file downloading, focus on the information related to joining your computer's Wi-Fi network — the rest of the appendix deals with connecting the camera to a smartphone or tablet. After you do the necessary setup work, you should be able to press the Wi-Fi button on the back of the camera to start the connection process.

For Wi-Fi transfer, the camera displays a message asking you to launch EOS Utility. If you're connecting via cable, the program may start automatically; if not, launch it the way you start any program on your computer. The initial program window looks like the one shown in Figure 10-16. (Figures show the Windows versions of software screens, but the Mac versions offer the same options, although the specific window design is slightly different.)

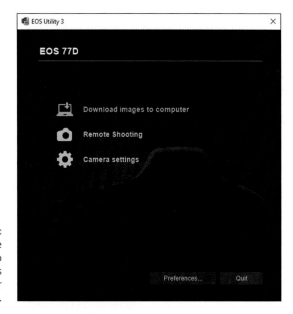

FIGURE 10-16: You must use EOS Utility to transfer files via Wi-Fi or USB cable.

With EOS Utility ready to go, follow these steps to set up and preform the file transfer:

1. **Click Download Images to Computer.**

   You see a screen offering two options: Start Automatic Download and Select and Download.

2. Click Select and Download.

The program displays a file browser window similar to the one in Figure 10-17, with thumbnails of images and movies on your memory card. Click the magnifying glass icons in the lower-right corner of the window to enlarge or reduce the thumbnail size.

Selection filters

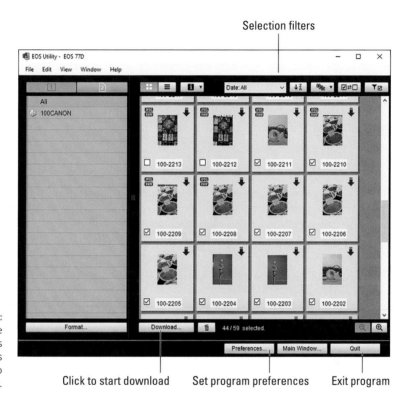

FIGURE 10-17:
Select the
thumbnails
of the files
you want to
transfer.

Click to start download   Set program preferences   Exit program

3. Select the files you want to copy to the computer.

Each thumbnail contains a check box in its lower-left corner. To select an image for downloading, click the box to put a check mark in it. To select multiple files, click the first image and then hold down the Ctrl key (Windows) or Cmd key (Mac) as you click each subsequent thumbnail.

TIP

At the top of the screen, in the area labeled "Selection filters," are tools that enable you to automatically select all images or to filter the list of selected images based on various criteria, such as an assigned image rating or the date you recorded the photo or movie.

4. **Click the Download button, labeled in Figure 10-17.**

   A screen appears that tells you where the program wants to store your downloaded pictures, as shown in Figure 10-18.

5. **Verify or change the storage location for your pictures.**

   If you want to put the pictures in a location different from the one the program suggests, click the Destination Folder button and then select the storage location and folder name you prefer.

6. **Click OK to begin the download.**

   A progress window appears, showing you the status of the download.

When the download is complete, disconnect your camera from the wireless network by choosing the Disconnect, Exit option from the menu screen displayed on the camera monitor. (You may need to press the Wi-Fi button to display the screen.) If the camera is connected via USB cable, turn the camera off and then remove the cable.

A couple of additional tips about this process:

>> **Setting download preferences:** While the camera is connected and turned on, click the Preferences button at the bottom of the browser window (refer to Figure 10-17) to open the Preferences dialog box, where you can specify many aspects of the transfer process.

>> **Auto-launching a photo program after download:** You can set things up so that after the download is complete, the computer automatically launches Canon Digital Photo Professional 4 or another image-editing program. Visit the Linked Software panel of the EOS Utility's Preferences dialog box to specify which software you want to use. Choose None to disable auto-launch altogether.

>> **Closing the EOS Utility:** The browser window doesn't close automatically after the download is complete. You must return to it and click the Quit button, labeled in Figure 10-17, to shut it down.

Downloading from a card reader

When you opt to use a card reader to transfer files, you can't use the automated download tool found in Canon EOS Utility. However, if you open Digital Photo Professional 4, you can use the old-fashioned drag-and-drop technique to move files from your memory card to a folder on your hard drive, as shown in Figure 10-19.

FIGURE 10-19: You can drag and drop files from your memory card to a drive on your computer using Canon Digital Photo Professional 4.

Memory card   Image folder

Your screen may not look exactly like the one you see in the figure; you can customize the window by using options on the View and Window menu. If you don't see the folder list, open the View menu, select Open/Close Pane, and then select Left. To change the thumbnails display, choose one of the Thumbnails options from the View menu.

In the folder list, the memory card appears with the label EOS Digital, as highlighted in the figure. To get to the files it holds, open the DCIM folder and then the image folder, named 100Canon by default. Then just select the files you want to copy and drag them to the destination folder.

TIP

After clicking on a thumbnail in Digital Photo Professional 4, you can display the image *metadata*, or hidden data that stores the settings you used to take the picture. Open the View menu and then choose Info to display the metadata, as shown in Figure 10-20. Many other photo programs can also display metadata, but Canon's own software provides the most detailed information.

Not so confident in your computer skills? Try out the built-in photo programs provided by the Windows and Mac operating systems — in the latest versions of those systems, both programs go by the name Photos. After opening the program, look for a menu option or toolbar button labeled *import*, which tells the program that you have new files to send to the computer. Through your computer's system preferences, you can also tell the computer to launch your favorite download program whenever you insert a memory card that contains images or movies. (Ask your neighborhood tech guru for help if you need it.)

FIGURE 10-20:
You can view image metadata by choosing Info from the View menu in Digital Photo Professional 4.

Converting Raw Images in Digital Photo Professional 4

Chapter 2 introduces you to the Raw file format, which enables you to capture images as raw data. The downside of Raw is that you can't have your photos printed at most retail outlets or share images online until you *process* them — which just means to convert them to a standard file format, such as JPEG. The upside is that if you use a capable Raw conversion tool, you can more precisely control image attributes such as color, exposure, and sharpness than you can when you capture images in the JPEG format.

Canon Digital Photo Professional 4 is not the only way to convert Raw images. If you already own a program that offers a good Raw converter, such as Adobe Photoshop or Adobe Lightroom, you can use that program to do your Raw processing. You may need to download updates that enable the software to deal with the Raw files from your camera. If you don't already have Photoshop or Lightroom, however, give Digital Photo Professional 4 a try. It's free, has good image-viewing tools, and enables you to edit and convert Raw photos from your Canon camera very nicely.

The following steps provide a brief overview of how to process a Raw file in Digital Photo Professional 4. For additional details on this feature, as well as other file-management and picture-editing tools, download the program manual from the Canon website.

1. **Open the program and locate the file you want to process.**

   You can customize the program window by using options on the View and Windows menus, but by default, you should see the Folder pane, which contains a list of folders on your hard drive, and thumbnail views of the images in that folder. In Figure 10-19, the Folder pane is on the left side of the window, with the thumbnails to the right.

2. **Click the thumbnail of the image you want to process and then click the Edit Image button.**

   By default, the button appears just above the Folder pane. If you don't see the button, you can open the View menu and choose Edit Image Window.

   Either way, your photo appears inside an editing window, as shown in Figure 10-21. Along the right side of the window is the Tool palette, which contains most controls for setting image colors, exposure, and so on. If you don't see the pane, open the View menu and choose Tool Palette.

Drag to scroll palette

Exit editing window   Click tabs to display more controls

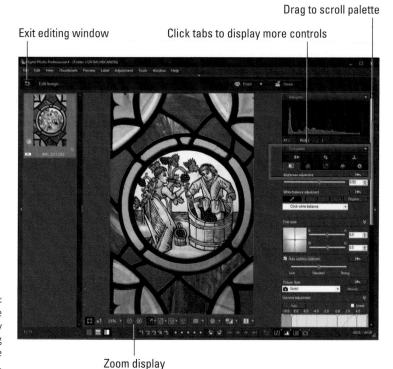

FIGURE 10-21:
Adjust the image by selecting options on the Tool palette.

Zoom display

3. **Adjust the image using controls in the Tool palette.**

The Tool palette offers multiple tabs, each offering its own assortment of adjustment tools. The tab shown in the figure is the Basic tab, which appears by default when you first open the window. To explore another tab, click its icon. The icons are near the top of the palette, in the area surrounded by the red box in the figure. You may need to drag the scroll bar, also labeled in the figure, to access all the options on a particular tab.

As you change the various settings, the preview updates to show you the results. You can magnify the display by using the controls underneath the preview, highlighted in Figure 10-21. When the preview is magnified, place your cursor inside the preview area and drag to scroll the display.

At any time, you can revert the image to the original settings by opening the Adjustment window and selecting Revert to Shot Settings.

4. **Open the File menu and choose Convert and Save.**

You see a standard file-saving dialog box with a few additional controls. Here's a rundown of the critical options:

- *Save As Type:* Choose Exif-TIFF (8bit). This option saves your image in the TIFF file format, which preserves all image data. Don't choose the JPEG format; doing so is destructive to the photo because of the lossy compression that's applied. (Chapter 2 explains JPEG compression.)

A *bit* is a unit of computer data; the more bits you have, the more colors your image can contain. Some photo-editing programs can't open 16-bit files, or else they limit you to a few editing tools, so stick with the standard, 8-bit image option unless you know that your software can handle the higher bit depth. If you prefer 16-bit files, you can select TIFF 16bit as the file type.

- *Output Resolution:* This option does *not* adjust the pixel count of an image, as you might imagine. It only sets the default output resolution to be used if you send the photo to a printer. The final resolution will depend on the print size you choose, however. See the next section for more information about printing and resolution.

- *Resize:* Clear this check box so that your processed file contains all its original pixels.

- *Embed ICC Profile in Image:* Select this check box to include the color-space data in the file. If you then open the photo in a program that supports color profiles, the colors are rendered more accurately. *ICC* refers to the International Color Consortium, the group that created color-space standards.

5. **Enter a filename, select the folder where you want to store the image, and then click Save.**

   A progress box appears, letting you know that the conversion and file saving is going forward. Close the progress box when the program announces that the process is complete.

6. **Click the exit button (labeled in Figure 10-21) to close the editing window.**

   You're returned to the main program window.

REMEMBER

When you close the program, you see a dialog box that tells you that your Raw file was edited and asks whether you want to save the changes. Choose Yes to store your raw-processing "recipe" with the Raw file. The Raw settings you used are then kept with the original image so that you can create additional copies of the Raw file easily without having to make all your adjustments again.

Again, these steps give you only a basic overview of the process. If you regularly shoot in the Raw format, take the time to explore the Digital Photo Professional instruction manual so that you fully understand all the program's Raw conversion features.

Preparing Pictures for Online Sharing

Have you ever received an email message containing a photo so large that you can't view the whole thing on your monitor without scrolling the email window? This annoyance occurs because monitors can display only a limited number of pixels. The exact number depends on the screen resolution setting, but suffice it to say that most of today's digital cameras produce photos with pixel counts in excess of what the monitor can handle.

Thankfully, the newest email programs incorporate features that automatically shrink the photo display to a viewable size. But that doesn't change the fact that a large photo file means longer download times and, if recipients hold onto the picture, a big storage hit on their hard drives.

Sending a high-resolution photo is the thing to do if you want the recipient to be able to generate a good print. But for simple onscreen viewing, a good practice is to limit the image size to about 1,000 pixels on the longest side. That ensures that people who use an email program that doesn't offer the latest photo-viewing tools can see the entire picture without scrolling the viewer window.

REMEMBER

Because you need lots of pixels if you want to produce decent prints — and adding pixels after the fact lowers image quality — always shoot your originals at the Image Quality (Large, Medium, S1, or S2) that will enable you to have a high enough resolution for the size of the print you want to have. You can then create a low-res copy of the picture for email sharing or for other online uses, such as posting to Facebook. (Posting only low-res photos to Facebook and online photo-sharing sites also helps dissuade would-be photo thieves looking for free images for use in their companies' brochures and other print materials.)

In addition to resizing high-resolution images, also check their file types; if the photos are in the Raw or TIFF format, you need to create a JPEG copy for online use. Web browsers and email programs can't display Raw or TIFF files.

For Raw photos or JPEG images already on your computer, you can do both bits of photo prep using Canon Digital Photo Professional 4. When you process the Raw file, just choose JPEG as the file type and set the image dimensions you want to use. Set the level of JPEG compression by dragging the Quality slider; a higher Quality value produces a larger file and better image quality. To resize a JPEG file, click the thumbnail and choose Convert and Save from the File menu. Keep the file type set to JPEG, set the image dimensions, and set the Quality slider. But before you click the Save button, be sure to give the file a new name so that you don't overwrite the original.

For JPEG images you haven't yet downloaded, you can do the job using the Resize option built into the camera. However, the smallest size copy the camera can create is 2400 x 1600 pixels, or 3.8 megapixels. That's the same size as the S2 Image Quality setting, and it's still pretty large for online use. But if you can't get to your computer, sending an S2 sized copy is better than uploading a maximum resolution original.

Like other post-capture tools, the Resize option is available through the playback version of the Quick Control screen, shown on the left in Figure 10-22, or Playback Menu 2, as shown on the right.

FIGURE 10-22:
You can create low-resolution copies of JPEG images using the camera's Resize tool.

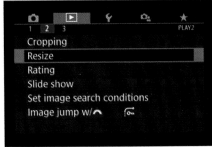

Whichever way you go, you're presented only with size options that result in a smaller file than the original. After you choose a setting, tap the Set icon or press the Set button. On the confirmation screen that appears, choose OK. During playback, you can distinguish the resized copy by looking in the lower-right corner of the screen. For the copy, you see the edited photo symbol, as shown in Figure 10-23, while the neighboring value displays the Image Quality of the copy (S2, in the figure).

Keep in mind that if you have a smartphone or tablet compatible with the Canon Camera Connect app, you may want to use the app to resize JPEG photos and send them online. The app enables you to create lower-resolution copies than the in-camera Resize tool. See the appendix for details.

Edited photo

Image Quality

FIGURE 10-23:
The edited photo symbol appears on the resized copy, along with the value indicating the Image Quality setting.

4

The Part of Tens

IN THIS CHAPTER

» Changing the functions of a few buttons

» Turning off the AF Assist beam

» Creating custom folders and a custom menu

» Tagging files with copyright data and cleaning instructions

Chapter 11 Ten More Customization Options

Earlier chapters discuss major ways to customize your camera, such as changing the data displayed during picture playback and adjusting autofocusing performance. This chapter details ten customization options that aren't quite as critical but may come in handy on occasion.

Changing the Furniture Around

If you like, you can change the function of the Set button, shutter button, AE Lock button, and the AF-ON button when shooing in the P, Tv, Av, or M exposure modes. Please *don't* take advantage of these options, though, until you're thoroughly familiar with how the camera works using the original function settings. If you modify a control, it's not going to behave the way our instructions in the book indicate that it should.

Navigate to Custom Function 14 in Setup Menu 4. Press the Set button to get started. Then highlight the control you want to customize, as shown on the left in Figure 11-1. The icons are, as you can see, somewhat cryptic, so it's nice that as you highlight each one, the name of the button appears, along with its default function.

FIGURE 11-1:
Custom
Function 14
enables you
to modify the
functions of
four camera
controls.

TIP

As you select the different controls, the camera graphic on the left side of the screen highlights the button you're adjusting. In the figure, for example, the shutter button is lit.

After highlighting a control, tap Set or press the Set button to display the options available for that button. For example, the right side of Figure 11-1 shows the options available for the shutter button. As you scroll through the choices, the label above the icons shows you what the button will accomplish at that setting. Make your choice and tap Set or press the Set button to return to the initial setup screen. Then press the Menu button or tap menu to exit.

Silencing the Camera

By default, your camera beeps after certain operations, such as after it sets focus when you use autofocusing and during the timer-countdown when you use the Self-Timer Drive mode. If you need the camera to hush up, set the Beep option on Setup Menu 3 to Disable. This option is available in all shooting modes.

Note that if the option is set to Enable (which is the default setting), you also hear a tone when you tap touch screen–controlled options. If you don't want to hear that tone but still want the non–touch screen beeps, set the option to Touch Silence, which is shown in the menu as a speaker with a slash through it on the menu.

Disabling the AF-Assist Beam

In dim lighting, your camera may emit an AF (autofocus) assist beam from the built-in flash when you press the shutter button halfway — assuming that the flash unit is open, of course. This pulse of light helps the camera "see" its target better, improving autofocus performance.

If you're shooting in a situations where the beam may be distracting, you can disable it — but again, only when using the P, Tv, Av, or M exposure modes. Make the change via Custom Function 5. Along with the basic Enable and Disable settings, you get two options related to using an external flash. Enable External Flash Only permits an external flash to emit the beam but prevents the built-in flash from doing so. The other setting, IR AF Assist Beam Only, allows a flash that has infrared (IR) AF-assist to use only the IR beam, which is less noticeable than the regular light.

These and other external flash options work only with certain flash units; your camera manual provides specifics on compatible models.

Preventing Shutter Release without a Memory Card

By default, you can take a picture without any memory card in the camera. But the image you shoot is only temporary, appearing for a few seconds on the monitor and then dissolving into digital nothingness. The option is designed mainly for use in camera stores, enabling salespeople to demonstrate cameras without having to keep a memory card in every model. But for those of us not in that biz, leaving the option on only invites trouble. So open Shooting Menu 1 and set the Release Shutter without Card option to Off, as shown in Figure 11-2.

FIGURE 11-2:
Turn this option off to prevent shutter release when no memory card is installed.

Reducing the Number of Exposure Stops

By default, major exposure-related settings are based on one-third stop adjustments. If you prefer, you can tell the camera to present exposure adjustments in half-stop increments so that you don't have to cycle through as many settings each time you want to make a change. Make your preferences known via Custom Function 1, Exposure Level Increments. (You can get to the option only when using the P, Tv, Av, and M exposure modes.) Be aware that the exposure meter will reflect this change and, thus, appear differently than shown in the figures in this book.

Creating a Custom Menu

Through the My Menu feature, you can create a custom menu containing up to five tabs, each of which can hold six menu items. The idea is to enable you to group your favorite menu options together in a way that makes more sense to you than the standard menu organization. In Figure 11-3, for example, the first tab contains six exposure options that appear on separate tabs in the normal menu configuration.

FIGURE 11-3:
The My Menu feature lets you create a custom menu.

Having this kind of control may appeal after you're fully aware of how all your camera settings work and which features you use the most. But when you're just beginning, stick with the standard menu structure so that what you see on your camera matches the instructions found in this book and other resources.

Two other issues to note about the My Menu feature: First, you can access it in the P, Tv, Av, and M exposure modes only. If you want to shoot in any other exposure mode, your custom menu doesn't appear, which means that you have to learn two sets of menu layouts instead of just one. You also have to switch from the default guided menus and displays to the standard versions, which you do via the Display Level menu. (Chapter 1 has information on that menu.)

Should you decide that you're ready to step up to a custom menu, check the section in the camera manual related to customizing the camera.

Adding Custom Folders

Normally, your camera automatically creates folders to store your images. The first folder has the name 100Canon; the second, 101Canon; and so on. Each folder can hold 9,999 photos. However, you can create a new folder before the existing one is full at any time. You might take this organizational step so that you can segregate work photos from personal photos, for example. To create the folder, open Setup Menu 1, choose Select Folder, and then choose Create Folder, as illustrated in Figure 11-4.

FIGURE 11-4: You can create a new storage folder at any time.

The camera asks for permission to create the folder; choose OK and press Set. The folder is automatically assigned the next available folder number and is selected as the active folder — the one that will hold any new photos you shoot. Press the Set button or tap the Set icon to return to Setup Menu 1.

To make a different folder the active folder, choose Select Folder again, choose the folder you want to use, and press or tap Set.

Turning Off the Shooting Settings Screen

When you turn on your camera, the monitor automatically displays the screen that shows shooting settings for normal, through-the-viewfinder photography. If you prefer not to see the display upon startup, set the Mode dial to P, Tv, Av, or M, select Custom Functions from Setup Menu 4, and bring up Custom Function 12. Change the setting from the default, Display On, to Previous Display Status.

WARNING

The setting name reflects the fact that the camera remembers the current display status when you turn the camera off. Then it returns to that previous status the next time you turn the camera on. So if you don't want the display to appear on startup, press the Info button to shut off the display before powering down the camera.

Although disabling the automatic display saves battery power, having to remember to turn the display off each time you shut down the camera is a pain. So we stick with the default setting and then press the Info button to toggle the screen on and off if the battery is running low. Also note that if the camera is set to any of the Basic Zone modes when you turn on the camera, the display appears regardless of the setting you choose for the Custom Function.

Embedding Copyright Notices

If you sell your photography (or hope to), this is one customization feature definitely worth enabling. You can embed a copyright notice into the *metadata* — hidden text data — that's included in every photo or movie you capture. Anyone who views your picture in a program that can display metadata can see your copyright notice. (Chapter 10 explains how to view it in Canon Digital Photo Professional 4.)

REMEMBER

You can enter copyright data only when the camera is set to P, Tv, Av, or M exposure mode, but the information you enter is added to all new files you create, regardless of which exposure mode you used to capture them.

Follow these steps to create your copyright notice:

1. **Open Setup Menu 4 and choose Copyright Information, as shown on the left in Figure 11-5.**

   You see the screen shown on the right.

FIGURE 11-5:
Enter your name and other copyright information that you want tagged to your images.

2. **Choose Enter Author's Name to display the digital keyboard shown in Figure 11-6.**

3. **Enter your name.**

   The easiest option is to use the touchscreen: Just tap the letters you want to enter; the characters you select appear in the text box above the keyboard.

Tap the symbol labeled *change keyboard* in the figure to cycle the keyboard display from all uppercase letters, to all lowercase letters, and then to numbers and symbols.

To move the cursor in the text box, tap inside the box or tap the arrows at the end of the text box. To erase the character to the left of the cursor, tap the Delete character icon, also labeled in the figure.

If you prefer button pushing to touchscreen tapping, press the Q button to toggle between the keyboard and the text box. When the keyboard is active, use the Quick Control keys, the Quick Control dial, or the Main dial to highlight a character and press the Set button to enter that character in the text box. To delete a character, press the Q button to activate the text box, move the cursor in front of the character you want to delete, and press the Erase button. Press Q again to jump back to the keyboard.

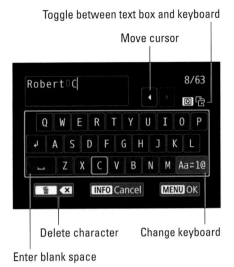

Toggle between text box and keyboard

Move cursor

Delete character   Change keyboard

Enter blank space

FIGURE 11-6:
Enter the text you want to include in your copyright notice.

4. **Tap the Menu icon or press the Menu button; then confirm your decision to save the information and return to the main setup screen (right screen in Figure 11-5).**

5. **Choose Enter Copyright Details to return to the keyboard and add any additional data you think necessary.**

    You might want to add the year or your email address, for example. (You don't need to enter the word *Copyright* — it's added automatically.)

6. **Tap the Menu icon or press the Menu button once to exit the setup screen; then tap OK or highlight it and press the Set button to complete the process.**

7. **Press the Menu button to return to the menu system.**

Disable copyright tagging by choosing the Delete Copyright Information option, also found on the main setup screen. (The option is unavailable, as in Figure 11-5, until you add copyright data.)

Adding Cleaning Instructions to Images

If small spots appear consistently on your images — and you know that dirt on your lens isn't the cause — your sensor may need cleaning. The Dust Delete Data feature, designed for use with Canon Digital Photo Professional 4, provides a stop-gap measure until you can take the camera to a service shop for sensor cleaning.

You start by recording a data file that maps the location of the dust spots on the sensor. To do this, you need a white piece of paper and a lens that offers a focal length of 50mm or longer. Put the camera in the P, Tv, Av, or M exposure mode, set the lens to manual focusing, and then set the focus distance at infinity. (If you're holding the camera in the horizontal position, turn the lens focusing ring counter-clockwise until it stops.) Next, open Shooting Menu 4, choose Dust Delete Data, and select OK.

Position the paper 8 to 12 inches from the camera, make sure that the paper fills the viewfinder, and then press the shutter button all the way. No picture is taken; the camera just records the Dust Delete Data in its internal memory. When you see the message "Data obtained," select OK. The current date appears on the initial Dust Delete Data screen.

After you create your Dust Delete Data file, the camera attaches the data to every image you shoot. To clean a photo in Digital Photo Professional 4, select the image thumbnail, open the Adjustment menu, and then click Apply Dust Delete Data. The program's instruction manual, available for download from the Canon website, offers additional details.

IN THIS CHAPTER

» Shooting time-lapse movies and video snapshots

» Capturing long exposures using Mirror Lockup

» Investigating printing features and special-effects filters

» Setting up slide shows and photo books

» Trimming frames from the beginning and end of a movie

» Setting up time-lapse still photos

Chapter **12**

Ten Features to Explore on a Rainy Day

onsider this chapter the literary equivalent of the end of one of those late-night infomercial offers — the part where the host exclaims, "But wait! There's more!" Options covered here aren't the sort of features that drive people to choose one camera over another, and they may come in handy only for certain users, on certain occasions. Still, they're included at no extra charge with your camera, so check 'em out when you have a spare moment. Who knows? You may discover just the solution you need for one of your photography problems.

Because Part of Tens chapters are meant to offer bite-size nuggets of information, this chapter doesn't provide full-length explanations of every feature. So, if you want more details, consult the camera manual. You can download the manual from the Canon website if you can't find your paper copy.

Shooting a Time-Lapse Movie

After you put the camera in Movie mode, you can access the *time-lapse movie* feature, which records single frames at periodic intervals and then stitches the frames into a movie.

If you're shooting in the P, Tv, Av, or M exposure modes, choose Time-Lapse Movie from Shooting Menu 5; in other exposure modes, from Shooting Menu 3. Change the setting from Disable to Enable, which displays the following recording options:

>> **Interval and No. of Shots:** The first option sets the delay between captures; the second option determines how many frames are captured. You can set that value from 2 to 3600. As you change the interval and number of shots, values at the bottom of the screen indicate how long it will take the camera to record all the frames and the length of the resulting movie.

>> **Auto Exposure:** Choose Fixed First Frame to record all frames using the exposure settings the camera selects for the first frames. Choose Each Frame if you want the camera to reset exposure for before each shot.

>> **LCD Auto Off:** By default, the monitor stays on during shooting but automatically turns off about 30 minutes after the first image is captured. If you want to save battery power, you can shut the monitor off automatically about 10 seconds after the first frame is captured by setting this option to Enable. Press the Info button to bring back the display at any time. Note that you can't record a time-lapse movie while the camera is connected to an external display, so the onboard monitor provides your only visual reference.

>> **Beep as Image Taken:** By default, the camera beeps after each frame is captured, which is a very good way to annoy everyone within earshot. If you don't want to lose friends and family members, set this option to Disable.

 After exiting the menu screen, frame your shot and the press the shutter button halfway to initiate autofocusing and exposure metering. Make sure that focus is accurate — the camera won't adjust focus between frames. To begin capturing frames, press the Live View button. Recording stops automatically after all frames are captured and the movie is created.

TECHNICAL
STUFF

For video-spec lovers: Time-lapse movies are created in the MOV format, using the Full HD video setting (1920 x 1080 pixels) at 30 frames per second (for NTSC systems) or 25 frames per second (for PAL systems). Frames are compressed using ALL-I compression rather than the IPB compression used for regular movies. If you want to know more about these specifications, see Chapter 8.

Enabling Mirror Lockup

One component in the optical system of a dSLR camera is a mirror that moves when you press the shutter button. The vibration caused by the mirror movement can result in image blur when you use a very slow shutter speed, shoot with a long telephoto lens, or take extreme close-ups. To eliminate this possibility, your camera offers *mirror lockup,* which delays the shutter release a little longer than normal so that the picture isn't recorded until after the mirror movement is completed. Of course, you should also mount the camera on a tripod so that camera shake caused by handholding the camera doesn't create blur.

You can take advantage of mirror-lockup shooting only in the P, Tv, Av, or M exposure modes. Enable it through Custom Function 10, as shown in Figure 12-1.

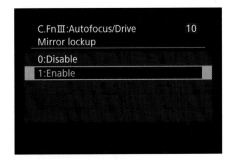

REMEMBER

Mirror-lockup shooting requires a special picture-taking process: Press the shutter button once to lock up the mirror, release the button, and then press it all the way down again to take the picture.

FIGURE 12-1:
Mirror lockup eliminates the chance that mirror movement blurs the photo.

Exploring DPOF Printing

DPOF (dee-poff) stands for *Digital Print Order Format.* If your printer supports this technology, you can select and print specific pictures stored on your memory card without having to first download the images to your computer. Choose Print Order from Playback Menu 1 to tag the images you want to print and to specify how many prints you want of each image. Then, if your printer has an SD card slot, take the memory card out of the camera and put it in the printer's card slot. The printer checks your "print order" and outputs just the requested prints. If your printer doesn't have a card slot, you can purchase a USB cable from Canon that enables you to connect the camera to the printer for this purpose. It's the same cable used for downloading pictures to the computer (Canon IFC-400PCU, about $12). You can also connect to a printer using Wi-Fi. Check out the Appendix for more information on setting up Wi-Fi.

Adding Special Effects to Photos

During playback, you can add special effects to your photos by using the Creative Filters feature. The camera creates a copy of your image and applies the filter to the copy; your original remains intact. Figure 12-2 offers a look at three filter effects along with the original shot.

Original

Fish-Eye

Toy Camera

Miniature Effect

FIGURE 12-2: Here's a look at how three Creative Filters affected a city scene.

You can choose from these effects:

>> **Grainy B/W:** Creates a noisy (grainy) black-and-white photo.

>> **Soft Focus:** Blurs the photo to make it look soft and dreamy.

>> **Fish-Eye:** Distorts the picture to produce the look of photos taken with a fish-eye lens.

>> **Art Bold:** Produces a vivid, high-contrast oil-painting effect.

>> **Water Painting:** Softens colors and focus to mimic the look of a watercolor painting.

>> **Toy Camera:** Creates an image with dark corners — called a *vignette* effect. Vignetting is caused by poor-quality lenses, like those found in toy cameras — thus, the effect name. You can also add a warm (yellowish) or cool (blue) tint when you apply the filter.

>> **Miniature:** Blurs all but a very small area of the photo to create a result that looks something like one of those miniature dioramas you see in museums. This effect works best on pictures taken from a high angle, like the one featured in Figure 12-2.

The easiest way to apply the filters is to put the camera in Playback mode, display the photo you want to alter, and then press the Q button to bring up the Quick Control screen. Select the Creative Filters option, as shown on the left in Figure 12-3, to display symbols representing the available filters at the bottom of the screen. Select a filter and press the Set button (or tap the Set icon) to display a preview of your picture along with options for adjusting the effect, as shown on the right in the figure. For most of the filters, you can increase or decrease the strength of the filter (after you have selected it by pressing the Set button) by rotating the Quick Control dial, using the right/left Quick Control keys, or tapping directly on the to Effect scale. For the Miniature effect, a narrow focus box appears. Move the box over the portion of the photo that you want to keep in sharp focus; press the Info button to change the orientation of the box.

If you like what you see, press Set to save the filtered copy as a new file. Or, to cancel out of the operation and check out a different filter, press the Menu button or tap the Menu symbol. You're taken back to the initial filter-selection screen (left screen in Figure 12-3).

You also can get to the special effects by choosing Creative Filters from Playback Menu 1. Scroll to the picture you want to doctor and press Set. From there, everything works as just described.

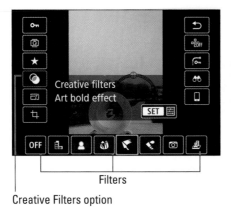

FIGURE 12-3:
During playback, apply Creative Filters through the Quick Control screen.

Creative Filters option

Filters

Effect strength

Adding Effects During Shooting

To apply effects as you record pictures or movies, set the Mode dial to Creative Filters, as shown in Figure 12-4. (This is the only way to create a movie with effects.) In this case, you don't wind up with an unfiltered original and a special effects version; you get only the special-effects image or movie.

You're offered different filters depending on how you have the camera set up. Here's a quick rundown of the filters that are available when shooting stills and movies through the viewfinder or using Live View:

FIGURE 12-4:
Choose this exposure mode to add special effects to photos as you shoot.

>> **Viewfinder (P, Tv, Av, or M exposure modes):** None

>> **Viewfinder and Live View (Creative Filter exposure mode):** Ten filters available:

- Grainy B/W

- Soft focus

- Fish-eye

- Water painting

- Toy camera

- Miniature

- HDR art standard

- HDR art vivid

- HDR art bold

- HDR art embossed

>> **Live View (P, Tv, Av, or M exposure modes):** Seven filters are available:

- Grainy B/W

- Soft focus

- Fish-eye

- Art bold

- Water painting

- Toy camera

- Miniature

>> **Movie mode (Creative Filter, P, Tv, Av, or M exposure modes):** Five filters are available:

- Dream

- Old Movies

- Memory

- Dramatic B&W

- Miniature effect

The process of applying a filter is very similar. Press the Q button to put the camera in Quick Control mode and then look for the Creative Filters option on the screen. The left side of Figure 12-5 shows you where to find the option during viewfinder shooting; the right screen shows the option as it appears during Live View and Movie shooting.

After highlighting the Creative Filters option, press Set to display the screen shown in Figure 12-6. Scroll the display up and down to check out all the available effects. When you find one you like, press the Set button to return to the Quick Control screen. For some effects, the screen now offers a second option that enables you to adjust the impact of the filter. For example, the adjustment option for the Grainy Black and White filter are labeled in Figure 12-5.

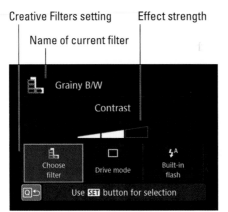

Creative Filters setting · Effect strength · Creative Filters setting

Name of current filter · Effect strength

FIGURE 12-5:
Use the Quick
Control screen
to select and
adjust an
effect.

A few other quick pointers:

>> For still photos, all images are stored
in the JPEG format, even if the Image
Quality option is set to Raw.

>> During Live View and Movie
shooting, you can also access
creative effects when the Mode dial
is set to P, Tv, Av, or M. Just display
the Quick Control screen and look
for the Creative Filters symbol on
the right side of the screen. The
symbol looks like the one that marks
the Creative Filters setting on the
Mode dial. If the symbol is dimmed, another setting is interfering; for example,
you can't apply a filter when the Multi-Shot Noise Reduction option is enabled.

FIGURE 12-6:
After you choose the Creative Filters option,
you see a screen offering an illustration and a
bit of information about each filter.

Tagging Pictures for a Photo Book

Many online and retail photo-printing sites make it easy to print books featur-
ing your favorite images. The Photobook Set-Up option on Playback Menu 1 is a
nod to this popular trend. Using this feature, you can tag photos that you want
to include in a photo book. Then, if you use the Canon EOS Utility software to
transfer pictures to your computer, tagged photos are dumped into a separate
folder so that they're easy to find.

Just two restrictions: This feature works only when you download pictures by connecting the camera to the computer. In addition, you can't tag Raw files for photo book selection.

Creating Video Snapshots

The Video Snapshot feature captures short video clips that are stitched into a single recording, called a *video album.* You can set the clip length to 8, 4, or 2 seconds long (but all clips in an album must be the same length).

Given the brevity of the individual clips, we doubt you'll find much use for this feature. But it's worth mentioning anyway if only to explain that when you put the camera in Movie mode, a Video Snapshot symbol appears, as shown in Figure 12-7. (If you don't see any data onscreen, press the Info button to change the display style.)

Video Snapshot option

To record a snapshot album, press Q to enter Quick Control mode and select the Video Snapshot icon. Exit Quick Control mode and press the Live View button to record the first clip. You're then prompted to create a new album to store the clip or to choose an existing album. After that bit of business is completed, you can record your second clip.

FIGURE 12-7:
The Video Snapshot feature joins brief video clips into a single movie.

By default, the camera records 4-second clips, but you can alter the clip length and set a few other recording choices from the Video Snapshot menu item. In the P, TV, Av, and M exposure modes, the option is found on Shooting Menu 5; in other modes, it's on Shooting Menu 3. Control audio recording via the normal movie-recording sound options, covered in Chapter 8.

You can't record normal movies when the Video Snapshot feature is enabled, so be sure to re-enter Quick Control mode to disable it after you create your album.

Trimming Movies

Your camera's movie-edit feature makes it possible to remove unwanted material from the beginning or end of a movie. To access the editing tools, set the camera to Playback mode, display the movie file, and then tap the Set symbol or press the Set button to display the controls shown on the left in Figure 12-8. Select the scissors symbol, labeled Edit in the figure, and press Set. On the next screen (not shown), choose the leftmost icon at the bottom of the screen, which represents the Cut Beginning option. The display then changes to appear as shown on the right in Figure 12-8, with the Cut Beginning icon highlighted and the other three icons dimmed. The bar at the top of the screen indicates the original movie length.

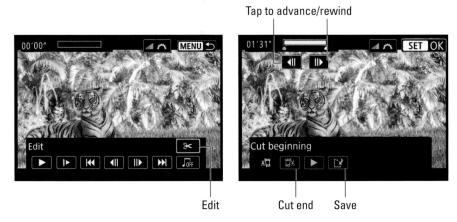

FIGURE 12-8: From the playback screen, select the scissors icon to get to the movie-editing functions.

Advance the movie to reach the first frame you want to keep by rotating the Quick Control dial to the right, pressing the right Quick Control key, or tapping the advance/rewind symbols, labeled in the figure. If you go too far, rotate the Quick Control dial to the left, tap the left arrow, or press the left Quick Control key. Also note that the white bar above the advance/rewind symbols — it represents the entire movie. As you advance the playback, the orange marker moves to the right to show you the position of the current frame. The other marker indicates the endpoint of the movie.

When you reach the first frame you want to keep, press Set. When you do, the four symbols at the bottom of the screen become accessible again. Choose the one marked Save in the figure. You're then given the choice to save the movie as a new file, overwrite the existing file, or cancel the edit altogether. To trim the end of a movie, follow the same process, but choose the Cut End icon (labeled in Figure 12-8) instead of the Cut Beginning icon. Now the orange marker indicates the last frame that will appear in the edited movie.

Presenting a Slide Show

The Slide Show feature automatically displays photos and movies one by one for a period of time that you specify. You can view the show on the camera monitor or connect your camera to a TV, as explained next, to display your work on the TV screen.

REMEMBER

Your first step in setting up a slide show is to consider whether you want all photos and movies to be included in the show. If not, head to Chapter 9 and read the section related to the Image Search feature. Through that option, you can limit playback to files that meet certain criteria, such as the date they were created or a rating that you assigned. If you don't set up a search, all files on the memory card are displayed during the show.

With that step out of the way, open Playback Menu 2 and choose Slide Show to display the screen shown on the left in Figure 12-9. The thumbnail previews the first image or movie that will appear; you also see the total number of files that are included. Choose Setup to specify how long you want each photo to appear (movies always play in their entirety) and whether you want the show to repeat automatically after it ends. You also can choose to add one of five transition effects and add background music. The background music thing is a bit complex, though: You have to use Canon EOS Utility software to download music to the memory card. The EOS Utility program instruction manual provides details. (You can download the program and manual from the Canon website.)

After selecting playback options, tap Menu or press the Menu button to return to the screen shown on the right in Figure 12-9. Choose Start to begin playing the show. You can then control playback as follows:

>> **Pause playback.** Press the Set button or just tap anywhere on the touch-screen. While the show is paused, you can rotate the Quick Control dial or press the right or left Quick Control key to view the next or previous photo. Press Set again or tap the Set icon to continue playback from the current slide.

>> **Change the information display style.** Press the Info button.

>> **Adjust sound volume.** Rotate the Main dial.

>> **Exit the slide show.** Press the Menu button to return to the menu display. To instead return to normal picture playback, press the Playback button. Remember that any search you set up before the show is still in force. See Chapter 9 to find out how to cancel the search so that you can once again access all files on the memory card.

FIGURE 12-9:
Choose Slide
Show and then
either start it
or customize
the settings.

Exploring Interval Timer Shooting

Finally, your 77D offers automatic *time-lapse photography*, which enables you to record a series of shots over a specified period of time without having to stick around to press the shutter button for each shot. You can space the shots minutes or even hours apart, and you can record as many images as your memory card can hold. Canon calls this feature *Interval Timer*, and it's located in Shooting Menu 5 when the camera is set to P, Tv, Av, or M exposure modes; in other exposure modes, from Shooting Menu 1.

Enable the feature, as shown in Figure 12-10, then tap Info or press the Info button to configure the detailed settings. Set the interval between shots and the total number of photos you want to take.

Several restrictions apply: This feature won't work in Live View or Movie modes, nor can you set the camera to Bulb mode. You have to take the first shot yourself, and you'll get better mileage if you use a sturdy tripod and the optional Canon AC Adapter and DC Coupler instead of a battery.

FIGURE 12-10:
After you enable the Interval Timer feature, press Info to configure the settings.

Appendix

Exploring Wireless Connections

Your camera enables you to connect wirelessly to a computer, smartphone, or tablet. After you make the wireless link, you can download files to your computer or smart device, control your camera remotely, and perform a number of other functions. Before you can enjoy these features, however, you need to do the following:

» **Install Canon EOS Utility software on your computer.** This free program, introduced in Chapter 10, serves as the concierge for wireless communication with a computer. It's available for download from the Canon website.

» **Install the Canon Camera Connect app on your smartphone or tablet.** This app, available for Android and iOS devices, is needed to connect your camera to a smartphone, tablet, or other "smart" device. Go to Google Play for the Android app; head to the App Store for the Apple iOS version. Before downloading, check the listed system requirements to make sure that your device can run the app.

Unfortunately, we don't have room in this book to provide detailed information on the wireless functions because things work differently depending on your computer or smart device, the kind of security your wireless network employs, whether you're using the Android or iOS version of the app, and so on. If you need more help after scanning the general overview provided in this appendix, download the electronic version of the Wi-Fi Function Instruction Manual, which offers a whopping 170 pages of details. (Visit www.canon.com/icpd and follow the instructions for downloading the Wi-Fi manual for your camera.)

Preparing the Camera

In addition to installing the EOS Utility software and Canon Camera Connect app on your computer and smart device, you have to do a bit of setup work on the camera before you can make a connection. Follow these steps:

1. **Press the Wi-Fi button or open Setup Menu 1 and choose Wireless Communication Settings, as shown on the left in Figure A-1.**

   The settings screen shown on the right in the figure appears.

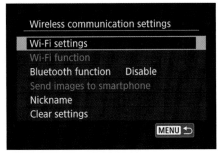

FIGURE A-1: The wireless communication options are located on Setup Menu 1.

2. **Choose Wi-Fi Settings and then set the option to Enable.**

   You see the screen shown on the left in Figure A-2, asking you to give your camera a nickname. Choose OK to display the screen shown on the right in the figure.

FIGURE A-2: You need to assign a nickname to your camera.

3. **Give your camera a nickname.**

   This name is used to identify your camera when you make a wireless connection. The name EOS77D is assigned by default. To use a different name, use the keyboard techniques covered in Chapter 10 to erase the existing name and replace it with another. Then press the Menu button or tap the Menu icon. The camera tells you that the name you entered will be assigned; choose OK.

The Wi-Fi Settings screen reappears, showing Wi-Fi enabled, as shown on the left in Figure A-3.

FIGURE A-3:
Verify that
Wi-Fi is
enabled
(left), exit the
screen, and
then choose
Wi-Fi Function
(right).

4. **Tap the Menu icon or press the Menu button.**

The initial Wireless Communications Settings screen reappears, with all wireless functions now accessible, as shown on the right in Figure A-3.

5. **Choose Wi-Fi function or press the Wi-Fi button to display the screen shown in Figure A-4, where you select which Wi-Fi function you want to use.**

The various options are labeled in the figure.

Upcoming sections provide more information about computer and smartphone connections. You also can connect to another camera (to send pictures from your memory card to a friend's memory card); send a file to a printer that has Wi-Fi connectivity; and connect to Canon Image Gateway, which is a free online photo sharing and storage site. For help with these features, check the aforementioned Wi-Fi instruction manual and pay a visit to the Canon Image Gateway website (www.canon.com/cig).

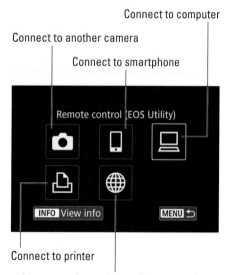

FIGURE A-4:
Select the icon representing the type of connection you want to make.

Connecting to a Computer

After performing the setup steps just described and installing the EOS Utility Software, you're ready to connect the camera to a computer. But you need to know one more bit of background information: In addition to being able to connect to a regular wireless network, the camera can act as an independent *access point.* That means that you can connect directly to the camera instead of going through your regular network.

However, if your computer is connected to your network via cable and doesn't have built-in Wi-Fi — which is the case with many desktop computers — you have to join the network that the computer is on.

The following steps show how to use the second method; the information you need to use the camera's access point appears after the steps.

1. **Press the Wi-Fi button to display the screen shown in Figure A-4.**

2. **Tap the computer icon or highlight it and press Set.**

You see the screen shown on the left in Figure A-5.

FIGURE A-5:
To connect a new computer, select the register option (left) and then choose the wireless network you want to use (right).

3. **Choose Register a Device for Connection.**

The screen shown on the right in Figure A-5 appears. Ignore everything except the Switch Network symbol in the lower-right corner. Select that option to display the screen shown on the left in Figure A-6. The screen displays a list of available wireless networks, which should include yours. A lock symbol indicates that you need to enter a network password, so go find the scrap of paper on which you jotted that down before you take the next step.

FIGURE A-6:
Choose your
wireless
network and
then enter
the network
password.

4. **Select your network and then enter the network password on the keyboard, as shown on the right in Figure A-6.**

This keyboard is the same one detailed in the Chapter 10 section about adding copyright information; check out that section if you can't figure out how to enter your password. Press the Menu button or tap the Menu icon after you put in all the necessary characters.

5. **On the next screen, shown on the left in Figure A-7, choose Auto Setting and then choose OK.**

FIGURE A-7:
After selecting
Auto Setting
(left), choose
OK; when
prompted to
start pairing
devices (right),
choose OK
again.

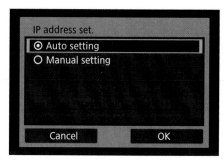

Now you see the screen shown on the right, which suggests that you start pairing devices. *Pairing* is computer speak for linking two devices wirelessly.

6. **Choose OK to display the screen shown on the left in Figure A-8.**

7. **On your computer, launch Canon EOS Utility.**

When the program starts, click the Pairing over WI-FI/Lan option. You see a list of devices that the program has recognized; click Canon EOS 77D and then click Connect.

8. **When you see the camera screen shown on the right in Figure A-8, choose OK.**

The camera then shows the screen shown in Figure A-9. Ignore it until you're ready to disconnect from the computer. From this point forward, everything is handled by the EOS Utility software, covered a little later in this appendix.

FIGURE A-9:
This screen appears after the wireless connection is established.

Now for the promised details on using the camera as an access point instead of joining a standard network: Follow the preceding steps until you see the screen shown on the right in Figure A-5. Then, on your computer, find the setting that enables you to choose a wireless network. The list of available networks should include the name shown in the SSID portion of the camera screen. Select that network and then enter the password shown on the camera screen. You can then start EOS Utility on the computer. Again, the screen shown in Figure A-9 appears at the end of the connection process.

Disconnecting and reconnecting

When you're ready to end the connection between your camera and computer, choose the Disconnect option from the camera screen shown in Figure A-9. Then press the Menu button or tap the Menu icon. To exit the menu system, just press or tap Menu as needed to back your way out of all the setup screens and return to shooting mode.

To reconnect, press the Wi-Fi button or make your way back to Setup Menu 1, choose Wireless Communications Settings, and then choose Wi-Fi function. A screen appears showing the name of your computer and any other devices you've already *registered* (connected to), as shown on the left in Figure A-10. Choose your computer name and then just sit back and wait for the camera to make the connection. Depending on the program preferences you establish in the EOS Utility program, the software either launches automatically or the camera prompts you to start the software. You'll know the connection is active when you see the screen shown in Figure A-9 again.

FIGURE A-10: Press the Wi-Fi button to display this screen; select your computer to reestablish the connection.

If you want to take advantage of one of the other Wi-Fi functions, such as using Wi-Fi to connect to a smart device, tap the right scroll arrow or press the right Quick Control key to get back to the main function screen (refer to the right screen in Figure A-10). Keep scrolling to cycle through the options and return to the screen showing your computer name.

TIP

Reviewing EOS Utility functions

And now for the fun part: Exploring the stuff you can do with EOS Utility while your camera is connected to your computer:

» **Downloading photos and movies to your computer:** From the main program window, choose Download Images to Computer (shown in Figure A-11). Chapter 10 details the rest of this process.

» **Controlling your camera from your computer:** Choose Remote Shooting (the second option in Figure A-11) to open a window where you can adjust shooting settings, trigger the shutter release, display the captured image on your computer monitor, and even set up automatic image download to your computer, to the memory card, or both.

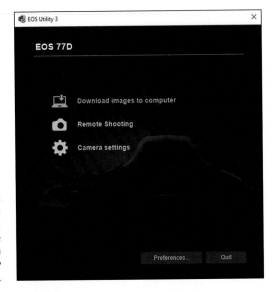

FIGURE A-11:
Choose the
function you
want to use
from the main
EOS Utility
window.

If you put the camera in Live View mode, you can view the live preview on your computer display. Options for adjusting shooting settings are also accessible from the screen.

In photo lingo, this feature is known as *tethered shooting* — except that instead of having your camera connected to the computer via a cable as photographers have done for a while, it's tethered via Wi-Fi. Tethered shooting is especially useful for situations where you need to show your subject or a group of clients the results of each shot. You can view the images on your computer monitor instead of passing around the camera.

>> **Transferring firmware updates, lens registration data, background music files, and other data to your camera.** Choose the Camera Settings option to access these and other options, including one that enables you to establish options for your Canon Image Gateway account.

For more information about using these and other EOS Utility features, consult the program's instruction manual, available for download from the Canon website.

Connecting to a Smartphone or Tablet

After installing the Canon Camera Connect app and taking the steps outlined in the earlier section "Preparing the Camera," you can connect the camera to your smartphone or tablet — hereby known collectively as a *smart device.*

In fact, depending on your device, you can connect in a number of different ways. As with a computer connection, you can either set up the link via a private wireless network or use the camera's own Wi-Fi access point. If your phone offers Bluetooth or NFC technology, you can make the connection that way.

How about some specifics, you say? Again, covering all the variations here would require way more pages than this book can hold. More important, you don't need to see those specifics here because the app provides its own connection guide. The guide steps you through the process of choosing your preferred method of connection, selecting the necessary settings on the camera, and selecting related options on your device. Launch the guide from the home screen of the app, shown in Figure A-12. Note that this figure and Figure A-13 show the Apple iOS version of the app, but the Android version is laid out the same.

After you connect the camera to your smart device, you can then access the app features from the home screen, as shown in Figure A-13. Here are the features you're most likely to use on a regular basis:

Tap to launch setup guide

FIGURE A-12:
Tap this option to let the app guide you through the camera connection process.

>> **Viewing photos without transferring them from the memory card:** Especially on a tablet, this feature enables you to get a larger view of your images than provided by the camera monitor. Choose the Images on Camera option to display your photos.

>> **Transferring selected files from the camera to the device:** After you display images, you can select the ones you want to transfer. The original files stay on the memory card; the camera sends copies to your device. You can choose to transfer full-resolution copies or opt for low-resolution versions that are more suitable for online sharing and take up less storage space on your device.

TIP

After transferring photos, you can upload them to Facebook or other social media sites, send them via email, or just enjoy showing them off when you don't have your camera with you.

» **Using your device as a wireless remote control:** Although you can't control nearly as many camera settings through the app as you can using EOS Utility, it's still a handy way to trigger the camera shutter remotely. Choose Remote Live View Shooting from the home screen to display the remote control window.

Although the app does a good job of guiding you through the setup process, it doesn't offer a built-in instruction manual, as some apps do. However, you should be able to figure things out if you just tap the various onscreen symbols. You may also want to visit the Canon website and just type **Canon Camera Connect** in the search box. There's a section of the site devoted entirely to this app.

FIGURE A-13:
To view and transfer photos, choose Images on Camera; to use your device as a remote control, choose Remote Live View Shooting.

Decoding the Wireless Symbols

One last piece of information about the wireless functions: The camera uses the symbols labeled on the left in Figure A-14 to represent the current wireless status. In Live View and Movie modes, the symbols don't appear in the default display style; press the Info button to change to the detailed data display.

When you're connected to a private network, you see one symbol indicating that the camera is connected via Wi-Fi and another symbol that shows the network's signal strength. That symbol doesn't appear if you use the camera as the wireless access point. The Bluetooth symbol appears when Bluetooth is enabled on the camera. (Choose Wireless Communication Settings from Setup Menu 1 to access the Bluetooth Function setting.) If Bluetooth is enabled but not being used for the current connection, the symbol appears dimmed, as in the left screen of the figure. When the connection is being handled via Bluetooth, the symbol turns white, as shown in the figure on the right. On that same screen, the word *Off* next to the Wi-Fi symbol means that although Wi-Fi is enabled, it's not being used to make the connection.

If none of these symbols appears, wireless communication is disabled.

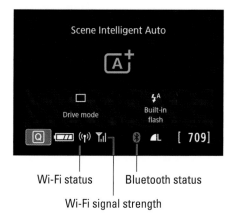

Wi-Fi status

Bluetooth status

Wi-Fi signal strength

Index

About the Authors

Julie Adair King: Julie has been teaching and writing about digital photography for more than two decades. She is the author of the best-selling book *Digital Photography For Dummies,* as well as a series of *For Dummies* guides to Canon, Nikon, and Olympus cameras. Other works include *Digital Photography Before & After Makeovers, Shoot Like a Pro!: Digital Photography Techniques,* and *Digital Photo Projects For Dummies.*

Robert Correll: Robert is the author of the comprehensive photography book *Digital SLR Photography All-In-One For Dummies,* now up to the third edition. He has authored and co-authored many other *For Dummies* guides to Canon and Sony cameras. Some of his other creative titles include *Photo Restoration: From Snapshots to Great Shots, Digital Holga Photography,* and *Photographing Rivers, Lakes, and Falling Water.* When not writing and taking photos, Robert enjoys family life and playing the guitar. He graduated from the United States Air Force Academy.

Authors' Acknowledgments

We are deeply grateful for the support of the team that made this book possible. Many thanks to our skilled editor, Elizabeth Kuball, as well as Steve Hayes, Mary Corder, and the other publishing professionals at John Wiley & Sons. Thank you all.

Publisher's Acknowledgments

Executive Editor: Steven Hayes

Project Editor: Elizabeth Kuball

Technical Editor: Theano Nikitas

Sr. Editorial Assistant: Cherie Case

Production Editor: Antony Sami

Cover Image: Courtesy of Robert Correll